Sociology and Classical Liberalism in Dialogue

Sociology and Classical Liberalism in Dialogue

Freedom is Something We Do Together

Edited by Fabio Rojas and Charlotta Stern

LEXINGTON BOOKS
Lanham • Boulder • New York • London

Published by Lexington Books
An imprint of The Rowman & Littlefield Publishing Group, Inc.
4501 Forbes Boulevard, Suite 200, Lanham, Maryland 20706
www.rowman.com

86-90 Paul Street, London EC2A 4NE

British Library Cataloguing in Publication Information Available

Library of Congress Cataloging-in-Publication Data Available

Names: Rojas, Fabio, 1972- editor. | Stern, Charlotta, 1967- editor.
Title: Sociology and classical liberalism in dialogue : freedom is something we do together / edited by Fabio Rojas and Charlotta Stern.
Description: Lanham : Lexington Books, [2024] | Includes bibliographical references and index.
Identifiers: LCCN 2024003223 (print) | LCCN 2024003224 (ebook) | ISBN 9781666961331 (cloth) | ISBN 9781666961348 (epub)
Subjects: LCSH: Liberalism--Social aspects. | Political sociology. | Free enterprise--Social aspects.
Classification: LCC HB95 .S64 2024 (print) | LCC HB95 (ebook) | DDC 330.12/2--dc23/eng/20240301
LC record available at https://lccn.loc.gov/2024003223
LC ebook record available at https://lccn.loc.gov/2024003224

Contents

Introduction

Sociology and Classical Liberalism in Dialogue: Freedom is Something We Do Together

Fabio Rojas and Charlotta Stern

The world cries for freedom.[1] People may seek relief from the legacy of European colonization, or they may resist laws and customs meant to restrict women and sexual minorities. Around the world, communities struggle against the disruptions of mass incarceration and the brutal costs of border controls. Social liberation is a steady drumbeat and modernity is often a story of repressed peoples seeking relief from social coercion and asserting liberty.

Economic liberalization is another aspect of freedom. One of the most important aspects of contemporary life is the emergence of the market as the way to organize material production. The globalization of production requires that people participate in complex chains of production and exchange that cross national borders. These markets have generated levels of material wealth that would have been difficult to imagine in previous generations. People today have access to material goods, from electronics to life -saving medicines, that enrich the lives of millions.

Classical liberalism looks at both social and economic liberty and says, "this is good." It is a framework that focuses on freedom as a unifying idea for social analysis. Classical liberals see freedom as a virtue in social life, whether it be the workplace, the family, or church. In ethical terms, classical liberals view any form of coercion with deep suspicion, and they are quick to praise institutions that encourage tolerance and voluntary cooperation. Classical liberals often make pragmatic arguments for freedom as well. People who are allowed to organize their own affairs are happier and wealthier. Freedom works.

In contrast, the academic field of sociology is often highly skeptical of classical liberal arguments. At times, sociologists will praise liberation movements, especially if they assert the rights of people who have been violated by Western imperialist projects such as colonialism, slavery, and apartheid. Similarly, sociologists tend to be very supportive of women's rights and the diversity of sexual identity. However, sociologists are wary of other forms of freedom. Sociologists are concerned that liberalized markets lead to concentrations of wealth, increases in economic inequality, poverty, and corruption (e.g., Burawoy 2005). The sociological concern about freedom isn't limited to the economic sphere. Social freedoms have been critiqued by sociologists as well. At times, sociologists have argued that free speech enables exploitative neoliberal politics and sociologists have often praised political regimes that explicitly reject social freedoms (Moore and Bell 2019).

As a result of these concerns, there is a large and noticeable gap between classical liberal social thought and academic sociology. Classical liberals have often dismissed sociology as a field that has something valuable to say, while sociologists have rejected classical liberalism as a strain of social thought that does nothing of service and defends the rich and powerful from critique.

We think another way is possible. The main thesis of this volume is that classical liberalism and sociology have a great deal to say to each other. There is value in creating points of contact between these two areas of inquiry and promoting trade in ideas. One key idea is that freedom sets free cultural processes reaching beyond mere materialism. Classical liberal writers have often argued that freedom and ownership under the rule of law foster voluntary action, by exchanges among free people, fosters a culture of tolerance, trust, and civility. Sociologists are often concerned about the effects of political and social institutions on the poorest and most marginalized in society, and classical liberals have much to say about which institutions improve, or damage, those groups. Conversely, sociologists have a lot to teach classical liberals because they have a rich language for understanding the link between culture and institutions. Sociological theory can teach classical liberals to ask better questions about how culture and social structure allow people to build voluntary institutions and prosper.

To help establish a productive dialogue between sociology and classical liberalism, we have invited scholars in sociology and allied areas such as demography, political science, and public policy to write chapters that explore this approach as it applies to traditional sociological research areas such as racial inequality, health, and poverty. We strived to include a wide range of views, from those who strongly identify with classical liberalism to those who are critics. This introductory chapter provides context for the classical liberal-sociology dialogue by documenting the gap between these two groups, discussing earlier manifestations of classical liberalism in sociology, and identifying the object of study for classical liberal sociologists. Then, we preview each of the individual chapters and situate them in a larger scholarly context. Taken together, we think the book will be of interest to scholars in both sociology and classical liberalism who are curious and open minded toward ideas outside each area's mainstream.

MIND THE GAP

But you may ask, "Is there really a gap between classical liberalism and sociology?" The answer is clearly yes. Casually, we note that classical liberal scholars are hardly ever found in sociology. There is not a school of classical liberal, or libertarian, sociology, nor do sociological journals routinely, if ever, publish scholarly works with a classical liberal flavor. More systematic research confirms this observation. A 2003 survey conducted by Daniel Klein and one of the editors of this volume studied the political attitudes of sociologists (Klein and Stern 2004). Out of 351 people surveyed who were members of the American Sociological Association, only one (!) identified as libertarian and zero indicated membership in the Libertarian Party. This is not an isolated finding. In their book, *Passing on the Right*, Jon A. Shields and Joshua M. Dunn, Jr. (Shields and Dunn 2016) interviewed dozens of non-progressive academics but they were unable to find a single libertarian sociologist.

This is not the case in disciplines adjacent to sociology. In neighboring social sciences, like economics, political science, or political philosophy, there are small, but vibrant, communities of classical liberals and libertarian scholars. There are Austrian economists who develop the ideas of classical liberals like Ludwig von Mises and F.A. Hayek. Other economists argue and debate the ideas of free market advocates like Milton Friedman. Within political philosophy, there is ample debate and discussion of figures like Robert Nozick, David Schmidtz, and Jerry Gaus. Political science is the home of scholars who cultivate classical liberal ideas such as Chandran Kukathas and Jacob Levy.

Why have sociology and classical liberalism been so distant? The social institutions favored by classical liberals, such as property rights, contracts, free speech, constitutional rights, and limited government have had a central role in the rise of wealthy liberal democracies. Surely, this would mean that sociologists would have a sustained interest in freedom as an important feature of modern society.

One can think of a number of reasons for this rejection. Perhaps classical liberal scholarship has been rejected because sociologists would prefer to stay clear of scholarship with ideological associations. A simple test refutes that hypothesis. A Google Scholar search on "Marxist sociology" reveals close to

8,000 hits and the American Sociological Association has a section dedicated to Marxist sociology. Expand the search to include traditions deeply influenced by Marxist theory, such as "public sociology" or "critical sociology," the numbers quadruple. The lack of classical liberal thinking has to do with type of ideology, not ideology per se.

Another explanation of the classical liberal absence in sociology is the disciplinary division of labor. If economists labor on individual actors making rational choices in the marketplace, then sociologists labor on collectives fostered by social norms in civil society. This explanation has some merit. At least since Smith wrote of the famous baker in *The Wealth of Nations* (A. Smith 2009), economists have taken to heart that individuals free to pursue honest income does not merely contribute to their own wealth, but also their neighbors' and nation's. Under the rule of law, free individuals' exchange and trade, are entrepreneurial, pursue new ideas, innovate and discover (Hayek 1978, Schumpeter 1983, A. Smith 2009, Weber 1976). Markets, or what most sociologists would call capitalism, has created unparalleled wealth (McCloskey 2016).

The division of labor explanation for the sociology-classical liberalism gap would suggest that classical liberal ideas mostly pertain to wealth creation. That is simply not empirically correct. Ideas of individual freedom and individual rights also contribute toward cultures of free speech, equality before the law, meritocracy, toleration of differences in taste, religion, and ideas in a likewise unparallel manner, also in civil society (Berggren and Nilsson 2016, Mill 1982). Freedom seems rather pertinent to sociological interests.

However, sociology's focus on social norms, traditions of groups and collectives, emphasize how norms and traditions interfere with individual freedom of choice in various ways (e.g., Sen 2001). The sociological individual may be formally free but fettered by informal pressures by her peers (Gambetta 2019). Those pressures are partly due to her entanglement with others in her local context; she cares a lot about both their views and well-being. Such complexity, formal and informal constraints, does not deter sociologists from studying norms and traditions. Freedom just does not make it into the sociological imagination, it seems.

Perhaps another reason is that sociology, as a discipline, emerged after the classical liberal era of Smith, Hume, and de Tocqueville. When sociology emerged as a discipline in the late nineteenth century, ideas of communism, socialism, and social-democracy had started to gain ground in Europe. Classical liberal ideas lost influence, partly because those ideas became taken for granted, partly because new generations replaced old. The lack of a classical liberal sociology identity could have historical roots.

Still, if one holds classical liberal ideas of individualism and freedom in high esteem, the dearth of classical liberal and libertarian scholars working on sociological topics suggests important ideas are lost in the field. Sociology is poorer because a whole tradition of ideas is left out of consideration. Likewise, as there are few classical liberal sociologists, classical liberal scholarship lacks sociological insights. These two traditions, classical liberal social thought and academic sociology, need each other.

The editors of the present book are both part of a rare breed of sociologists wedded to classical liberal ideas. We believe there is merit to tell of an untold story of classical liberal sociology. The purpose is to show how really great classical liberal thinkers, such as Smith, de Tocqueville, and Hayek coupled individualism and freedom with social sensibilities in a fashion that is all but lost in contemporary scholarship. Scholars today think they need to choose between utilitarian individualism and constructivist collectivism, while the proto-sociologists of the classical liberal tradition upheld individualism and freedom without discounting the importance of social context. In the section below, such a story is told. It is told as a sketch fitting an introductory chapter of an edited volume, putting forward some key points and leaving behind any aspiration to do justice to the rich classical liberal tradition.

THE LOST HERITAGE OF CLASSICAL LIBERALISM IN SOCIOLOGY

Classical liberalism may be an unclaimed parcel in the sociological inventory, but that doesn't mean that current scholars need to develop their ideas *ex nihilo*. Long before sociology was established as an academic discipline, sociological topics were studied by classical liberal scholars. For instance, in Adam Smith's *Theory of Moral Sentiments* (TMS) (A. Smith 1982), written before *The Wealth of Nations*, Smith presented moral sentiments as deeply social facts. Key concepts such as "the impartial spectator" or "the man within the breast," describe a man (yes, Smith talks of Man) who naturally relates to "others" in judging himself and his social actions. Other sociologically pertinent concepts in TMS are sympathy and fellow feeling, and Smith shows a deep understanding of how humans both care for themselves as well as for others. Moral sentiments, Smith argues, come naturally to us, an insight lately caught on in Behavioral economics (Ashraf et al. 2005). In TMS, Smith illustrates the biases and imbalances of moral reasoning by imagining a man faced with the choice of cutting off his pinky to prevent an earthquake in China. The agony the man faces in sacrificing his pinky, although realizing it is a small sacrifice and the right thing to do, illustrate human's deep self-interestedness, but also how natural is our inclination to care for others well-being (Smith 1982, 136–137), even if these others happen to be Chinese.

Smith's account of how sympathy becomes weaker over social distance does not imply a lack of moral sentiment. Rather, it teaches us a lesson about the real world that more sociologists should take to heart, which is that social relations are often local and contextualized. As you are part of society, and the part you know best, caring for yourself is virtuous. Your next duty is caring for your family, since after yourself the people you know best are close to you, etc. Your moral responsibilities as well as your feelings of sympathy extend outwards but diminish with distance. To Smith, there is no conflict between self-interest and fellow-feeling. As a matter of fact, Smith's "local duties first" make sense, as social affairs have well-known knowledge problems (Hayek 1945).

Similarly, Alexis de Tocqueville's in *Democracy in America* found what he termed enlightened individualism—Americans caring for themselves, and their families, but also expanding efforts in the local communities (Tocqueville 2000, 500–503). The democratic freedom in the new world not only made industrious men, it also created virtuous men. Americans belonged to prospering civil societies where community members came together to build schools and churches. Smith and Tocqueville are two examples of classical liberal thinkers who understood that freedom under the rule of law fosters not only individualism, but also responsibility and dignity (e.g.. Klein 1997). For these early classical liberals, individuals were meant to be respected so long as they did not harm others. They believed that properly functioning communities and markets would cultivate virtues that would mitigate humanity's selfish tendencies.

There are other classical liberal thinkers whose ideas about individualism and freedom deserve to be better known by sociologists. Mary Wollstonecraft's individualist feminism, for instance, argued in 1792 that women were socialized into the role of the weaker sex by existing social expectations. She argued that if women were free and had the same rights and duties as men, they would be shown to have the same reasoning skills as men (Wollstonecraft 2004). Wollstonecraft insisted in the 1700s that women granted freedom in the shape of individual rights would develop into strong individuals free and able to pursue their own way of life. Wollstonecraft's vision contrasts rather sharply with contemporary sociological feminists who tend to think women need special government protections to increase her ability to be free. Ideas of the weaker sex seem to be reviving, and perhaps it is time to rediscover the merit of Wollstonecraft's insistence on freedom and equal rights in gender relations.[2]

The section above inferred sociological themes in reading seminal classical liberal texts. These classics had a following when sociology was formed, and there are scholars who self-identify as sociologists who were also classical liberals. One of the earliest was Herbert Spencer. Spencer was a best-selling author and a widely known writer and intellectual of his time. Spencer was a staunch defender of classical liberal ideas, most famously expressed in *The Man versus the State* (Spencer 1982). Spencer's provocative language, such as describing "deserving and undeserving poor," will not pass unnoticed on today's campus. However, Spencer was a classical liberal, early in exploring intuitions on social evolution. Like most early sociologists, Spencer's sociology was occupied with societal transformation and social solidarity. Spencer's theory stresses how population growth increased competition, competition increased societal division of labor and economic exchange. Division of labor and exchange in turn fostered organic solidarity.

These themes are familiar to most sociologists but attributed mostly to Durkheim (1997). Indeed, Durkheim wrote the Division of Labor primarily to argue with Spencer's sociology (Perrin 1995). Turner (1984) described *The Division of Labor* as "Durkheim's very noisy conversation with Spencer" (p. 21). Durkheim shaped how sociologists received Spencer, making him "the forgotten theoretical giant" (Turner 1981, see also Turner 1985). In retrospect, Spencer's sociology could be thought of as rational choice sociology (Hedström and Stern 2008, 2017). In terms of legacy, Durkheim saw Spencer as the sociological descendant of Adam Smith and J. S. Mill (Turner 1984, 30).

Turning to the United States, classical liberal sociology emerged with William Graham Sumner, who wrote on class, mores, and folkways (Sumner 1960, 1925). Sumner was a proponent of laissez-faire government policy, spontaneous order, and understood that liberal society is "unnatural" to human beings (Hayek 1976). Both Spencer and Sumner warned against the unintended consequences of enforcing collectivist instincts by government action. It seems both thinkers held what today would be viewed as modern evolutionary thinking, where collectivist instinct are part of our heritage from the band. Hayek offered a similar argument when writing about how the yearning for social justice was atavistic (Hayek 1976, 1978, 1979) and Klein (2005) argued that a collectivist atavism help us understand why people turn to governments as enforcers of "the people."

Today, Spencer and Sumner are both tainted by the accusation of social Darwinism made by Hofstadter (1965). Later scholarship has exonerated them from the charge as they themselves did in fact not advocate "the law of the jungle," to human society (Kaye 1997, pp. 33–34). In his book, Hofstadter is highly critical toward Spencer's and Sumner's views on limited government, the merits of individualism and competition but fails to see that endorsing such views is not necessarily grounded on Darwinian premises (Wilson 1989). As a matter of fact, it seems Hofstadter used the epithet to discredit essential classical liberal ideas (Leonard 2009).

Sometimes argued to have been the first woman sociologist (Hoecker-Drysdale 1992), Harriet Martineau (1802–1876) is another example of an early sociologist who had strong classical liberal instincts. Active as a journalist and writer, she popularized political economy in *Illustrations of Political Economy* (1832), as well as wrote a condensed first English translation of August Comte (Postlethwaite 1989). Most relevant for the present text is that Martineau viewed prosperity as emerging from a harmonious blending of Labour and Capital, which later scholars have framed as a Smithian argument. In fact, she wrote that one of her goals as a writer was to present Smith's ideas for a lay audience:

She praised Smith's *Wealth of Nations*, "a book whose excellence is marvellous when all the circumstances are considered," but while she found the work "engaging [for] the learned," it was neither "fitted nor designed to teach the science to the great mass of the people." Political economy lacked the practical lessons to illustrate these principles for the masses, to explicate "the science in a familiar, practical form" (Martineau 1832: xi).

Her book, *How to Observe Morals and Manners* (Martineau 1838), is considered an early sociological treatise on methods. To observe morals and manners, according to Martineau, required neutral observations of social behavior across societies. Her approach to morals and manners was to understand, not judge, and it is not farfetched to think that her classical liberal bearings, grounded in freedom and individualism, contributed to make her a remarkable sociologist of the time. Writing on what to observe during travels with regard to freedom, she writes on the importance of markets:

> An observing traveler has said, "To judge at once of a nation, we have only to throw our eyes on the markets and the fields. If the markets are well supplied, the fields well cultivated, all is right. If otherwise, we may say, and say truly, these people are barbarous and oppressed." This, though a rather sweeping judgment, is founded in truth, and is well worthy of being borne in mind in traveling. (Martineau 1838: 154)

Martineau also offered an idea that is close to the heart of this volume, freedom is a cultural process: "It is obvious enough that the Idea of Liberty, which can originate only in the intercourse of many minds, as the liberty itself can be wrought out only by the labours of many united hands, is not to be looked for where the people live apart, and are destitute of any knowledge of the interests and desires of the community at large" (Ibid. 190).

She did not have an overly rigid notion of morality and recognized many facets of moral worth, but seemed to recognize that "liberality" could be expressed in many ways.

> For such a one it may be sufficient to bear about the general notions that lying, thieving, idleness, and licentiousness are bad; and that truth, honesty, industry, and sobriety are good; and for common purposes, such an one may be trusted to pronounce what is industry and what idleness; what is licentiousness and what sobriety. But vague notions, home prepossessions, even on these great points of morals, are not sufficient, in the eyes of an enlightened traveller, to warrant decisions on the moral state of nations who are reared under a wide diversity of circumstances. The true liberality which alone is worthy to contemplate all the nations of the earth, does not draw a broad line through the midst of human conduct, declaring all that falls on the one side vice, and all on the other virtue; such a liberality knows that actions and habits do not always carry their moral impress visibly to all eyes, and that the character of very many must be determined by a cautious application of a few deep principles. (Ibid. 17–18)

On morals, then, Martineau could be said to be a relativist. She was also an abolitionist, an atheist, and a feminist (Hoecker-Drysdale 1992; Postlethwaite 1989).

Martineau, Spencer, and Sumner share an intellectual tradition with Smith and de Tocqueville, but they are also names that we count among the founders of sociology. Another famous founder of sociology who is seldom heralded as a classical liberal thinker is Max Weber. Weber self-identified as a liberal in his party politics. His most famous book *The Protestant Ethic and the Spirit of Capitalism* (Weber 1976) is thought by some scholars to be a silent critique of Marx (Bendix 1998). The protestant ethic showcases how sociological notions of ideas and values (spirit) add to understanding of how a new economic order (capitalism) emerged. Weber argued that modern markets may depend on contracts, ownership, and the rule of law, but unique to Western societies was a (Christian/Calvinist) culture where earning money and being entrepreneurial was seen as legitimate. Weberian theorizing is mainstream in sociology, and his influence on yet another classical liberal sociologist, Edward Shils, is well known. Shils saw freedom as a key feature of modern society, and as such not at all natural to man (Shils 1997). According to Shils, to preserve freedom, as well as civil society, you need the virtue of civility. The virtue of civility means to practice care for the common good in social affairs, to avoid partisanship, and to consider society as a whole.

Much like de Tocqueville and Smith, Shilsian sociology builds on a concept of individual freedom without reducing individualism to selfishness. In the United States of the 2020s, with rampant political polarization, and reductions in social trust, the virtue of civility is no longer obvious in public discourse. Rather, we see a public discourse where opponents are seen and described as malevolent, and where common goods are reduced to members of one's ingroup. The erosion of liberal democratic values can be one consequence. After all, when the legitimacy of an institution is disparaged at the dinner table, or in church pews, there is a risk of it being challenged or even disbanded. In his seminal *Folkways*, sociologist William Graham Sumner (Sumner 1960) noted that policies that directly contradict folk understandings of the world are subject to resistance and failure.

The sociological ideas created by classical liberals would be seen by many as relevant to contemporary sociology. These ideas all point to the importance of the social, whether we call it culture, virtues, norms, mores, or ideology. In their own ways, classical liberals of the past and more recent sympathetic sociologists were all interested in how these social factors relate to individual autonomy and the ability to support a functional and beneficial open society.

THE DISCIPLINE OF DISCONTENT

To gain a deeper understanding of why these ideas have not found an audience in sociology, we consider the history of the field. On the European continent, sociology emerged side by side with the new social order. Thinkers like Marx, Tönnies, Simmel, Weber, and Durkheim witnessed social disorganization, anomie, alienation, and a loss of both social order and community in the wake of industrialization and urbanization. For this reason, sociology often understands itself as a discipline of critique and unmasking the sources of inequality and power.

Among these early sociologists, witnessing the evolution of traditional to modern societies meant witnessing increases in individual freedom and well-being but also eroding social norms and loss of community. As Storr explains, the theme of something lost is present in Hayek: For Hayek, there are tremendous differences between the sorts of interactions that occur within the extended order of the market and within the bands which comprise community. Habits of solidarity (e.g., living communally and sharing all that is produced equally), Hayek (1979, 162) writes, "had to be shed . . . to make the transition to the market economy and the open society possible." For Hayek, the evolution of modern markets was conditioned on the transition from personal exchange to impersonal exchange. (Storr 2010, 203).

In contrast to Spencer and Sumner, the continental thinkers held a more critical view of the new social order. Social problems became main topics, and, since the discipline emerged in liberal democracies, capitalism became the target for criticism. Then came the radical 1960–1970s, a period where the discipline flourished and new faculty brought in new ideas. Parsons's functionalist consensus theory became unfashionable, and Marxist conflict theory took over. Suddenly, capitalism came to be seen as the main source of social problems. Western liberal democratic societies came to be seen as oppressive, with rampant social problems.

This brief section above is a grave simplification and omits important nuances. The goal, however, is merely to point out that sociology as a discipline drastically increased the focus on topics such as poverty, inequality, and repression. Lost in that development was an appreciation of classical liberal ideas that described how societies generate wealth, promote individual well-being, and allow people to create beneficent institutions. As a consequence, freedom of speech and religion, property rights, and individualism as positive contributions to humankind are rarely treated. One can say that they are devalued. Likewise, voluntarism, or freedom from coercion by state intervention, is rarely a part of the sociological imagination.

IMAGINING THE SOCIOLOGICAL TOOLKIT FOR FREEDOM

If one buys the argument that there is a lamentable and unnecessary gap between classical liberalism and sociology, then what does the bridge look like? What ideas might be used to guide this discussion? No single author, or group of authors, could exhaust the possibilities and each author in this volume has their own answer. In this introduction, we map some of the terrain and offer ideas about how sociological theory can be used to enrich freedom-oriented social thought.

The Coercion-Freedom Axis: The starting point might be translating the core normative argument about the value of freedom into an empirical description of the social world. Human beings experience different levels of constraint that are imposed by the society to which they belong and we call this variation the coercion-freedom axis. Societies, or communities, that have institutions and social practices that are tolerant, promote well-being, and facilitate individual autonomy might be deemed "liberal societies," while societies that impose great constraints and harms on their members might be deemed "illiberal."

Classically liberal sociology would start by asking for an empirical description of liberal societies and then ask about the cultural or institutional factors that support open norms. For example, a sociologist interested in political dissidence would ask about the types of open critiques that are allowed by a government and then ask about the conditions that are associated with tolerance of political dissent. In this way, classical liberal sociology would use Weberian historical sociology as a template. Not only can we ask if certain religious beliefs facilitate capital accumulation, we can also ask how cultural factors, such as religions, inform and enable social and economic liberalism.

Conversely, sociologists also study the roots of illiberalism, intolerance and discrimination, the flip side of group belonging, since a We cannot exist

…em. Just like a real human being is other-centered and prone to …e, she is also prone toward outgroup bias. It is part of human nature. …ed point is that some social processes seem to necessitate an erosion …illiberal social practices. In this vein, a number of sociologists have noted that trade requires some degree of trustworthiness. Trade and commerce tears down group barriers, teaching us civility toward strangers. Sociologists such as Durkheim (1997), note that norms of being trustworthy come first. Without norms enforcing a contract, it is only a piece of paper.

If the purpose of classical liberal sociology is to examine the social contexts of openness, tolerance, and voluntary institutions, then what sort of answer might be found in the sociological toolkit? Culture, language, and beliefs are the answer. If cultural sociology has a motto, it is that "ideas matter" and studies shared ideas and how they translate into stable patterns of behavior. Rather than focus exclusively on simple aggregate levels of belief (e.g., what percentage of the population is Protestant), cultural sociology dwells on the social processes that shape collective belief. From this perspective, it is important to know how social interactions generate beliefs, the structure of public attitudes, and the ways that these ideas are "crystallized" into behavioral norms.

Cultural sociology suggests that institutional accounts of culture and freedom might be further developed by considering the larger "cultural environment" in which rules and norms are created (Bail 2014; McLean 2016). The term "cultural environment" denotes a broad range of things and processes. It refers to beliefs themselves, but also to the way in which beliefs are made, remade, categorized, framed, and connected to other beliefs and the individuals and organizations that drive this process. This larger cultural environment is relatively stable but can be affected by the collective action of the actors within the environment.

Second, there are "moves" or strategies that actors pursue within these fields that may, eventually, yield a change in the collective structure of public opinion (Bail 2016; Fligstein et al. 2015). Such actions include creating or challenging group boundaries or boundaries between what is and is not legitimate, introducing new ideas to the "stock of facts," creating rituals around how to address leaders, or how to introduce new members to help socialize people into particular belief systems, and attempting to use discursive strategies to frame ideas or people in particular ways. Such rituals are varied, and include political speeches, cultural performances, and scientific conferences. These practices, and many others, are meant to change what an audience believes to be true and re-orient behavior.

By focusing on the cultural environment and how institutions are "anchored" in this environment (Bourdieu 1975; Foucault 1994; Martin 2003; Wuthnow 1993; cf. Bail 2014), the vocabulary of cultural sociology allows a richer understanding of the relationship between freedom and culture. After all, what a community values, or views, as legitimate impacts the operation of institutions. To take a corporate example, how leadership is practiced at Volvo in Sweden, in contrast to Toyota in Japan, shapes the production of cars. The public's attitudes and beliefs have their own organization, practices, and rituals that are important for understanding how institutions are created and maintained.

Contemporary sociology provides us with a rich vocabulary for describing and understanding various sorts of cultural processes that yield liberal or illiberal communities. First, the idea that societies have a "stock of facts," a collection of things that are deemed to be true through group interactions (Berger and Luckmann 1967). Second, the idea of "symbolic boundary." Third, the idea of the "interaction ritual chain" which are routine gatherings of people where values, beliefs, and attitudes are created and transmitted. Together these three ideas identify "where" and "how" freedom happens.

The Stock of Facts: Communities develop a collection of "facts" that reflect their beliefs about the world. In some cases, this may simply reflect beliefs about the natural world, such as the belief that the sun revolves around the earth (pre-Copernicus) or the earth revolves around the sun (post-Copernicus). In other cases, a fact may reflect a belief about the nature of the social world. For example, scholars of communist societies such as the German Democratic Republic (GDR) have noted that they developed an ideology of perpetual conflict with capitalist nations (Glaeser 2011). Within these societies, there was a widespread belief that a class of capitalists, fascists, and other counter-revolutionary elements was actively undermining their states. This collection of facts within a community represents the "institutionalization" of beliefs (Berger and Luckmann 1967). In other words, social norms, laws, and religions. Over time, a "stock of facts" appears that reflects a community's collective judgment about what is real, important, and valuable.

Symbolic Boundaries: The socially accepted "stock of facts" includes facts about what is appropriate or permissible, which in turn often rests in deeply felt social categories. The anthropologist Mary Douglas (2003) argued that people tend to use categories to understand the world and that institutions, or rules of society, are designed to make sure that people, or things, stay within their categories. People feel outrage or discomfort when boundaries are violated and expend great effort in "policing" symbolic boundaries (e.g., Gamson 1997; Gieryn 1999; Grodal 2018). The nature of these symbolic boundaries in many cases reflects what people think is legitimate or appropriate. Institutional change occurs when people openly dispute social categories and the rules that enforce them (e.g., Mike 2017). The movement for same sex marriage challenged the symbolic boundaries of marriage as a heterosexual identity (Fetner 2008).

It is helpful to compare the cultural sociology approach to institutions with Vernon Smith's (2003) distinction between constructivist and ecological rationality. For Smith (p. 486), a constructivist rationalist "uses reason to deliberately create rules of action, and create human socioeconomic institutions that yield outcomes deemed preferable, given particular circumstances, to those produced by alternative arrangement." In contrast, Smith asserts that ecological rationality:

> uses reason—rational reconstruction—to examine the behavior of individuals based on their experience and folk knowledge, who are 'naïve' in their ability to apply constructivist tools to the decisions they make; to understand the emergent order in human cultures; to discover the possible intelligence embodied in the rules, norms, and institutions of our cultural and biological heritage that are created from human interactions but not by deliberate human design. People follow rules without being able to articulate them, but they can be discovered. (470)

Cultural sociology makes a similar shift in argument. Instead of seeing freedom of action as either a right granted from an authority to an individual (e.g., the government guarantees freedom of speech) or a conscious and direct translation of values (e.g., laws governing speech are liberal because Americans value freedom), the actual institution that governs a particular activity emerges from a decentralized, often "naïve" interactional process where beliefs, social facts, morals, and social boundaries are discussed and reinforced.

The Ritual Chain Process: The sociologist Randall Collins (2005) adds two important elements to Berger and Luckmann's stock of facts. First, the development of a socially shared reality often occurs in fairly routine settings that are interconnected. For example, a church holds weekly services with substantial overlap of participants and content; scientific communities have laboratory meetings or annual conferences filled with ritualistic social practice, where meanings are articulated, negotiated, and enacted.

Second, drawing on Emile Durkheim's ([1915] 1976) analysis of religious ritual as an emotionally charged process, Collins argues that attendance in ritual events triggers strong emotions that align the individual with the broader institution. For example, a graduate student may feel pride when they present a paper at a scientific conference. Then, they are rewarded for continued participation in the scientific community and will thus spend effort in the future to create and maintain scientific practices. Collins's ritual chain theory reminds us that socially derived meaning depends on social structure. For example, "science" consists of decentralized "micro-cultures," scientific practices defined in a collection of interrelated events and communities, such as lab groups, college classes, science journal editorial meetings, and scientific conferences (e.g., Knorr Cetina 1999; Leahey 2008). Ritual chain theory also draws attention to the highly emotional component behind social construction.

Ritual chains can also produce change, as Teles's (2008) study of ideological change in the U.S. courts produced by the Federalist Society describes. Law professors and students founded the Federalist Society, which hosted debates with a conservative focus. These events eventually became focal points for emerging conservative jurisprudence. Judges and professors who attended these events and identified with their cause were then able to transport those ideas to the bench. Formal rituals allow people to assert truth and shape values, rather than just transmit or receive them. While many rituals exist to transmit information and coordinate, many are places of discussion, interaction, and dispute.

Sociological concepts of culture would add to classical liberal thought and could lead to a "warmer" liberalism (contrasting it to "cold" materialism). It would benefit the world if classical liberalism's emphasis on freedom were more closely coupled to social issues of sociologists. Just as ideas of freedom and voluntariness would infuse the sociological imagination with new (well) ideas, sociology would reinvigorate and modernize classic themes from Smith and de Tocqueville. In the end, social science would be richer.

OVERVIEW OF THE CHAPTERS

We have gathered sociologists, criminologists, demographers, and political scientists that care about classical liberal ideas, or are willing to engage their sociological thinking with classical liberal ideas. Not all authors would identify themselves as classical liberals; some embrace these ideas while others openly dispute them or think they belong to a bygone era. What unites them is a belief that the nexus of classical liberalism and sociology is worth exploring and that both sides can gain something.

Chapters sometimes start with classical liberal ideas and discuss sociological topics through the lens; what is seen with regards to class, gender, or race relations when using a different perspective? Sometimes, the chapters work out the intersection of sociology and classical liberalism, exploring where viewpoints conflict and where they align. The chapters also cover standard sociological topics such as class, gender, and race, as well as important fields such as social movements, political sociology, health, toleration, and criminal justice.

Here we give a brief synopsis of each chapter to entice the reader. John Iceland and Eric Silver's chapter delves into the extensive empirical evidence documenting the link between liberalized markets, economic growth, and poverty reduction. On a similar note, Fabio Rojas's chapter on racial inequality argues that economic and social liberalism create the resources needed for the struggle for civil rights. Brandon Rudolph Davis, a political scientist and policy scholar, explores the possibility that many African Americans live under the shadow of a "predatory state," where the criminal justice system impoverishes their lives. Charlotta Stern asks whether individualist feminism might be a sounder foundation for the sociology of gender than more egalitarian forms of feminist social theory. Lauren Hall asks how liberalizing the healthcare system might improve medical outcomes for people in marginalized communities, while Mikayla Novak examines social movements as vehicles for freedom.

Two chapters focus on cultural aspects of classical liberalism. Patrik Aspers's contribution is an exploration of what freedom means in economic sociology, and Jack A. Goldstone, a leading political sociologist, wonders if classical liberalism is a lost ideal, better suited for a previous age. Last but not least, Ilana Redstone's chapter is a thoughtful and personal exploration of what disagreement and debate mean in a free society.

CODA

We end this introduction with two personal notes about this volume. First, we are humbled by our collaborators. When we first formulated the idea for this book, we were concerned that there were not enough sociologists who would be interested in submitting contributions. We were deeply moved when many of our colleagues said they would be delighted to help out. We were impressed once again when we organized a workshop for the contributors and they provided fascinating drafts. The conversation was lively and critical, and everyone responded by revising their manuscripts in response to this conversation. The reader will see the intelligence, thoughtfulness, and care that went into each chapter.

Second, we have a particular vision for success. It is not enough, in our eyes, to have a steady stream of books and journals that focus on a new set of buzzwords like "liberal culture," "viewpoint diversity," or "open institutions." Rather, classical liberal sociology should mirror the open society itself. Multiple frameworks can be applied to this topic and scholars should have sharp debates over the merit of the entire enterprise itself. Classical liberal sociology should be a joyful noise, not a quiet sterile room in the ivory tower of academia. If this modest edited volume can help the discipline of sociology move in that direction, we will consider this undertaking to be a most profitable investment.

REFERENCES

Ashraf, Nava, Colin F. Camerer, and George Loewenstein. 2005. "Adam Smith, Behavioral Economist." *Journal of Economic Perspectives* 19 (3): 131–45.

Bail, Christopher. 2014. "The Cultural Environment: Measuring Culture With Big Data." *Theory and Society* 43 (July).

Bail, Christopher Andrew. 2016. "Combining Natural Language Processing and Network Analysis to Examine How Advocacy Organizations Stimulate Conversation on Social Media." *Proceedings of the National Academy of Sciences* 113 (42): 11823–28.

Bendix, Reinhard. 1998. *Max Weber: An Intellectual Portrait*. New York: Psychology Press.

Berger, Peter L., and Thomas Luckmann. 1967. *The Social Construction of Reality: A Treatise in the Sociology of Knowledge*. New York: Anchor.

Berggren, Niclas, and Therese Nilsson. 2016. "Tolerance in the United States: Does Economic Freedom Transform Racial, Religious, Political and Sexual Attitudes?" *European Journal of Political Economy* 45 (December): 53–70.

Bourdieu, Pierre. 1975. "The Specificity of the Scientific Field and the Social Conditions of the Progress of Reason." *Social Science Information* 14 (6): 19–47.

Burawoy, Michael. 2005. "American Sociological Association Presidential Address: For Public Sociology." *The British Journal of Sociology* 56: 259–94.

Collins, Randall. 2005. *Interaction Ritual Chains*. 2. print., and First paperback print. Princeton Paperbacks. Princeton, NJ: Princeton Univ. Press.

Douglas, Mary. 2003. "Purity and Danger: An Analysis of Concepts of Pollution and Taboo." Routledge & CRC Press. 2003. https://www.routledge.com/Purity-and-Danger-An-Analysis-of-Concepts-of-Pollution-and-Taboo/Douglas/p/book/9780415289955.

Durkheim, Émile. 1915. *The Elementary Forms of the Religious Life: A Study in Religious Sociology*. New York: Macmillan.

———. 1976. *The Elementary Forms of the Religious Life*. 2. ed. London: Allen and Unwin.

———. 1997. *The Division of Labor in Society*. New York: Free Press.

Fetner, Tina. 2008. *How the Religious Right Shaped Lesbian and Gay Activism*. 1st edition. Minneapolis: Univ. of Minnesota Press.

Fligstein, Neil, and Doug McAdam. 2015. *A Theory of Fields*. Oxford, New York: Oxford University Press.

Foucault, Michel. 1994. *The Order of Things: An Archaeology of the Human Sciences*. Reissue edition. New York NY: Vintage.

Gambetta, Diego. 2019. *Were They Pushed or Did They Jump?: Individual Decision Mechanisms in Education*. Routledge.

Gamson, Joshua. 1997. "Messages of Exclusion: Gender, Movements, and Symbolic Boundaries." *Gender & Society* 11 (2): 178–99.

Gieryn, Thomas F. 1999. *Cultural Boundaries of Science: Credibility on the Line*. Chicago: University of Chicago Press.

Glaeser, Andreas. 2011. *Political Epistemics: The Secret Police, the Opposition, and the End of East German Socialism.* Chicago Studies in Practices of Meaning. Chicago: University of Chicago Press.

Grodal, Stine. 2018. "Field Expansion and Contraction: How Communities Shape Social and Symbolic Boundaries." *Administrative Science Quarterly* 63 (4): 783–818.

Hayek, Friedrich A. von. 1945. "The Use of Knowledge in Society." *The American Economic Review* 35 (4): 519–30.

———. 1976. *Law, Legislation and Liberty: A New Statement of the Liberal Principles of Justice and Political Economy. Vol. 2, The Mirage of Social Justice*. London: Routledge.

———. 1978. *New Studies in Philosophy, Politics, Economics and the History of Ideas*. Chicago: University of Chicago Press.

———. 1979. *Law, Legislation and Liberty: A New Statement of the Liberal Principles of Justice and Political Economy. Vol. 3 The Political Order of a Free People.* London: Routledge.

Hedström, Peter, and Charlotta Stern. 2008. "Rational Choice and Sociology." In *The New Palgrave Dictionary of Economics*, 2nd ed.

———. 2017. "Rational Choice Theory." In *The Wiley-Blackwell Encyclopedia of Social Theory*, 1–7. John Wiley & Sons, Ltd.

Hoecker-Drysdale, Susan. 1992. *Harriet Martineau, First Woman Sociologist.* Berg Women's Series, 99-0576310-4. Oxford [England]; Berg.

Hofstadter, Richard. 1965. *Social Darwinism in American Thought*. Beacon Paperback, 99-0102495-1. Boston: Beacon Press.

Illustrations of Political Economy (3rd ed) in 9 vols. (London: Charles Fox, 1832).

Kaye, Howard L. 1997. *The Social Meaning of Modern Biology: From Social Darwinism to Sociobiology.* New Brunswick, N.J.: Transaction Publishers.

Klein, Daniel B. 1997. "Liberty, Dignity, and Responsibility." *Independent Review* 1 (3): 325.

Klein, Daniel B. 2005. "The People's Romance: Why People Love Government (as Much as They Do)." *The Independent Review* 10 (1): 5–37.

Klein, Daniel B. and Charlotta Stern. 2004. "Democrats and republicans in anthropology and sociology: How do they differ on public policy issues?" *American Sociologist*, 35, 79–86

Knorr Cetina, Karin. 1999. *Epistemic Cultures: How the Sciences Make Knowledge*. Cambridge, MA: Harvard University Press.

Leahey, Erin. 2008. "Methodological Memes and Mores: Toward a Sociology of Social Research." *Annual Review of Sociology* 34 (June).

Leonard, Thomas C. 2009. "Origins of the Myth of Social Darwinism: The Ambiguous Legacy of Richard Hofstadter's Social Darwinism in American Thought." *Journal of Economic Behavior & Organization* 71 (1): 37–51.

Martin, John Levi. 2003. "What is Field Theory?" *American Journal of Sociology* 109 (1): 1–49.

Martineau, Harriet. 1832. *Illustrations of Political Economy. No.1. Life in the Wilds. A Tale.* Philadelphia: Littell.

———. 1838. *How to Observe Morals and Manners*. London: Charles Knight & Co.
McCloskey, Deirdre N. 2016. *Bourgeois Equality: How Ideas, Not Capital or Institutions, Enriched the World*. Chicago: The University of Chicago Press.
McLean, Paul. 2016. *Culture in Networks*. John Wiley & Sons.
Mike, Károly. 2017. "The Intellectual Orders of a Market Economy." *Journal of Institutional Economics* 13 (4): 899–915.
Mill, John Stuart. 1982. *On Liberty*. Edited by Gertrude Himmelfarb. Harmondsworth: Penguin.
Moore, Wendy Leo and Joyce M. Bell. 2019. "The Limits of Community: Deconstructing the White Framing of Racist Speech in Universities." *American Behavioral Scientist*, 63(13), 1760–1775
Perrin, Robert G. 1995. "Émile Durkheim's 'Division of Labor' and the Shadow of Herbert Spencer." *The Sociological Quarterly* 36 (4): 791–808.
Postlethwaite, Diana. 1989. "Mothering and Mesmerism in the Life of Harriet Martineau." *Signs: Journal of Women in Culture and Society* 14 (3): 583–609.
Schumpeter, Joseph Alois. 1983. *The Theory of Economic Development: An Inquiry into Profits, Capital, Credit, Interest, and the Business Cycle*. Edited by John E. Elliott. Translated by Redvers Opie. New Brunswick, (U.S.A.): Transaction Publishers.
Sen, Amartya. 2001. *Development as Freedom*. Oxford: Oxford University Press.
Shields, Jon A., and Joshua M. Dunn. 2016. *Passing on the Right: Conservative Professors in the Progressive University*. New York: Oxford University Press.
Shils, Edward. 1997. *The Virtue of Civility*. Indianapolis, IN: Liberty Fund Inc.
Smith, Adam. 1982. The Theory of Moral Sentiments. Edited by D. D. Raphael and A. L. Macfie. *The Glasgow Edition of the Works and Correspondence of Adam Smith 1*. Indianapolis: Liberty Classics.
———. 2009. *The Glasgow Edition of the Works and Correspondence of Adam Smith. 2 1: An Inquiry into the Nature and Causes of the Wealth of Nations / Adam Smith.* General Editors R. H. Campbell. Edited by R. H. Campbell. 11. print. Indianapolis: Liberty Fund.
Smith, Vernon L. 2003. "Constructivist and Ecological Rationality in Economics." *American Economic Review* 93 (3): 465–508.
Spencer, Herbert. 1981. *The Man versus the State, with Six Essays on Government, Society and Freedom*, ed. Eric Mack, introduction by Albert Jay Nock. Indianapolis: LibertyClassics.
Storr, Virgil Henry. 2010. "The Social Construction of the Market." *Society* 47 (3): 200–206.
Sumner, William Graham. 1925. *What Social Classes Owe to Each Other*. New Haven, London.
Sumner, William Graham. 1960. *Folkways: A Study of the Sociological Importance of Usages, Manners, Customs, Mores and Morals*. Mentor Books. New York: New American library.
Teles, Steven Michael. 2008. *The Rise of the Conservative Legal Movement: The Battle for Control of the Law*. 2. Dr. Princeton Studies in American Politics

Historical, International and Comparative Perspectives. Princeton, NJ: Princeton Univ. Press.
Tocqueville, Alexis de. 2000. *Democracy in America*. Edited by Harvey C. Mansfield and Delba Winthrop. Chicago: University of Chicago Press.
Turner, Jonathan H. 1981. "The Forgotton Theoretical Giant: Herbert Spencer's Models and Principles." *Revue Européenne Des Sciences Sociales* 19 (59): 79–98.
———. 1984. "Durkheim's and Spencer's Principles of Social Organization: A Theoretical Note." *Sociological Perspectives* 27 (1): 21–31.
———. 1985. *Herbert Spencer: A Renewed Appreciation. Masters of Social Theory*, Beverly Hills: SAGE.
Weber, Max. 1976. *The Protestant Ethic and the Spirit of Capitalism*. Translated by Talcott Parsons. London: Allen & Unwin.
Wilson, R. Jackson. 1989. *Darwinism and the American Intellectual: An Anthology*. 2nd edition. Chicago: Dorsey Press.
Wollstonecraft, Mary. 2004. *A Vindication of the Rights of Woman*. London; New York: Penguin Books.
Wuthnow, Robert. 1993. *Communities of Discourse: Ideology and Social Structure in the Reformation, the Enlightenment, and European Socialism*. Cambridge, MA: Harvard University Press.

NOTES

1. We gratefully acknowledge funding from the Templeton Foundation and the Institute for Humane Studies (grant no. IHS016527). Also, IHS staffers Aaron Ross Powell, Maria Rogacheva, and Joanna McCool helped organize the workshop which brought all of the contributing authors together in Arlington for a wonderful weekend of work and good company. Also, a warm thank you to Bill Glod who read and commented on all chapters with good insights and suggestions. Portions of this chapter were initially presented at the 2019 Sociality and Austrian Economics workshop sponsored by the Free Market Institute at Texas Tech University. We thank Daniel D'Amico, Adam Martin, and Daniel Bromley for their supportive comments and constructive criticisms.

2. Today, the weakness of women is not stated in terms of their feeble minds, but their victimhood under patriarchal burdens that require government intervention to be resolved.

Chapter 1

Does Economic Liberalism Reduce Poverty?

John Iceland and Eric Silver

A common sociological critique of capitalism is that it increases poverty and income inequality. Karl Marx, one of the early and most influential critics of capitalism, argued that capitalists exploit their workers by pocketing the "surplus value" generated by their work.[1] He predicted that the working class would become increasingly impoverished and alienated under capitalism, which would spur class consciousness that would eventually lead to the overthrow of the capitalist system and the establishment of an egalitarian, classless society (Marx and Engels 2015). In sociology, the Marxist understanding of inequality gained popularity into the twentieth century, especially under the broader umbrella of what has been termed *conflict theory*, which rose in prominence in the late 1950s and 1960s (Turner, Beeghley, and Powers 2012). Conflict theory describes how interest groups mobilize and compete for scarce resources (Collins 1993). Conflict theory, and related theories that center conflict between those with and without power (such as critical theory and strands of feminist theory), remains an important orienting theoretical approach in sociology, though often extended beyond the economic realm to areas such as a race and gender (Ritzer and Stepnisky 2018).

Classical liberalism offers a fundamentally different view of markets, and by extension poverty and inequality, than conflict theory. The orienting principle of economic liberalism is the *freedom* of individuals to invent, create, accumulate, and engage in voluntary trade with others (Friedman 1962). While capitalism obviously involves competition between economic actors seeking customers for their products and services, it also relies heavily on *cooperation* between buyers and sellers. Sellers succeed only if they can empathize with and meet the needs of potential buyers. As a result, trade typically is mutually beneficial: buyers receive the goods and services they desire, and sellers receive remuneration that they can use to consume other goods and services or to further invest in their business. These activities reinforce civil society and individual autonomy, thereby contributing to a democratic political order (Novak 2018). In advanced economies with an extensive division of labor, individuals ideally work in occupations of their choosing that are commensurate with their interests or talents, rather than, say, occupations designated to them by birth or assignment by those in power.

A key distinction between conflict theories and economic liberalism is that while the former view economic transactions in capitalist systems—especially those between employers and employees—as fundamentally exploitative in a zero-sum competition for power, the latter sees the economic system as increasing the aggregate well-being of all involved. In other words, while conflict theory focuses on the unequal distribution of economic rewards—or distribution of the slices of the economic pie—economic liberalism highlights the overall growth of the pie under a system of free economic exchange.

In the rest of this chapter we briefly describe the basic tenets of economic liberalism, outline its main critiques with regard to its effect on poverty and inequality, examine overall trends in economic well-being, discuss how supporters of economic liberalism address the critiques, and conclude with observations of how further consideration of economic liberalism in sociology could enhance our understanding of poverty and inequality.

WHAT IS ECONOMIC LIBERALISM?

Free markets and free people are the cornerstone of economic liberalism (Buchanan 2000). Free markets are dynamic, unplanned, and unpredictable, and are shaped by constant input from millions of individuals, each with their own goals and values. Prices, which emerge spontaneously, reflect the going rate at which people are willing to exchange some items for others. In free markets, prices also reflect scarcity, such that increasing prices show where demand for a good or service is outstripping its supply. This induces suppliers to produce more of this good or service. If prices fall, this indicates that supply is outstripping demand, which leads suppliers to cut back on production. Free markets thus efficiently coordinate exchange and create value for participants (Butler 2015).

Economic liberalism is grounded in predictable rules of behavior among participants. Individuals are motivated by self-interest and profit, but activity is regulated by factors such as competition, contracts, property rights, and justice. Property rights are critical because they allow individuals to exchange items they own for ones they seek. Property rights also permit individuals to build capital—such as by investing in tools and equipment—to produce more and better goods without worrying that their investments or wealth will be confiscated by those with more power. It also generates a division of labor as people specialize in areas where they may have a comparative advantage, which further increases economic efficiency, productivity, and growth (A. Smith 2008). Free competition is necessary for people to provide goods and services at a price and quantity that reflects their demand. One of the functions of the state is to uphold these rules so that markets continue functioning in a beneficial way (Butler 2015).

Adam Smith described how markets generate prosperity in his 1776 book, *Wealth of Nations* (2008), and his classical economic liberal ideas (as we now refer to them) swept through Europe in the mid-nineteenth century. While economic liberalism was in retreat in the early decades of the twentieth century, especially during the ruinous Great Depression in the 1930s, it resurged thereafter, championed by influential economists such as Friedrich von Hayek and Milton Friedman in the 1940s, 1950s, and 1960s, and later by political leaders, including Ronald Reagan and Margaret Thatcher, in the 1970s and 1980s (Helleiner 2003; Birch 2015; Hayek 1960; Friedman 1962). The increase in income inequality in many countries in recent decades has led to calls for another retreat from economic liberalism and for the adoption of socialism, or one of its variants, such as "democratic socialism" (Piketty 2021).

CRITIQUES: HOW ECONOMIC LIBERALISM PRODUCES POVERTY

Critics argue that economic liberalism produces poverty in several ways. First, economic liberalism empowers businesses at the expense of workers. Second, it generally seeks to minimize government regulation to maximize freedom of commerce, which undermines support for a strong welfare safety net to reduce poverty. Third, economic liberalism produces economic inequality, such that those at the low end of the income spectrum suffer deprivation. We briefly review each of these arguments in turn.

The first critique, that economic liberalism confers power to exploitative business interests, was the one highlighted by Marx and it continues to be a common criticism today. Matthew Desmond, for instance, argues that tenant exploitation by landlords in neighborhoods with a high concentration of poor people and African Americans contributes to evictions and homelessness (Desmond 2016; Desmond and Wilmers 2019). Similarly, in a cross-national analysis of poverty, Brady et al. (2009: 277) conclude that one fundamental cause of poverty is that "Business, owners and managers have far more power because they control the means of production and thus the delivery of economic resources to the population. Ultimately, the default organization of markets becomes favorable for business, which triggers the exploitation of workers and subsequent economic insecurity in the broader population." A variant of this critique is what's known as "racialized capitalism," where business interests in the U.S. historically exploited African Americans—such as through slavery and, later, low wages or charging exorbitantly high rents—to increase their profits (Desmond 2023).

Thus, critics of economic liberalism, or what is sometimes pejoratively called "neoliberalism,"[2] argue that free markets legitimize business power. That is, economic liberalism fosters class- (and race-) based exploitation that benefits owners of capital at the expense of their workers and consumers. Those with economic clout are able to enact rules and regulations that serve their interests, ranging from the provision of self-serving tax breaks, to the discharge of toxic waste in low-income areas far away from where they themselves live, to the design of criminal sentencing policy that softens penalties for white-collar offenders (Barry 2005; Nkansah-Amankra, Agbanu, and Miller 2013). This critique of economic liberalism has been applied to the international dynamics of capitalism as well, where businesses of the imperial west are criticized for having exploited the labor and resources of less developed countries at the expense of those countries and their people (Wallerstein 1979).

A second critique of economic liberalism is that its emphasis on free markets and small government undermines the scope and effectiveness of the welfare state in reducing poverty. One of the foundations of economic liberalism is that individuals are rational actors who are responsible for securing their own well-being. Implicitly, then, according to critics, the poor are often blamed for their poverty. As Feldman (2019: 342) argues, "[N]eoliberalism constructs the poor, especially women, as deficient and immoral individuals who do not take full responsibility for their own fate. For example, the figure of the welfare queen, which identifies African-American mothers as cheats and delegitimizes welfare use by them, has become a cultural icon of the neoliberal era" (see also Gustafson, 2012; Schram, 2015). This argument has merit in that those who favor economic liberalism generally don't favor generous welfare programs, especially if they are seen as disincentivizing work (Murray 1984; Rachidi and Doar 2019). Critics of economic liberalism thus worry that weak safety nets, especially those that require work to access benefits, hurt the most disadvantaged—including those who can't work—thereby increasing poverty and exacerbating economic and racial inequality (Edin & Shaefer, 2015; Nkansah-Amankra et al. 2013). According to this view, the neoliberal welfare state is considered paternalistic (for making aid conditional on work) and punitive (for punishing those who can't work), and often criticized for excluding "undeserving" poor families of color from attaining economic wellbeing (Soss, Fording, and Schram 2011; Morgen and Maskovsky 2003). Following this logic, Desmond (2018) argues, there is no such thing as the "undeserving" poor and that "[w]e need a new language for talking about poverty. 'Nobody who works should be poor,' we say. That's not good enough. Nobody in America should be poor, period."

A third critique of economic liberalism is that it inevitably creates high levels of wealth and income inequality (Piketty 2014; Jacobs and Dirlam 2016; Kollmeyer 2018; Volscho 2007). Inequality may contribute directly to the suffering associated with poverty by reducing the income of those at the bottom of the income distribution in absolute terms, or indirectly by increasing their sense of deprivation relative to others who have more. Those who endorse using relative poverty measures, where people below some fraction of the national median household income are categorized as poor, argue that poverty is relative to a society's existing level of economic development. People with significantly fewer resources than others, even if they are physically able to survive or even thrive, may nonetheless be unable to participate adequately in social organizations and networks (Sen 1999; Townsend 1993). This criticism, too, has merit in that those who favor economic liberalism are generally more concerned with absolute deprivation than with relative deprivation.

These critiques of economic liberalism have influenced many people in the United States to support socialist ideals, especially in recent years. Bernie Sanders, a self-described democratic socialist, was the runner-up in the Democratic Party's presidential primary in 2016 and 2020. Likewise, membership in the Democratic Socialists of America spiked from just a few thousand in 2016 to close to 100,000 in 2021, and several new magazines with growing readerships, such as *Jacobin* and *Current Affairs,* are now devoted to promoting socialist ideas and policies (Kenworthy 2022).

So is this indictment of economic liberalism justified? Is the liberal economic system responsible for high levels of poverty and inequality in the United States and abroad? We argue that while economic inequality is a feature of economic liberalism and an issue that warrants attention and a policy response, a central problem with many critiques is that they overlook the fact that the advent and spread of economic liberalism has coincided with dramatic increases in standards of living, not only in the United States and the European Union, but globally. While critics focus on the uneven distribution of resources between the powerful and the powerless, they too often overlook the facts that economic liberalism has fostered the development of more wealth that any other known system, and that it does not inherently produce more inequality than other known systems. Economic growth generated by economic liberalism has benefited a vast majority of people, not only through the monetary resources they increasingly have at their disposal, but also in the form of longer, healthier, and often happier lives.

GENERAL TRENDS IN WELL-BEING

Several economic trends support the notion that economic liberalism increases prosperity. To begin with, figure 1.1 shows the trend in the U.S. gross domestic product (GDP) per capita, a common measure of economic productivity (U.S. Bureau of Economic Analysis 2022). The figure shows that GDP per capita grew from $14,128 in 1947 to $58,478 in 2021 (in 2012 dollars), despite drops during economic recessions, such as in the early 1980s and late 2000s. Data before 1947 are not available from the U.S. Bureau of Economic Analysis, but other estimates indicate that U.S. GDP per capita also increased considerably over the nineteenth and early twentieth centuries, from about $1,257 in 1820 to $2,445 in 1870 to $5,301 in 1913 (in constant $1990) (Maddison 2001).

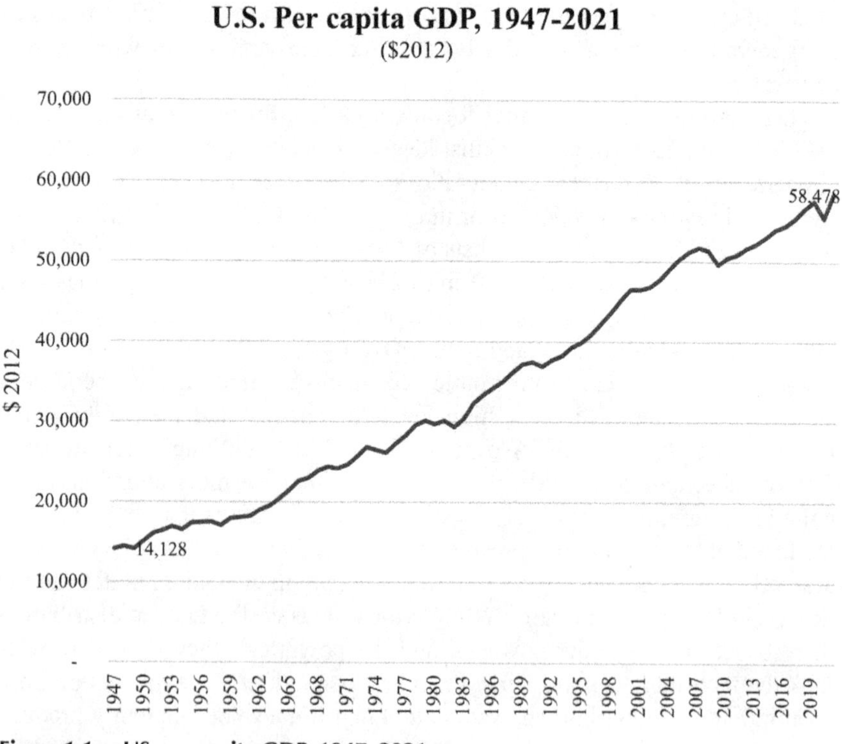

Figure 1.1. US per capita GDP, 1947–2021.
US Bureau of Economic Analysis 2022

GDP per capita is just one measure of living standards, and any single measure is bound to have limitations. But regardless of how it's measured, the data show that living standards in the United States have increased dramatically when measured over a long period of time. Median household incomes have increased from $50,803 in 1967 to $70,784 in 2021 (in constant $2021) (U.S. Census Bureau 2020c). The official poverty rate decline from 22.4 percent in 1959 to 11.4 percent in 2020 (U.S. Census Bureau 2020a). Using an arguably more refined poverty measure than the official one that more fully considers both the cost of economic necessities and the resources households have to meet them (often referred to as the "supplemental" poverty measure), there's an even more pronounced decline (Center on Poverty & Social Policy 2021). Notably, these declines in poverty have occurred across a wide variety of groups, with the decline in poverty and material hardship (such as living in dilapidated housing) among blacks and Hispanics exceeding the decline observed among whites, though poverty and hardship remain considerably higher among the former two groups (Iceland 2019; Baker et al. 2021; Iceland and Sakamoto 2022). This decline in poverty occurred during the period when neoliberalism was blamed by some critics for impoverishing families of color—a claim not consistent with the available evidence (Soss, Fording, and Schram 2011; Morgen and Maskovsky 2003).

Moreover, we have many conveniences today that were unheard of throughout most of the nineteenth century, such as indoor plumbing, electric lighting, cars, airplanes, and modern forms of communication, including perhaps the most impactful consumer items of the early twenty-first century, the personal computer and the smart phone. Our lives have been transformed not just by the proliferation of consumer goods and services, but also by improved health, morbidity, and life expectancy. Shortly after the nation's founding in 1789 life expectancy at birth was 35 years in the United States. It rose to about 49 years in 1900 and 64 years in 1940 (Gill, Glazer, and Thernstrom 1992). In 2020, life expectancy at birth was 77 years, having dipped from 79 in 2019 due to the COVID-19 pandemic (and after a decade of relatively little change) (S. L. Murphy et al. 2021).

Globalization and productivity growth—both offshoots of the liberal economy—have increased living standards and driven down poverty in most countries. Figure 1.2 shows that the share of the global population in extreme poverty, measured as below $2.15 per day, declined from 38 percent in 1990 to 8 percent in 2019. The change in East Asia was particularly striking, declining from 66 percent in 1990 to 1 percent in 2019 (Our World in Data 2022b). Much of this was driven by declines in poverty in China due to its large size. Notably, the Chinese poverty rate declined mainly after Deng Xiaoping introduced pro-market reforms in 1978 (Ravallion and Chen 2004; Nee and Opper 2012). India, likewise, has experienced increasing growth and

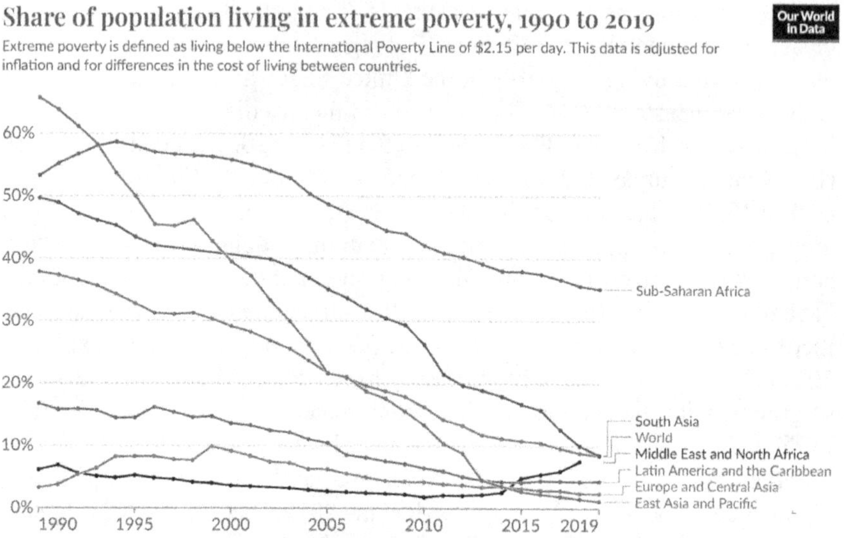

Figure 1.2. Share of population living in extreme poverty, 1990 to 2019.
World Bank Poverty and Inequality Platform. ourworldindata.org/poverty

declining poverty after liberalizing its economy (National Research Council 2010). Poverty declined even in the poorest global region, Sub-Saharan Africa, from 53 percent in 1990 to 35 percent in 2019 (Roser and Ortiz-Ospina 2022). Economic growth due to global economic liberalism is thus strongly correlated with reductions in poverty and suffering worldwide (World Bank 2015).

Global economic prosperity is also strongly correlated with improvements in other important outcomes across a wide variety of countries, including education and life expectancy (Shleifer 2009). Global life expectancy at birth increased from 62 years in 1981 to 73 years in 2019. In Africa, where life expectancies are lowest, they also increased from 50 to 63 over the same period (Roser and Ortiz-Ospina 2022). Moreover, both within and across countries, income is positively associated with happiness (Ma and Zhang 2014).[3] As Veenhoven and Vergunst (2014: 311) conclude in their analysis of this issue, "Both GDP and happiness have gone up in most nations, and average happiness has risen more in nations where the economy has grown the most . . . "

In short, a vast amount of research supports the notion that economic liberalism has been a driving force behind the growth in global prosperity. As economist Andrei Shleifer (2009: 135) concludes in his review of global economic trends over the 1980 to 2005 period, "On strategy, economics got the right answer: free market policies, supported but not encumbered by government, deliver growth and prosperity. And while a lot has been accomplished in the last quarter century, a lot remains to be done."

RESPONDING TO CRITIQUES OF ECONOMIC LIBERALISM

So far we have shown that global patterns and trends in poverty are consistent with the notion that economic liberalism increased living standards. Now we return to the specific critiques of economic liberalism, beginning with Marx's contention that economic liberalism disproportionately benefits the owners of capital. This is no doubt true. But what Marx got wrong was his contention that capitalism would inevitably impoverish the middle class and increase the ranks of the poor and working classes. He saw capitalists and workers as engaged in a zero-sum struggle for power. Instead, however, as we have shown, the growth of capitalism and the industrial revolution it produced greatly increased global prosperity. This is because the market system incentivizes innovation that leads to new products and services—such as automobiles and medicines—that benefit everyone. As a result, wherever liberal economies developed, the middle class grew and flourished. Indeed, most of the people who today are considered poor in the U.S. enjoy absolute standards of living substantially higher than was the case in the nineteenth century (Patterson 2000).

Contemporary critics of capitalism likewise highlight the role of exploitation in producing poverty. As noted earlier, Desmond, in his analysis of evictions, argues that landlords exploit vulnerable renters, causing evictions and often homelessness (Desmond 2016). By one estimate, from 2014 to 2016, about 900,000 renters were evicted from their homes each year, representing a national eviction rate of 2.6 percent (Robustellli et al. 2020). While Desmond rightly points to the struggles of many low-income Americans, he fails to acknowledge the larger picture of how many fewer people face dire poverty today than they did 50 years ago, let alone 100 years ago (Patterson 2000). Economic growth generated by the liberal economy has greatly reduced the number of Americans who struggle just to survive. After adjusting for the full range of transfers families receive and the under-reporting of income, only about 0.24 percent of households in the United States lived on $2 per person per day, which is close to the World Bank measure of extreme poverty shown in figure 1.2 (Meyer et al. 2021). And while homelessness is a tragedy when it occurs and is a persistent problem in some American cites, nevertheless, we should not overlook that the homeless population constitutes a mere 0.18 percent of the U.S. population (580 thousand homeless people out of a total population of 330 million in 2020). The number of homeless is down 17 percent from 2007, when the these data were first reported (National Alliance to End Homelessness 2022).

Thus, while many Americans undoubtedly struggle to make ends meet in our affluent society, we should not lose sight that the experience of poverty in the U.S. today is far better than what it was historically, or what it is in most other countries today. So while relative deprivation remains an important issue in the U.S. today, it is nothing near the problem of absolute deprivation that plagued the nation in years past. As Delsol (2017: 7) notes, "A poor American has the same access to basic foods as Bill Gates. The idea of not being able to eat meat more than once a week or once a month, common for the vast majority of people a century ago, has become foreign to us (at least in the countries that have chosen the path to development). It takes fewer hours of work to pay for similar goods than a generation ago."

Even though economic liberalism has done much to reduce poverty, that doesn't mean that business owners, hedge fund managers, and corporate CEOs don't wield more power than the rest of us. They clearly do and often use that power to further their interests. Those who believe in economic liberalism generally also believe that there is a role for government to prevent the rise of monopolies, which undermine free markets, and to regulate businesses to prevent misconduct, such as instituting environmental protections or disallowing companies to make false claims about their products (Friedman 1962). The point of contention often comes down to *how much* regulation there should be; supporters of economic liberalism generally prefer a lighter government touch so as to interfere as little as possible with the coordination and productivity of markets, while those who are skeptical of economic liberalism generally prefer heavier regulation.

Proponents of economic liberalism argue that excessive regulation can be regressive, by increasing the cost of goods and services or of starting a new small business. For example, the mandate issued by the National Highway Traffic Safety Administration in 2014 requiring automakers to install rear-view cameras in all new passenger vehicles only minimally improved safety but added about $200 to the cost per vehicle (Thomas 2019). Likewise, heavy regulation of the housing market in California—such as in the form of zoning rules to reduce housing or commercial building density that many residents find undesirable—greatly increased the cost of housing (Quigley and Raphael 2005), which in turn was partly responsible for low employment growth and the outmigration of many middle-class households from the state in recent decades (Chakrabarti and Zhang 2015; Johnson 2022).

With regards to the second critique—that economic liberalism, by favoring small government, undermines the welfare state's ability to reduce poverty—the debate tends to center around the size and function of the government and the reach of transfer programs. Supporters of economic liberalism offer a range of opinions on these issues. Many would prefer, in the abstract, that private charities—that are seen as being closer to the needs of local community members—should support those in poverty rather than an impersonal, inefficient government bureaucracy (Friedman 1962). Nevertheless, most supporters of economic liberalism advocate for at least some government welfare assistance for poor and vulnerable families. Milton Friedman, for example, favored a negative income tax at a time when a such a program (today known as the Earned Income Tax Credit) did not exist. He favored this approach because it would reduce poverty through tax rebates for low income earners, would be relatively easy and inexpensive to implement with a low administrative burden, and would not provide a significant disincentive to work, given that one had to be working to receive it (Friedman 1962).

While critics of economic liberalism highlight the fact that there have been periodic cutbacks in some welfare programs, such as cash welfare (Nkansah-Amankra et al. 2013; Morgen and Maskovsky 2003), the fact is that federal spending on welfare benefits has increased significantly over the past several decades. This increase in spending is facilitated by the economic growth generated by economic liberalism. According to a 2012 Congressional Budget Office (CBO) report, spending on federal means-tested programs and tax credits increased from $55 billion in 1972 to $588 billion in 2012 (in $2012). This increase in spending was due to both more participants in welfare programs and higher average spending per participant (Congressional Budget Office 2013). State and local government spending on public welfare also rose, from $146 billion in 1977 to $744 billion in 2019 (in $2019)—a 411 percent increase (The Urban Institute 2022).

Some proponents of economic liberalism also argue that, despite increases in recent decades, public expenditures on transfer programs have yielded only modest results (Tanner 2021). There is no dispute that accounting for these transfers reduces the estimated extent of poverty, in that the percentage of people who are categorized as poor increases significantly if one subtracts these benefits from household incomes. For example, Wimer and colleagues (2016) estimate that the sum of all transfers, including Social Security, Supplemental Nutrition Assistance Program benefits, and the like, reduced poverty in 2012 from 28.7 percent if transfers were not included in household income to 16.0 percent if they were. However, critics of this estimation procedure (usually proponents of smaller government) counter that these estimates don't consider the behavioral responses to the availability of government transfers. As researcher Michael Tanner from the libertarian Cato Institute argued (2021: 8), "[W]e should also consider the counterfactual. What actions would the poor have taken in the absence of welfare, and how would their lives have changed as a result? We know that incentives matter, and there is a vigorous debate about the degree to which the availability of welfare creates incentives toward poverty-inducing behavior by discouraging work and encouraging non-marital births." The evidence on this issue is mixed. Economists generally find that welfare provides a disincentive to work and marriage, though the estimated effects are modest (Moffitt 2008; Teitler et al. 2009). The consensus is that government transfers can and do reduce poverty, but the design and implementation of anti-poverty programs also affect behavioral responses (Kenworthy 2011; Moffitt 2002).

Critics of the more stringent libertarian approach to classical liberalism also assert, with merit, that there is no strong evidence that safety net programs per se necessarily hinder overall economic growth. After all, investment in the well-being of poor children, for example, could increase their economic productivity later in life (Kenworthy 2004; Heckman and Masterov 2007; Alesina and Rodrik 1994). Thus, questions about the effects of the welfare state on poverty and economic growth do not yield simple answers. Design and implementation (i.e., "where the rubber meets the road") matters. A welfare state that invests effectively in people, provides a safety net that does not disincentivize socially productive behavior, and facilitates innovation and investment, makes good sense to many supporters of economic liberalism who are not maximalist libertarians (Cowen 2018).

Beyond the issue of the size of the welfare state, supporters of economic liberalism argue that government ownership of economic enterprises (i.e., socialism) hinders innovation, productivity, and economic growth over the long run. They not only point to examples of socialist countries that failed to achieve sustained economic growth, such as the former Soviet Union, North Korea, and China before its economic reforms, but also western countries that experimented with government ownership of large sectors of the economy that later retreated from this approach after poor results, including the United Kingdom and Sweden. While Sweden levies high taxes and redistributes a considerable amount of income today, it undertook a series of economic reforms in the early 1990s that deregulated many of its public monopolies, including telecommunications, railways, and domestic air travel, and provided tax incentives for innovation and entrepreneurship. These and other measures (such as investment in research and development) resulted in strong economic growth (Edquist and Henrekson 2013).

The third critique is that economic liberalism increases income inequality, and this heightens relative deprivation and reduces social cohesion (Piketty 2014; Reeves 2017; Jacobs and Dirlam 2016; Kollmeyer 2018; Volscho 2007). The generalization that proponents of economic liberalism are more accepting of income inequality than progressives is undoubtedly true. After all, the guiding principle of economic liberalism is freedom. Some degree of inequality is expected in a society that cherishes liberty, as people vary in their values, interests, and endowments. This variability means that we should expect a range of individual outcomes, including income, because of the abilities people have and the interests they pursue. An advantage of economic liberalism is that it harnesses self-interest—a quality embedded in human nature—for the broader good, as people strive to provide goods and services that others may desire, to advance their own economic interests and in the process, raise standards of living for all.

In addition, it is not at all clear that, empirically, economic liberalism causes more income inequality than its alternatives, given that inequality is a feature of all systems where standards of living are above subsistence. Figure 1.3 plots GDP per capita and income inequality. If anything, we see that higher income countries, which tend to have liberal economies that produced prosperity, have lower levels of income inequality, on average, than lower-income countries (Our World in Data 2022a). In addition, measures of inequality that take into account inequality between countries show an overall decline in global inequality, especially as many previously very poor countries have seen substantial gains in GDP per capita (and corresponding declines in poverty) that exceed those in rich countries (Firebaugh 2003). We

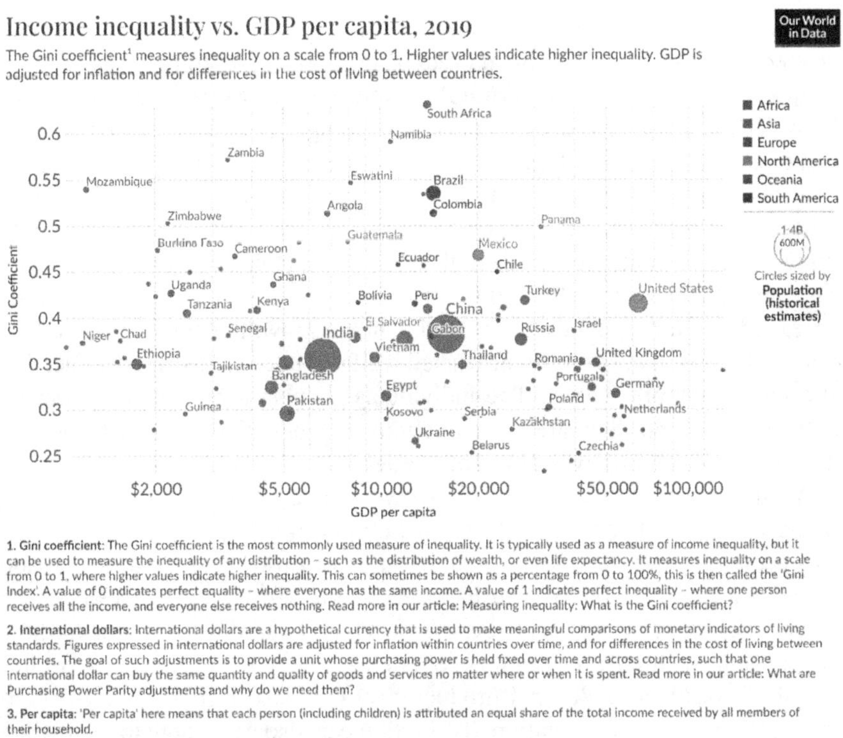

Figure 1.3. Income inequality vs. GDP per capita, 2019.
World Bank PIP; data compiled from multiple sources by World Bank. ourworldindata.org/income-inequality

also see declining global inequality in recent decades in other realms, including life expectancy at birth and education (Eberstadt 2017). Economic liberalism itself often produces the affluence necessary to meaningfully invest in poor people.

With regards to increasing income inequality within the United States, some argue that it is a result of economic liberalism and weak social safety net (Brady 2009; Danziger and Gottschalk 1995; Piketty 2020). While it is true that the Gini coefficient for households, a common summary measure of income inequality, increased from 0.397 in 1967 to 0.489 in 2020 (U.S. Census Bureau 2020b), this rise is wholly a function of larger increases in income among households at the high end of the income distribution than households at the lower end of the distribution, which, like those at the top, also experienced increases in income (Iceland 2013; Burkhauser 2017). Moreover, conventional measures of income inequality, such as the Gini coefficient, overstate the trend in the increase in income inequality because they miss some of the income and transfers that many households receive, such as employer-provided health insurance benefits (Auten and Splinter 2016; Gramm and Early 2021).

Even so, proponents of economic liberalism generally recognize that poverty and inequality are problems requiring a policy response, especially if inequality results from the purposeful exclusion of groups, such as by race (Novak 2018). The critical challenge is offering that assistance in a manner that does not undermine freedom, markets, and long-term prosperity, such as by ceding too much economic activity and power to governments. As economist Tyler Cowen (2018: 81) argues, "[W]e should redistribute wealth only up to the point that it maximizes the rate of sustainable economic growth. This may mean more redistribution than we currently undertake, and sometimes redistribution of a different kind, namely growth-enhancing redistribution . . . For instance, a well-constructed welfare state can distribute education and nutrition more widely. The individuals supported by this state are not only better off, but they are more likely to be productive and pay taxes, and they are less likely to overturn public order."

As illustrated in the quotation, Cowen, a champion of free markets, acknowledges that some wealth redistribution can help promote social order and positive regard toward the nation. He also, however, argues that too much wealth redistribution can harm economic growth by disincentivizing work, and encouraging dependency, corruption, and rent-seeking (where people gain wealth by, for example, obtaining government grants or subsidies that don't result in additional productivity) (see also Barro, 1991). Due to rent-seeking, too much wealth redistribution can also contribute to inequality, as business interests with more political power are often best-positioned to benefit from government policies and subsidies (B. K. M. Murphy, Shleifer, and Vishny 1993).

Perhaps more than most sociologists, Lane Kenworthy recognizes the importance of economic growth produced by economic liberalism while also appreciating the importance of redistribution to reduce poverty. This leads him to advocate for "social democratic capitalism" over "democratic socialism" (Kenworthy 2022). In a review and analysis of different economic strategies and redistributive policies, he argues that capitalism more effectively increases standards of living than socialism, and that some redistribution of resources helps reduce poverty and enhance opportunity. He concludes (Kenworthy, 2022: 185): " . . . over the coming half century, my best guess is that the dominant socioeconomic model among the world's rich democratic nations will be social democratic capitalism. It has proven effective at reducing poverty, economic insecurity, and inequality of opportunity. And it gets these desirable outcomes without sacrificing any of the multiple other things we want in a good society, from freedom to economic growth to health, happiness, and more."

CONCLUSION

As sociologist Gary Fine noted in a 1993 article in the *Annual Review of Sociology* (62), "A standard ploy of textbook writers is to divide sociology into three parts: functionalism, conflict theory, and symbolic interactionism." In the article Fine mourns the demise of the third of these three theoretical traditions, symbolic interactionism. The same also could be said for the first, functionalism. Functionalism highlights the importance of social order for preserving a strong society, as well as the importance of socialization, social integration, and prosocial behavior by individuals. Functionalism, however, has been out of fashion in sociology for decades (J. Smith 1975; Turner 2002), replaced by a proliferation of theories whose common theme is that social conflict and power override individual agency to produce social inequality (Olsson et al. 2015; Turner 2002; Turner et al. 2012). Thus, Social Justice and its promotion of equity is now a dominant theme in the discipline (Turner 2019; C. Smith 2014).

The goal of this chapter has *not* been to show that conflict and related theories are of little worth. They offer valuable insights into the causes and consequences of poverty and inequality. They point to structural conditions that can limit individual agency. People born into privilege have more choices than people born into poverty. Some take advantage of the market system to become wealthy without providing much of value. Policy choices sometimes produce benefits for one group at the expense of others. Poverty can have a pernicious effect on people's well-being and income inequality can undermine individual happiness and social cohesion. These are all valid criticisms of a classical liberal economic system.

However, as sociologists, we see merit in acknowledging the ways in which economic liberalism has contributed to human flourishing. Its guiding principle—freedom—is a value most people cherish, though it sometimes competes with other important values such as equality. In addition to promoting freedom, economic liberalism has done a remarkable job of raising standards of living, reducing poverty, and improving health and well-being across the globe. As such, it is *not* a system that depends on a zero-sum distribution of goods and services, as conflict theorists often assume. Rather, it is a system that produces a net benefit for most people.

For centuries economic liberalism has contributed vitally to economic and social progress in the U.S. and other developed and developing nations. Understanding its contribution is therefore crucial in any consideration of reforming or remaking our economy, as trade-offs are inevitable. So while much can be done to improve the functioning of our economic system, such as reducing crony capitalism and investing in poor families, we should not lose sight of the benefits we enjoy due to the historical rise and reach of economic liberalism.

Imagine how different the sociological study of poverty and inequality would be if we anchored our analyses in an appreciation of economic liberalism's immense contributions to economic growth and wellbeing. Rather than focus only on how people's life chances are determined and limited by nefarious economic and political forces we would also focus on the ways that a free society with free markets empowers those in the lower and middle classes to express their grievances and to take concrete steps to improve their lives and the lives of their families. We might pay more attention to the success stories that constantly surround us and weave from them a theoretical narrative that provides hope while also suggesting ways to lower or remove barriers to success. This more optimistic—and as we would argue, realistic—framing of sociological questions would go a long way toward helping sociology to achieve a more complete and balanced understanding of the distribution and trajectory of poverty and inequality today.

SUGGESTED READINGS

Cowen, T. (2018). *Stubborn Attachments: A vision for a society of free, prosperous, and responsible individuals*. Stripe Press.

Friedman, M. (1962). *Capitalism and Freedom*. The University of Chicago Press.

Hayek, F.A. (1960). *The Constitution of Liberty*. The University of Chicago Press.

Kenworthy, L. (2022). *Would Democratic Socialism Be Better?* Oxford University Press.

Smith, A. (2008). *An Inquiry into the Nature and Causes of the Wealth of Nations* (Oxford Wor). Oxford University Press.

REFERENCES

Alesina, Alberto, and Dani Rodrik. 1994. "Distributive Politics and Economic Growth." *Quarterly Journal of Economics* 109 (2): 465–90.

Auten, Gerald, and David Splinter. 2016. "Using Tax Data To Measure Long-Term Trends in U.S. Income Inequality." In *ASSA Annual Meeting*, 1–34. www.aeaweb.org/conference/2017/preliminary/paper/NkfkQ2ak%0Ahttps://www.aeaweb.org/conference/2017/preliminary/paper/NkfkQ2ak.

Baker, Regina S., David Brady, Zachary Parolin, and Deadric T. Williams. 2021. *The Enduring Significance of Ethno-Racial Inequalities in Poverty in the U.S., 1993–2017. Population Research and Policy Review*. Springer Netherlands. https://doi.org/10.1007/s11113-021-09679-y.

Barro, R. J. 1991. "Economic Growth in a Cross Section of Countries." *Quarterly Journal of Economics* 106 (2): 407–43. https://doi.org/10.2307/2937943.

Barry, Brian. 2005. *Why Social Justice Matters*. Cambridge, UK: Polity.

Birch, Kean. 2015. "Neoliberalism: The Whys and Wherefores . . . and Future Directions." *Sociology Compass* 9 (7): 571–84. https://doi.org/10.1111/soc4.12277.

Brady, David. 2009. *Rich Democracies, Poor People: How Politics Explain Poverty*. Oxford: Oxford University Press.

Brady, David, Andrew S. Fullerton, and Jennifer Moren Cross. 2009. "Putting Poverty in Political Context: A Multi-Level Analysis of Adult Poverty across 18 Affluent Democracies." *Social Forces* 88 (1): 271–300. https://doi.org/10.1353/sof.0.0221.

Buchanan, James M. 2000. "The Soul of Clas Liberalism." *The Independent Review* 5 (1): 111–19.

Burkhauser, Richard V. 2017. "The Rich, and Everyone Else, Get Richer." In *Anti-Piketty: Capital for the 21st Century*, edited by Jean-Philippe Delsol, Nicolas Lecaussin, and Emmanuel Martin, 77–80. Washington, D.C.: Cato Institute.

Butler, Eamonn. 2015. *Classical Liberalism: A Primer*. London: Institute of Economic Affairs.

Center on Poverty & Social Policy. 2021. "Historical Supplemental Poverty Measure Data." Columbia University. 2021. https://www.povertycenter.columbia.edu/historical-spm-data.

Chakrabarti, Ritashree, and Junfu Zhang. 2015. "Unaffordable Housing and Local Employment Growth: Evidence from California Municipalities." *Urban Studies* 52 (6): 1134–51. https://doi.org/10.1177/0042098014532854.

Collins, Randall. 1993. "What Does Conflict Theory Predict about America's Future?: 1993 Presidential Address." *Sociological Perspectives* 36 (4): 289–313. https://doi.org/10.2307/1389390.

Congressional Budget Office. 2013. "Federal Means-Tested Programs and Tax Credits." 2013. https://www.cbo.gov/publication/43935.

Cowen, Tyler. 2018. *Stubborn Attachments: A Vision for a Society of Free, Prosperous, and Responsible Individuals*. San Francisco: Stripe Press.

Danziger, Sheldon, and Peter Gottschalk. 1995. *America Unequal*. New York: Russell Sage Foundation.

Delsol, Jean-Philippe. 2017. "The Great Process of Equalization of Conditions." In *Anti-Piketty: Capital for the 21st Century*, edited by Jean-Philippe Delsol, Nicolas Lecaussin, and Emmanuel Martin, 5–17. Washington, D.C.: Cato Institute.

Desmond, Matthew. 2016. *Evicted: Poverty and Profit in the American City*. New York: Broadway Books.

———. 2018. "Americans Want to Believe Jobs Are the Solution to Poverty. They're Not." *The New York Times*, September 11, 2018.

———. 2023. *Poverty, By America*. New York: Crown.

Desmond, Matthew, and Nathan Wilmers. 2019. "Do the Poor Pay More?" *American Journal of Sociology* 124 (4): 1090–1124. https://doi.org/10.2307/1249191.

Eberstadt, Nicholas. 2017. "Longevity, Education, and the Huge New Worldwide Increases in Equality." In *Anti-Piketty: Capital for the 21st Century*, edited by Jean-Philippe Delsol, Nicolas Lecaussin, and Emmanuel Martin, 19–28. Washington, D.C.: Cato Institute.

Edin, Kathryn J., and H. Luke Shaefer. 2015. *$2.00 a Day: Living on Almost Nothing in America*. Boston: Mariner Books.

Edquist, Harald, and Magnus Henrekson. 2013. "Product Market Reforms and Incentives to Innovate in Sweden." 986. Stockholm.

Feldman, Guy. 2019. "Neoliberalism and Poverty: An Unbreakable Relationship." In *Routledge International Handbook of Poverty*, edited by Bent Greve, 340–50. London: Routledge. https://doi.org/10.4324/9780429058103–27.

Fine, Gary Alan. 1993. "The Sad Demise, Mysterious Disappearance, and Glorious Triumph of Symbolic Interactionism." *Annual Review of Sociology* 19: 61–87.

Firebaugh, Glenn. 2003. *The New Geography of Global Income Inequality*. Cambridge, MA: Harvard University Press.

Friedman, Milton. 1962. *Capitalism and Freedom*. Chicago: The University of Chicago Press.

Gill, Richard T., Nathan Glazer, and Stephan A. Thernstrom. 1992. *Our Changing Population*. Englewood Cliffs, NJ: Prentice Hall.

Gramm, Phil, and John Early. 2021. "Incredible Shrinking Income Inequality." *Wall Street Journal*, 2021. https://www.wsj.com/articles/incredible-shrinking-income-inequality-11616517284.

Gustafson, Kaaryn S. 2012. *Cheating Welfare: Public Assistance and the Criminalization of Poverty*. New York City: New York University Press.

Hayek, F.A. 1960. *The Constitution of Liberty*. University. Chicago: The University of Chicago Press.

Heckman, James J., and Dimitriy V. Masterov. 2007. "The Productivity Argument for Investing in Young Children." 13016. NBER Working Paper Series. Cambridge, MA.

Helleiner, Eric. 2003. "Economic Liberalism and Its Critics: The Past as Prologue?" *Review of International Political Economy* 10 (4). https://doi.org/10.1080/0969229031000160l948.

Iceland, John. 2013. *Poverty in America: A Handbook: Third Edition. Poverty in America: A Handbook: Third Edition.*

———. 2019. "Racial and Ethnic Inequality in Poverty and Affluence, 1959–2015." *Population Research and Policy Review* 38 (5): 615–54. https://doi.org/10.1007/s11113-019-09512-7.

Iceland, John, and Arthur Sakamoto. 2022. "The Prevalence of Hardship by Race and Ethnicity in the USA, 1992–2019." *Population Research and Policy Review* 41 (5): 2001–36.

Jacobs, David, and Jonathan C. Dirlam. 2016. "Politics and Economic Stratification: Power Resources and Income Inequality in the United States." *American Journal of Sociology* 122 (2): 469–500. https://doi.org/10.1086/687744.

Johnson, Hans. 2022. "Who's Leaving California—and Who's Moving In?" https://www.ppic.org/blog/whos-leaving-california-and-whos-moving-in/.

Kenworthy, Lane. 2004. *Egalitarian Capitalism: Jobs, Incomes, and Growth in Affluent Countries*. New York City: Russell Sage Foundation.

———. 2011. *Progress for the Poor*. Oxford: Oxford University Press.

———. 2022. *Would Democratic Socialism Be Better?* Oxford: Oxford University Press.

Kollmeyer, Christopher. 2018. "Trade Union Decline, Deindustrialization, and Rising Income Inequality in the United States, 1947 to 2015." *Research in Social Stratification and Mobility* 57 (June): 1–10. https://doi.org/10.1016/j.rssm.2018.07.002.

Ma, Y. Zee, and Ye Zhang. 2014. "Resolution of the Happiness–Income Paradox." *Social Indicators Research* 119 (2): 705–21. https://doi.org/10.1007/s11205-013-0502-9.

Maddison, Angus. 2001. *The World Economic: A Millenial Perspective*. Paris: OECD.

Marx, Karl, and Friedrich Engels. 2015. *The Communist Manifesto*. London: Penguin Classics.

Meyer, Bruce D., Derek Wu, Victoria Mooers, and Carla Medalia. 2021. "The Use and Misuse of Income Data and Extreme Poverty in the United States." *Journal of Labor Economics* 39 (S1): S5–58. https://doi.org/10.1086/711227.

Moffitt, Robert. 2008. "Welfare Reform: The US Experience." No. 2008–13. *Institute for Labour Market Policy Evaluation*. https://www.econstor.eu/bitstream/10419/45781/1/573610746.pdf.

Moffitt, Robert A. 2002. "Welfare Programs and Labor Supply." In *Handbook of Public Economics*, edited by Alan J. Auerbach and Martin Feldstein, Voume 4, 2393–2430. Amsterdam: North-Holland.

Morgen, Sandra, and Jeff Maskovsky. 2003. "The Anthropology of Welfare 'REFORM': New Perspective on U.S. Urban Poverty in the Post-Welfare Era." *Annual Review of Anthropology* 32: 315–38. https://doi.org/10.1146/annurev.anthro.32.061002.093431.

Murphy, By Kevin M., Andrei Shleifer, and Robert W. Vishny. 1993. "Why Is Rent-Seeking So Costly to Growth?" *The American Economic Review Papers and Proceeding* 83 (2): 409–14.

Murphy, Sherry L., Kenneth D. Kochanek, Jiaquan Xu, and Elizabeth Arias. 2021. "Mortality in the United States, 2020." *NCHS Data Brief.*

Murray, Charles. 1984. *Losing Ground: American Social Policy, 1950–1980*. New York City: BasicBooks.

National Alliance to End Homelessness. 2022. "State of Homelessness: 2022 Edition." 2022. https://endhomelessness.org/homelessness-in-america/homelessness-statistics/state-of-homelessness/.

National Research Council. 2010. *The Dragon and the Elephant Understanding the Development of Innovation Capacity in China and India: Summary of a Conference*. Washington, D.C.: The National Academies Press.

Nee, Victor, and Sonja Opper. 2012. *Capitalism from Below: Markets and Institutional Change in China*. Cambridge, MA: Harvard University Press.

Nkansah-Amankra, Stephen, Samuel Kwami Agbanu, and Reuben Jonathan Miller. 2013. "Disparities in Health, Poverty, Incarceration, and Social Justice among Racial Groups in the United States: A Critical Review of Evidence of Close Links with Neoliberalism." *International Journal of Health Services* 43 (2): 217–40. https://doi.org/10.2190/HS.43.2.c.

Novak, Mikayla. 2018. *Inequality: An Entangled Political Economy Perspective*. Cham: Palgrave Macmillan.

Olsson, Lennart, Anne Jerneck, Henrik Thoren, Johannes Persson, and David O'Byrne. 2015. "Why Resilience Is Unappealing to Social Science: Theoretical and Empirical Investigations of the Scientific Use of Resilience." *Science Advances* 1 (4): 1–12. https://doi.org/10.1126/sciadv.1400217.

Our World in Data. 2022a. "Income Inequality vs GDP per Capita, 2019." 2022. https://ourworldindata.org/grapher/gini-vs-gdp-per-capita.

———. 2022b. "Share of Population Living in Extreme Poverty, 2019." 2022. https://ourworldindata.org/grapher/share-of-population-in-extreme-poverty.

Patterson, James T. 2000. *America's Struggle Against Poverty in the 21st Century*. Cambridge, MA: Harvard University Press.

Piketty, Thomas. 2014. *Capital in the Twenty-First Century*. Cambridge, MA: Belknap.

———. 2020. *Capital and Ideology*. Cambridge, MA: Harvard University.

———. 2021. *Time for Socialsim: Dispatches from a World on Fire, 2016–2021*. New Haven: Yale University Press.

Quigley, John M., and Steven Raphael. 2005. "Regulation and the High Cost of Housing in California." *AEA Papers and Proceedings*, no. May: 323–28. http://mcdc2.

Rachidi, Angela, and Robert Doar. 2019. "Work, Family, and Community: A Framework for Fighting Poverty." *The Annals of the American Academy of Political and Social Science* 686 (1): 340–51. https://doi.org/10.1177/0002716219884867.

Ravallion, Martin, and Shaohua Chen. 2004. "China's (Uneven) Progress Against Poverty." WPS3408. Washington, D.C.

Reeves, Richard. 2017. *Dream Hoarders: How the American Upper Middle Class is Leaving Everyone Else in the Dust, Why That is a Problem, and What to Do about It*. Washington, D.C.: The Brookings Institution.

Ritzer, George, and Jeffrey Stepnisky. 2018. *Modern Sociological Theory*. Eighth Ed.. Los Angeles: Sage.

Robustellli, Tim, Yuliya Panfil, Katie Oran, Chenab Navalkha, and Emily Yelverton. 2020. "Displaced in America: Mapping Housing Loss Across the United States." Washington, D.C.

Roser, Max, and Esteban Ortiz-Ospina. 2022. "Global Extreme Poverty." OurWorldInData.Org. 2022.

Schram, Sanford F. 2015. *The Return of Ordinary Capitalism: Neoliberalism, Precarity, Occupy*. New York City: Oxford University Press.

Sen, Amartya. 1999. *Development as Freedom*. New York: Anchor Books.

Shleifer, Andrei. 2009. "The Age of Milton Friedman." *Journal of Economic Literature* 47 (1): 123–35. https://doi.org/10.7757/persnewmusi.49.2s.0365.

Smith, Adam. 2008. *An Inquiry into the Nature and Causes of the Wealth of Nations*. Oxford Wor. London: Oxford University Press.

Smith, Christian. 2014. *The Sacred Project of American Sociology*. New York: Oxford University Press.

Smith, Joan. 1975. "The Failure of Functionalism." *Philosophy of the Social Sciences* 5: 33–42. https://doi.org/10.1177/004839317500500103.

Soss, Joe, Richard C. Fording, and Sanford F. Schram. 2011. *Disciplining the Poor: Neoliberal Paternalism and the Persistent Power of Race*. Chicago: University of Chicago Press.

Tanner, Micael D. 2021. "Cato's Project on Poverty and Inequality in California: Final Report." Washington, D.C. https://www.cato.org/sites/cato.org/files/2021-10/California Project Final Report.pdf.

Teitler, Julien O., Nancy E. Reichman, Lenna Nepomnyaschy, and Irwin Garfinkel. 2009. "Effects of Welfare Participation on Marriage." *Journal of Marriage and Family* 71 (4): 878–91. https://doi.org/10.1111/j.1741–3737.2009.00641.x.

The Urban Institute. 2022. "Public Welfare Expenditures." State and Local Backgrounders. 2022. https://www.urban.org/policy-centers/cross-center-initiatives/state-and-local-finance-initiative/state-and-local-backgrounders/public-welfare-expenditures.

Thomas, Diana W. 2019. "Regressive Effects of Regulation." *Public Choice* 180 (1–2): 1–10. https://doi.org/10.1007/s11127-018-00634-8.

Thomas Sowell. 2013. "Thomas Sowell: There Are No Solutions, Only Trade-Offs." Fox News. https://www.youtube.com/watch?v=3_EtIWmja-4.

Townsend, Peter. 1993. *The International Analysis of Poverty*. Hemel Hempstead, UK: Harvester-Wheatsheaf.

Turner, Jonathan H. 2002. "Sociological Theory Today." In *Handbook of Sociological Theory*, edited by Jonathan H. Turner, 1–17. New York: Kluwer Academic/Plenum Publishers. https://doi.org/10.2307/3706911.

———. 2019. "The More American Sociology Seeks to Become a Politically-Relevant Discipline, the More Irrelevant It Becomes to Solving Societal Problems."

American Sociologist 50 (4): 456–87. https://doi.org/10.1007/s12108-019-09420-5.

Turner, Jonathan H., Leonard Beeghley, and Charles H. Powers. 2012. *The Emergence of Sociological Theory*. Seventh Ed. Los Angeles: Sage.

U.S. Bureau of Economic Analysis. 2022. "Real Gross Domestic Product Per Capita." Federal Reserve Bank of St. Louis, A939RX0Q048SBEA. 2022. https://fred.stlouisfed.org/series/A939RX0Q048SBEA/#.

U.S. Census Bureau. 2020a. "Table 2. Poverty Status of People by Family Relationship, Race, and Hispanic Origin." Historical Poverty Tables: People and Families–1959 to 2020. 2020. https://www.census.gov/data/tables/time-series/demo/income-poverty/historical-poverty-people.html.

———. 2020b. "Table H-4. Gini Ratios for Households, by Race and Hispanic Origin of Householder." Historical Income Tables: Households. 2020. https://www.census.gov/data/tables/time-series/demo/income-poverty/historical-income-households.html.

———. 2020c. "Table H-5. Race and Hispanic Origin of Householder—Households by Median and Mean Income." Historical Income Tables: Households. 2020. https://www.census.gov/data/tables/time-series/demo/income-poverty/historical-income-households.html.

Veenhoven, Ruut, and Floris Vergunst. 2014. "The Easterlin Illusion: Economic Growth Does Go with Greater Happiness." *International Journal of Happiness and Development* 1 (4): 311. https://doi.org/10.1504/ijhd.2014.066115.

Volscho, Thomas W. 2007. "Unions, Government Employment, and the Political Economy of Income Distribution in Metropolitan Areas." *Research in Social Stratification and Mobility* 25 (1): 1–12. https://doi.org/10.1016/j.rssm.2006.09.003.

Wallerstein, Immanuel. 1979. *The Capitalist World-Economy*. Cambridge, UK: Cambridge University Press.

White, Mark D. 2014. "The Problems with Measuring and Using Happiness for Policy Purposes." *Mercatus Working Paper*. Arlington, VA. https://doi.org/10.2139/ssrn.3191385.

Wimer, Christopher, Liana Fox, Irwin Garfinkel, Neeraj Kaushal, and Jane Waldfogel. 2016. "Progress on Poverty? New Estimates of Historical Trends Using an Anchored Supplemental Poverty Measure." *Demography* 53 (4): 1207–18. https://doi.org/10.1007/s13524-016-0485-7.

World Bank. 2015. "A Measured Approach to Ending Poverty and Boosting Shared Prosperity: Concepts, Data, and the Twin Goals." *Policy Research Report*. Washington, D.C. https://doi.org/10.1596/978-1-4648-0361-1.

NOTES

1. First and foremost we would like to thank Fabio Rojas and Charolotta Stern for their leadership in convening the workshop on classical liberalism in sociology and putting together this volume. We would also like to thank our fellow authors of

other chapters in this volume—Patrik Aspers, Jack Goldstone, Lauren Hall, Mikayla Novak, and Ilana Redstone—for their invaluable feedback on our work in progress. We also thank Bill Gold for providing additional comments and suggestions. Finally, a special thanks to the Instititue for Human Studies at Geroge Mason University and Program Director Aaron Powell for their critical support of this project.

2. We use the terms "capitalism," "economic liberalism," and "neoliberalism" interchangeably, though scholars sometimes use the term neoliberalism to refer to the extension of the economic logic of the market (i.e., economic liberalism) to nonmarket domains, such as government bureaucracies and nonprofit organizations, where individuals and organizations are considered as economic actors who are expected to compete in order to maximize profit or improve operations (Feldman 2019).

3. Happiness is challenging to measure, in part because people's understanding of this subjective concept varies across cultures (White 2014).

Chapter 2

Race, Freedom, and Social Change

Fabio Rojas

Classical liberalism makes a bold promise. If we vest people with individual rights and property, and offer the protective shield of tolerance, then we are better off. Under such a regime, classical liberalism argues that people will live longer and more meaningful lives and society, as a whole, will be wealthier. It is for these reasons that racial inequality represents a betrayal of this ideal. A society that creates classes of people who are systematically denied personal safety, or who are excluded from society's most important institutions, or who are denigrated in private and public settings, is deeply flawed.

Not surprisingly, classical liberals have levied strong critiques of racially based inequality. Adam Smith (2005, 113), for example, described slavery as a "love of power" and also labeled it a "perverse institution." In the nineteenth century, John Stuart Mill called slavery an "abhorrence" (1869, 117). In the twentieth century, we see denunciations of apartheid by the economist W. H. Hutt (1964), opposition to Japanese internment by libertarian newspaper publisher R. C. Hoiles (1942), and criticism of eugenics and nationalism socialism by Austrian economists Ludwig von Mises and F. A. Hayek (Magness 2019).

Recently, writers in the classical liberal and libertarian tradition have claimed that restrictions on immigration are unjust attempts by the majority to exclude foreigners (Caplan and Weinersmith 2019, Somin 2020). Within this broader conversation, racial inequality is a problem because it is inherently anti-individualist, violates human rights, and it is economically inefficient (Magness 2020a). In fact, prominent Civil Rights leaders have often incorporated individualist liberal rhetoric into their appeals for justice. Martin Luther King, Jr., famously called for people to be judged by the "content of their character" and not the color of their skin.

By drawing attention to racism in its many forms, classical liberal authors envisioned a world where racial distinctions were minimized and possibly eliminated. The central argument of these varied authors is that racial antagonism is at odds with individualism and it is an impediment to the institutions that classical liberals think are valuable, such as private property and limited government (Rojas 2022).

In contrast, many sociologists take a very different view of the relationship between racism and liberal institutions. Rather than seeing an inherent contradiction between liberal policies and racist social practices, they tend to see racism as an essential component of modernity (e.g., Clegg 2020, Corrigan 1977, Williams 1994, Virdee 2019, Morris 2022). It is routine among sociologists to claim that slavery, for example, was a causal factor for the rise of modern capitalism. For example, Matthew Desmond has claimed, at various times, that hierarchical business organization and accounting practices were invented to facilitate slavery (Desmond 2021). Another popular argument is that classical liberal approaches to racial conflict do not solve the problem but make it worse or distract attention from racial inequities. For example, Eduardo Bonilla-Silva's book *Racism without Racists* (2017) argues that race neutral ideology allows people to evade a much needed confrontation over race-based privilege. Sociologists Wendy L. Moore and Joyce Bell (2017) argued that free speech norms perpetuated a racially inequitable neo-liberal social order.

Sociologists and classical liberals reach markedly different conclusions about racial inequality and liberal social institutions. Classical liberals say freedom is the answer while critical sociologists often respond by saying that liberty is an illusion and individual rights are just a way to diffuse collective identities and interest. The promises of liberty, in their view, are just another tool in the oppressor's workshop.

The purpose of this essay is to articulate a puzzle that arises from this sociological literature. If contemporary societies are indeed organized in ways that rely so much on racial oppression, then why do we see tangible and substantial improvements in the well-being of racial and ethnic minorities? These would include large and successful movements for minority rights, increases in life expectancy and material wealth for minorities, the creation of programs to equalize work opportunities, the rise of popular culture that focuses on minority aesthetics, and the institutionalization of multiculturalism and antiracism in school curricula.

The claim is not that these developments have "solved" the problem of racial inequality. Indeed, there is ample evidence that racial inequality is a durable feature of American society. For example, there is much evidence that race is considered by employers in determining hiring and wages and it is consistent (e.g., Quillian, Pager, Hexel, and Midtbøen 2017). Rather, the issue is that many sociological theories suggest that large scale improvements rarely occur or that they bolster race-based privileges (Seamster and Ray 2018). Yet, the overall well-being of ethnic minorities in the US, and elsewhere, has increased in many important ways. Stasis is predicted, but that is not what is observed. Furthermore, liberal democracies appear to do better than their counterparts.

This chapter relies on sociological research to answer this "puzzle of minority improvement" and focuses on policies that are often associated with classical liberal policy prescriptions. The next section presents a standard account of how sociologists understand racial inequality with a focus on critical theories. Then, I discuss three resources that open societies with liberalized markets and norms of tolerance and free speech have for addressing racial inequality. Liberalized markets generate excess wealth that can be channeled into social change; the institution of free speech and assembly allows for open critique of racial and ethnic hierarchies; and open societies allow for exit from repressive environments. In other words, a classical liberal view recognizes that racial inequalities are an important and damaging feature of many societies, while pointing out that open societies create a dynamism that can result in large-scale improvements in the lives of millions.

SOCIOLOGICAL APPROACHES TO RACIAL INEQUALITY

Social scientists note that race and ethnicity are central features of most societies. It is extremely common for people to create social categories based on perceived appearances, shared heritage, and common cultural traits. These categories, in turn, often motivate social exclusion, repressive policies, and violence (e.g., Clair and Denis 2015). In extreme cases, racial and ethnic boundaries lead to violent conflict and are the foundation of repressive social systems such as slavery, apartheid, and mass incarceration.

In general, sociologists tend to make a number of arguments about the relationship between racial and ethnic hierarchies and other structures found in society, such as the state, the school system, and the workforce. First, racial hierarchies have a strong effect on relative status and life course outcomes (Hudson et al. 2013). That is, people from higher status groups tend to have better jobs, more income, and better life outcomes. In American society, for example, Whites will earn more money and be more likely to enter higher status occupations than Blacks. It is also true that race is correlated with life expectancy. Depending on the measurement, White men and women can live about five years longer than their Black counterparts (Harper et al. 2007).

The reason that race often has such a large impact on life course outcomes is that people use race as a criterion for judgment. It is very common for sociologists to argue that race as a "master status" that influences a wide range of human interaction. In every employment situation, people will be judged, in part at least, as a member of a racial or ethnic group, as well as an employee who might bring value to a firm. Social psychologists will often argue that racial statuses are applied nearly instantly in daily interactions and thus strongly shape how people evaluate each other, which leads to large-scale differences in outcomes (Ridgeway 2014). A related argument is that membership in a racial or ethnic group provides enhanced access to social or material resources. For example, sociologists of health will often ascribe superior outcomes to the fact that White health care providers are more attentive to the needs of White patients, while organizational sociologists will claim that racial minorities are rarely found in elite corporate settings because non-Whites are excluded, or rarely included, in the most influential cliques that lead firms (Ray 2019).

Second, many repressive social policies are created in order to harass or persecute others and allow higher status groups to profit from the exploitation of lower status groups. This argument is to be found in classical sociology, such as DuBois's seminal *Black Reconstruction in America, 1868–1880*, and in contemporary "critical race theory," which argues that modern social policies are dependent on racial hierarchies for their definition and operation (DuBois 1935, 1948, Ray 2022).[1]

Furthermore, historical sociologists note that racial and ethnic hierarchies are often integrated with other important institutions and that it is often impossible to properly assess these institutions without knowing how racial inequalities are manifested in particular societies. Well-known examples include plantation and hacienda systems in the Americas, the Indian caste system, and the South African apartheid system. In each of these cases, race was tied to labor and social practices, such as marriage and education. Recent sociological and historical literature has also tied law enforcement to racial hierarchy (Go 2020). Researchers have claimed that police departments were created to enforce racially based divisions, such as American slavery, or that policing practices were developed to maintain political power in colonies.

Overall, sociologists usually have mixed views on the prospects for racial and ethnic minorities. On the one hand, there is often a celebration of political struggles that overturn repressive social institutions. Social movement scholars, for example, routinely focus on the Civil Rights Movement as an example of a movement where repressed peoples used their own resources to successfully challenge racial repression (e.g., Morris 1983). Other developments in sociological theory complicate this celebratory story. Critical theory sociologists, such as Eduardo Bonilla-Silva (2017), Victor Ray (2022), and

Louise Seamster (Seamster and Ray 2018), argue that progress is illusory or offset by new forms of social repression. According to this line of thinking, people who belong to higher status groups will develop social practices and state policies that allow them to re-establish social superiority. For example, Bonilla-Silva's (2017) book, *Racism without Racists*, argues that Whites will deflect discussions of race so that they don't have to confront racial inequalities. Citing trends such as mass incarceration and continued Black-White inequality in income, Ray and Seamster (2018) argue against seeing history as an uncomplicated movement toward racial equality. Political sociologists will also spend considerable effort documenting the different ways that White majorities in America might undermine or limit Black political and economic gains.

Thus, the sociological discussion of race oscillates between occasional discussions of political victories, the role that racial differences have in the history of social institutions, and the push-back of White majorities. Theoretically, this constellation of positions draws on intersectional social theory, which suggests that racial inequality and capitalist repression are interwoven (Collins 2014, Crenshaw 1993). The main reason that it is impossible to completely eliminate racial inequality is that other social hierarchies, such as gender and class, are supported by racial hierarchies (e.g., capitalist firms often rely on the labor of exploited racial and ethnic minorities). The conclusion is that while it is possible to score impressive victories for equality, complete elimination of racial hierarchy is unlikely when racism is integral to so many of the institutions that define contemporary societies.

THE PUZZLE OF MINORITY IMPROVEMENT

If modern societies depend so much on the exploitation of minorities, then how is it possible that any improvement is possible? Why don't White majorities simply veto all social change so that they may maximize their own social status and material advantages? Much of the story of modern liberal societies is that relative differences in status often remain, but minorities nonetheless experience considerable improvements in well-being. Western nations were often responsible for highly destructive institutions, and they created hierarchies that persist to the present, but, at the same time, these very same nations later in their histories embark on extensive reform efforts, often as a result of internal debates about the grotesque nature of these institutions. The puzzle is why capitalist nations have reformed so much when sociological theory suggests that these reforms should not happen or be superficial in character.

For example, abolitionist historians note that most nations voluntarily abolished slavery in the eighteenth and nineteenth centuries (Mulligan and

Eric 2013). The resistance of the United States is an exception to an overall trend. Another important trend is that many nations have large and successful movements for minority and immigrant rights. Modern societies have also abolished statutes that directly impact the well-being of racial and ethnic minorities such as anti-miscegenation laws, which prohibit marriage between Whites and non-Whites and "Black Codes," which prohibited Black Americans from participating in many professions and occupations.

As minorities have gained fundamental political and economic rights, their material well-being has improved as well. Here, I will focus on the US as a motivating example. In 1900, Black life expectancy was 32 years, which is a result of extremely high rates of child mortality. In 2000, the life expectancy for Black men was 68, more than a doubling of the rate (Sanghi and Smaldone 2022). Poverty rates show large historical declines as well. In the 1950s, which is the point at which the US Census Bureau began measuring poverty, 40% of Blacks were classified as being in poverty. In 2020, 18% of Blacks fit into the definition of poverty. While income inequality persists, absolute improvements continue (US Census 2020). Black income levels have risen as well. In inflation adjusted dollars, Black households in the 40 to 60% of the income distribution received about $4,000 dollars in 1967. In 2020, that number has risen to $46,000 dollars per year (US Census 2022: Table H3).

Another important trend is that liberal societies often establish policies and statutes that institutionalize minority rights. For example, a wide range of countries have implemented affirmative action policies that encourage, and in some cases, guarantee the representation of ethnic minorities in schools, the professions, and workplaces. Another example can be found in school curricula (Guillebeau 1999). The United States, for example, has hundreds of colleges that offer degrees in various forms of ethnic studies. It is also common now for K-12 curricula to include material that focuses on the history and culture of ethnic minorities (Rojas 2007). These trends are most pronounced in the US, but the spread of this type of curriculum occurs in other nations as well.

There has also been significant cultural change that is worth documenting. In the last twenty or thirty years, English-speaking nations have experienced a groundswell in social justice and antiracist thinking (Dunivin et al. 2022). By examining large-scale databases of books, news media, and social media, sociologists have documented that antiracist discourse transitioned from academic writing to popular discourse in the early 2000s (Dunivin et al. 2022). Ideas such as "systemic racism" and "anti-blackness" are no longer confined to academic journals.

This vocabulary is now commonplace in media and entertainment. One indicator of the popularity of the new anti-racist discourse are best selling books such as Ibram X. Kendi's *How to Be an Antiracist* (2019) and *White*

Fragility: Why It's So Hard for White People to Talk about Racism by Robin D'Angelo (2018). Appearing on multiple best-seller lists, these books explain the problem of racism to the reader and encourage readers to employ various anti-racist strategies in their daily lives. It is worth noting that the message of these books is that social change can occur in a bottom-up fashion where personal reflection is the start of a larger change project and cultural forces are not epiphenomenal relative to repressive structures.

Another finding is that academic researchers increased their focus on racial discrimination. Multiple analyses have found that there has been a large increase in the number of academic journal articles that focus on racial discrimination. This suggests that racial inequality has become a more focal point within the academy as well as in popular culture. Academic journals have seen a large rise in articles that investigate many forms of discrimination, including racial discrimination. Journalist and sociologist Musa al-Gharbi's (2023) analysis of publication data shows that there were approximately 11,000 articles on racial discrimination in the year 2000 and over 26,000 in the year 2020.

The overall cultural shift associated with multiculturalism in the 1990s and antiracism today has facilitated the rise of social movements that are focused on racial inequality. These would include popular social movements like Black Lives Matter and various immigration rights movements such as the movements to curtail and end deportations. Black Lives Matter is particularly important because protests helped draw attention to antiracist ideas, resulted in some police reforms, and helped publicize more radical approaches to racial inequality such as prison abolitionism (e.g., CR10 Publications Collective 2008). Similarly, immigration rights movements highlight the racialization of immigration enforcement, which lead to calls to abolish or reform various immigration agencies.

These social trends indicate that accounts of very rigid racial hierarchies need some sort of modification. Critics might allege that these are superficial changes that distract from the fundamentally racist nature of American capitalism. Even if we grant the critics this premise, it would still be the case that minorities have experienced large and tangible gains in health, income, cultural prominence, and political status. This all occurred even in the face of a purportedly inflexible rigid structure. The purpose in reviewing these developments is not to undermine the importance of relative differences, or to downplay repressive policies and historical injustices, but to highlight the need to explain how relative inequality can co-exist with genuine improvements in the well-being of minorities.

THREE REFORM PROCESSES IN LIBERAL SOCIETIES

The argument of this chapter is that liberal ideas and institutions unleash processes that improve the lives of racial and ethnic minorities, even in the presence of antagonistic or apathetic majorities. The intuition is that social and economic liberalization helps communities acquire and develop the material and symbolic resources needed for the assertion of rights and sustained struggle. This chapter discusses three such processes—the creation of excess wealth; freedom of speech and assembly; and the freedom of exit and movement.

The first argument is that minorities benefit from liberalized economies because markets produce excess wealth that can be invested in social change. Even if there is a hostile racial majority, secure property rights means that minorities can invest financial and social resources in social institutions that will bolster their freedom and well-being. The second argument is that a regime of basic human rights focusing on speech and assembly allows minorities to voice critiques, coordinate action, and generate cultural change. The third argument is that the right of movement and exit helps minorities when faced with unusually repressive societies.

WEALTH CAN BE CHANNELED TO SOCIAL CHANGE

"There is no such thing as a free lunch" applies as much to social change as it does to anything else. One of the deep lessons of modern social movement research is that activism is expensive. According to the resource mobilization perspective, social movements rely on strategies that require substantial financial and social resources (McCarthy and Zald 1977). These strategies would include filing lawsuits, lobbying the government, paying for non-profit organizations, operating movement newspapers and websites, and paying for attorneys to defend activists in court. Furthermore, social change often requires a cohort of dedicated activists who need financial and social support, as well as organizations that sponsor their work.

This basic observation about social change leads to an important insight. Minorities who pursue social change in racist societies need access to resources which can pay for the tools of change. This leads to two additional hypotheses about the social conditions that might contribute to minority improvement. First, wealthier societies should have a "spillover" effect. Wealthy societies will have a larger fraction of the population that is willing to invest in social change than poorer societies. Second, societies that have firm property rights regimes will more easily channel their resources into social change.

These ideas point to a vital connection between economic liberalism and racial inequality. A consistent finding of economic research is that nations with economic freedom tend to have higher wealth levels and they are more likely to have large-scale reductions in poverty. For example, multiple studies show that the "Freedom Index," which assesses the degree to which people in a nation have economic freedoms, correlates with GDP and other measures of material well-being such as life expectancy (Carlsson and Lundström 2002). This general association suggests that economic liberalism has an important path to racial reform. Economically open societies generate additional wealth, which can be applied to activism and social change. As long as resources are "free" to move where people want, many will choose to use them for social change.

The literature on specific social movements provides many examples of privately held wealth invested in change. For example, Civil Rights organizations routinely received large grants from private foundations in support of their activities. This would include major organizations such as the Ford Foundation, which donated millions to the classical civil rights campaign. More recent scholarship has focused on other philanthropies such as the Voter Education Project which funneled considerable resources into the "big five" major Civil Rights organizations (Faulkenberry 2016).

Another example is the funding mechanism for the National Association for the Advancement of Colored People. One of the most important groups in the struggle against segregation, the NAACP had a simple fundraising model. In addition to larger donations made by wealthy individuals, people at lower income levels could purchase memberships in local NAACP chapters and the national organization. African Americans could purchase goods, such as newsletters and magazines published by the NAACP. It is important to note that this income was generated by African Americans of all income levels. According to the NAACP (2023), its peak membership level during the Civil Rights era was 600,000 members. Roughly, in 1946, nearly one out of twenty African Americans were dues paying members of the group. As long as economic growth allows people to have disposable income that they can use freely, many will support social change.

The dynamic suggested by these examples is as follows. Western nations were organized along racial lines but they also permitted a regime of property rights and stable economic institutions that encouraged economic growth and wealth accumulation. While most funds are used for consumption or reinvestment, significant resources are used to sponsor special interest groups and social movement organizations. In some cases, such as the Civil Rights movement, such investments in social change can have an enormous impact.

Aldon Morris's (1983) scholarship on the Civil Rights movement draws attention to another equally important process—the ability of repressed minorities to develop their own resources and deploy them in liberation struggles. Morris's major study of the movement focuses on the crucial role that "indigenous" resources had in underwriting social change. This would include the social resources of Black churches and the organizational skills of the pastors who helped mobilize millions of Black citizens.

Although Morris's seminal book does not focus on the institution of private property and disposable income, these factors appear frequently. For example, Black Americans contributed millions of dollars to key civil rights groups. He also notes that predominantly White unions frequently donated large sums of funds to the major Civil Rights organizations (57–58). Beyond providing the income needed to support social change by paying for social movement organizations, free economies contain additional tools that are needed to challenge repression. Morris's book has a very important example. Civil Rights activists were able to successfully stage bus boycotts because they had access to alternative privately controlled transportation.

The key issue for Civil Rights leaders was that boycotting segregated buses created a problem. Black workers might be at risk of losing their jobs if they could not show up for work. This problem was solved through a variety of strategies. In 1953, Civil Rights leaders addressed this issue during the Baton Rouge boycott by organizing a collective of Black car owners who would provide free transportation. Morris (19) then adds a very telling detail about the role of economic liberty. He notes that Black carpool participants could not accept funds or they would run afoul of taxi license regulations. This observation suggests that with more permissive rules for transportation that allowed payments, it would have been much easier to stage the boycott.

This issue re-appears in Morris's (57–59) account of how various organizations supported the famed 1955 Montgomery bus boycott. Again, a serious problem was that Black men and women needed to get to their jobs and this would be challenging without access to buses. In Montgomery, the Civil Rights leadership expanded the strategies developed in Baton Rouge. They engaged in a nationwide fundraising campaign to get funds to pay for alternative transportation. Initially, the Montgomery Improvement Association had relied on vehicles they purchased and Black taxi companies, who charged discounted fares. Then, Civil Rights leaders needed to switch to an all-volunteer transportation system because Montgomery's police commission did not permit Black-owned taxis to charge discounted rates that were equivalent to less expensive bus fares. The city government's prohibition of discounted taxi fares is another informative example of how economic regulations were used to undermine social change.

Though a small detail in Morris's narrative, the ability to create alternative transportation for Black workers during boycotts speaks to the role that excess wealth had in bolstering protest. Thousands of Black working men and women contributed modest amounts of money so that their compatriots could effectively boycott segregated buses. Furthermore, the ability to purchase alternative modes of transportation also speaks to the importance of having a free economy that allows individuals and communities to have free access to many services. There is also something important to be said about Black businesses, such as taxi companies, which donated labor and materials for the struggle. Without disposable income, private ownership of vehicles, and the contribution of Black businesses, the boycott would have been significantly reduced, if not completely impossible.

Critics might argue that there is something perverse in having repressed people fund their own liberation. While it may be true that economic liberalism generates the excess wealth needed for social change, a fundamental injustice remains until those who enacted repression and are sustained by repression are made to pay. This author concurs with this sentiment and has argued that reparations are a reasonable policy proposal that deserves serious consideration (Rojas 2023). However, a policy of reparation or restoration for racial inequality presumes that a society is at a point where marginalized people have achieved enough standing to make such a claim and that many people agree that historical injustices have occurred and merit redress. Such a society is one where a larger majority has already changed in fundamental ways that would allow the marginalized to assert their legal rights. In contrast, the sorts of social processes described here matter when the majority is still highly antagonistic and justice is in the hands of the marginalized and their allies.

FREEDOM OF SPEECH AND PRESS ENABLE CULTURAL CHANGE

Even though wealth is needed to create and sustain social change efforts, it would be a moot point if states could arbitrarily harass, imprison, and kill dissenters.Theoretically, this situation might be described as an equilibrium in a political conflict. A repressive society might have many people who disapprove of a regime that violently represses minorities, but when a few people speak out, they are harmed. This, in turn, suggests to other dissidents that the costs of speaking out are extremely high.

Indeed, this might be an apt characterization of highly repressive societies, including the US at many points in its history. For example, it's not a great distortion to say that the post-Reconstruction South operated in this way, by allowing extreme violence toward anyone who criticizes White domination over Blacks. Even up to the 1960s, there were instances of allies of the Civil Rights movement being murdered in response to their actions (Belknap 1984). Clearly, the purpose was to punish dissenters and send a signal that segregation would be defended.

The question becomes: how do societies, especially liberal societies, break out of this equilibrium? In addition to having the wealth to sponsor contention, liberal societies set up norms that slowly erode this equilibrium in numerous ways. Freedom of speech and the press allow dissenters to focus attention on issues. Even if imperfectly articulated or enforced, even a moderate degree of free speech and press can act as a focal point for social change.

In American history, there are ample examples of where freedom of the press was used to rally abolitionists, such as William Lloyd Garrison's *The Liberator*. Once again, this was made possible through donations from wealthy Black and White abolitionists (Garrison 1973). But also, it was made possible by freedom of press. Even though Garrison and his newspaper were physically attacked, American society allowed newspapers, including abolitionist papers, to operate much of the time. The presence of *The Liberator*, and other abolitionist publications, created a community of people who were deeply committed to ending slavery. Free speech norms allow dissenters to persist and build larger communities, even in the face of violent repression.

Freedom of the press and speech has other important cultural and discursive consequences. Here, I draw on the work of Hans Noel's (2014) book *Political Ideologies and Political Parties in America*. The crux of Noel's argument is that large-scale policy change often requires a preceding cultural change. That is, in order to assemble a large coalition that will implement policy change, political actors need to produce a set of ideas that will hold constituencies together. The new political ideology is discussed and debated in newspapers, and often precedes policy change by decades. Noel illustrates this with studies of various policy change movements, including the Civil Rights movement. In the decades before the Civil Rights movement, intellectuals, journalists, and opinion leaders began to articulate a critique of segregation that drew on ideas about equal access to the law and human rights. This new consensus appeared in newspapers of the era and laid the foundation for the mid-century push for integrationism (Lee 2002).

Here, I emphasize the importance of a free press in this entire process. During the Jim Crow era, with its attendant regime of violence, a larger cultural shift was taking place. It was not, for the most part, taking place in the South; it was taking place in the newspapers and lecterns of the era. Without the ability to publish and circulate these ideas, the Civil Rights movement would have been greatly impeded.

A third way that free speech norms spur social change is through cognitive dissonance. In other words, hypocrisy matters. Many observers have noted that the push for racial equality routinely employed many discursive tactics that highlight the difference between American ideals and actual practices of racial discrimination. In his most famous speech, Martin Luther King, Jr., accused White America of writing a check promising freedom that was rejected for "insufficient funds." King was not alone. A long-standing theme in both abolitionism and Civil Rights activism is that Americans were hypocritical because they violated Christianity's directive to treat others with love or the Constitution's promise that all Americans would receive equal treatment under the law.

The accusation of hypocrisy proved to be very important in American history as many legal challenges depended on having sympathetic Whites who recognized this profound problem. Contemporary historians also argue that the hypocrisy of White supremacy in that era was highlighted by a contrast with promises from socialist nations that they could do better (Skrentny 1998). This comparison points to a larger sociological dynamic. Open societies can, on occasion, be shamed into improvement. As long as there is discussion of alternatives, and tolerance of dissidence, critics can make plausible claims that competitor societies will be preferable.

MOVEMENT AND EXIT

This chapter has discussed how open societies have various features which make the mitigation of racial inequality a genuine possibility. Still, many minorities face extremely antagonistic majorities that refuse to grant any reprieve. In this case, minorities have one powerful option: exit. While exit can allow repressive regimes to escape criticism and reform, the option of leaving can have powerful and transformative effects on people who are persecuted by a vengeful majority (Somin 2020). Two examples illustrate this idea: the "Great Migration" in the US and the movement of Russian Jews from East Europe to the United States in the nineteenth and twentieth centuries.

The Great Migration occurred in the early twentieth century as millions of Black Americans moved from the South to the industrialized North to escape Jim Crow. Here, the focus is on relative difference, as the North also had its own forms of segregation. The issue is that the relative differences mattered a great deal. The North was less likely to have local and state governments that tolerated murders of its Black citizens and it was less likely to have the extremely punitive labor market regulations that completely excluded people from highly rewarding occupations. Also, industrial labor was much more lucrative than agricultural labor, and moving to the North allowed many Blacks to accumulate wealth. Thus, by simply allowing for free movement, millions of people were allowed to directly improve their well-being (Collins and Wanamker 2014, Derenoncourt 2022).

Another informative example comes from Europe, where Jews were the subject of extreme repression. One of the basic features of migration to the United States in the late 1800s and early 1900s is that millions of Jews took the opportunity to migrate from Russia and Eastern Europe to escape the pogroms of Tsarist Russia and, later, the violence of the National Socialist state (Somin 2020). Here, the point is about relative improvement. Jews arriving in America also faced significant levels of discrimination, as they were banned from many social institutions and people formed compacts that barred selling homes to Jews. Still, by allowing people to freely migrate, even to a society with its own discriminatory norms, millions of people were spared violent deaths and many were able to establish better lives in very concrete material terms.

This argument echoes and overlaps with those made by Albert O. Hirschman (1970) in his famous text, *Exit, Voice, and Loyalty*. The central thrust of Hirschman's book is that exit is an important mechanism for understanding the deterioration of states and firms. Firms that fail to help consumers and nations that abuse citizens will generate a flow of emigrants whose absence generates discussion within these organizations. The focus of the present discussion is that exit and the right of immigration are features of a open society with liberalized markets and tolerance that directly helped persecuted groups. Even if leaving results in no reform, movement dramatically increases the well-being of racial minorities. Improvements include escaping certain death, increased wages, and the ability to practice one's religious or cultural beliefs in peace.

SOCIAL CHANGE AND THE DISEQUILIBRIUM OF OPEN SOCIETIES

Critics of liberal societies correctly point out that majorities may have a great deal invested in the repression of ethnic minorities. They are also correct in that liberal societies emerged from a history of colonialism, slavery, and exploitation. It is very sobering to contemplate the fact that large majorities in the United States and Europe at various times condoned and actively supported such repressive institutions. As others in this volume have argued, states often acquire a predatory character aimed at lower-status minorities (Davis 2024).

This chapter has argued that the critics are mistaken in thinking this is a complete account of modern societies. The errors stem from ignoring the complexity and heterogeneity of contemporary life. Societies built on slavery, such as the United States, also created institutions that had the potential to undermine repression by amplifying and empowering diverse groups. A small fraction of the US population, for example, was able to finance organizations such as the NAACP, which helmed legal challenges to segregation. This would have been extraordinarily difficult in a society with low wealth, restrictions on speech, no commitment to legal equality, and rules that allow the government to easily attack and undermine dissident organizations.

The process at work is essentially one of heterogeneity, disequilibrium, and disruption in a larger complex society. Repressive majorities do in fact build social and political institutions that directly benefit them. These majorities seek institutions that are extremely stable and thus provide them with long-term benefits over generations. However, repressive social systems do not define the entire society, nor do they exist in isolation from competitors and critics. As long as individuals have economic and social rights, repression does not completely eclipse dissent. The importance of heterogeneity and disruption are important arguments for limited government. Overly intrusive states can limit the entry of people who can disrupt larger ethnic minorities and suppress the dynamism that might lead to much needed social change.

Theoretically, many sociological theories of racial inequality employ models that give excessive agency to racial and ethnic majorities. For example, critical sociologists will often explain social change by appealing to Derrick Bell's interest convergence argument. Black Americans will only experience improvement if it is in the interest of White majorities (Bell 1980). This argument uses the same logic as Duncan Black's famed Median Voter Theorem, which states that democracies will produce policies favored by the middle voter. If Whites are the majority, then policy will have to reflect the median White voter in some way. Furthermore, if Whites have an ideology of racial superiority, they will vote in ways that they believe will not jeopardize group privileges they may have. This argument does not consider heterogeneity among Whites, nor does it consider changes in social values.

Similarly, arguments about racism in labor markets often assume a variant of a monopsony model where White employers are treated as a uniform population of racially motivated actors who purchase labor. In such a model, racial discrimination would be rampant and unpunished by competition and wages would remain artificially low. Since most employers want to pay Blacks lower wages than Whites, Black employees have no plausible exit. These accounts often do not consider the sources of competition, either from non-racist or less-racist Whites, or from Black businesses and consumers. In fact a number of scholars have noted that people will often buy goods and services from racial minorities as an act of solidarity, which also has the effect of corroding economic barriers stemming from racial inequality. The argument is not that competition will completely erase Black-White income gaps. Rather, heterogeneity creates competition, an important factor that increases the economic position of minorities.

In addition to heterogeneity and competition, liberal institutions create disequilibrium by amplifying voices. Courts, for example, can amplify a position once considered marginal. In fact, it was this very property of courts that encouraged Civil Rights lawyers to focus so intently on the judicial system (Tauber 1999). If even a small number of judges agreed that Black Americans had the same speech rights and the same rights to jobs and housing, they could shift the legal system, and even the larger population, in their direction. Liberalized markets can also have this effect. A consistent theme in American popular culture is that many producers have used mass media to criticize and undermine racist attitudes. Such examples include productions such as *Guess Who's Coming to Dinner?*, *To Kill a Mockingbird*, and the television series *StarTrek*. Once again, this is not a claim that all forms of mass media will adopt an anti-racist stance or that these works are free from criticism. In fact, film critics will note that movies often affirm the racial attitudes of their era. Rather, cultural markets free from external regulation have the potential to create important critiques of illiberal attitudes. These may be relatively infrequent, but are nonetheless important.

CONCLUSION

W. E. B. DuBois (1903:1–2) famously wrote that "the problem of the twentieth century is the color line." DuBois lived in an era where the color line was incredibly stable and brutal. In his time, segregation was cemented in law and custom and the US Congress was unwilling to pass anti-lynching legislation. Globally, European empires ruled most of the earth. It is not difficult to see why DuBois, and many other Black intellectuals of his era, turned away from the promise of the open society and instead endorsed socialism.

This chapter offers an alternative to this assessment of open societies. While DuBois, and others, were correct to point out that racial repression existed within Western societies, they did not appreciate how unstable the global color line could be in the face of liberal, free institutions. The tools that were employed to combat and repeal brutal policies and shift public opinion were heavily embedded in a larger system of norms and expectations that define the open society. A free economy allows wealth to be applied to social change and free speech norms create cognitive dissonance in the larger society. Social change is not driven merely by material changes, but ideas matter as well. The ideals of equality and freedom can be used to illustrate the hypocrisy of the powerful. By understanding the dynamics of free institutions, we can gain a deeper appreciation of how freedom can erode the color line.

REFERENCES

Al-Gharbi, Musa. 2023. "The 'Great Awokening' of Scholarship May Be Ending." Heterodox Academy Blog. https://heterodoxacademy.org/blog/the-great-awokening-of-scholarship-may-be-ending/

Belknap, Michael. 1984. "The Vindication of Burke Marshall: The Southern Legal System and the Anti-Civil-Rights Violence of the 1960's." *Emory L. J.* 93.

Bell, D. A. 1980. "Brown v. Board of Education and the Interest-Convergence Dilemma." *Harvard Law Review*, 93(3), 518–33.

Bonilla-Silva, E. 2017. *Racism Without Racists: Color-Blind Racism and the Persistence of Racial Inequality in America* (5th ed). Oxford: Rowman & Littlefield.

Caplan, Bryan and Zach Weinersmith. 2019. *Open Borders: the Science and Ethics of Immigration*. First Second. New York.

Carlsson, F., and Lundström, S. 2002. "Economic Freedom and Growth: Decomposing the Effects." *Public Choice* 112, 335–344.

Cato Unbound. 2020. "Intersectionality and Classical Liberalism." https://www.cato-unbound.org/issues/may-2020/intersectionality-classical-liberalism/

Clair, M. and Denis, J.S. 2015. 'Sociology of racism,' *The International Encyclopedia of the Social and Behavioral Sciences,* 2: 857–63.

Clegg, John. 2020. "A Theory of Capitalist Slavery." *Journal of Historical Sociology* 33: 74–98.

Collins, Patricia Hill. 2014. *Black Feminist Thought: Knowledge, Consciousness, and the Politics of Empowerment*, 2nd edition. Routledge Press.

Collins, William J., and Marianne H. Wanamaker. 2014. "Selection and Economic Gains in the Great Migration of African Americans: New Evidence from Linked Census Data." *American Economic Journal: Applied Economics* 6 (1): 220–52.

Corrigan, Phillip. 1977. "Feudal Relics of Capitalist Monuments? Notes on the Sociology of Unfree Labor." *Sociology*, 11(3), 435–463. http://www.jstor.org/stable/42851926

Crenshaw, Kimberly. 1993. "Mapping the Margins: Intersectionality, Identity Politics, and Violence against Women of Color." 43 *Stan. L. Rev*. 1241 (1990–1991).

CR10 Publications Collective. 2008. *Abolition Now!: Ten Years of Strategy and Struggle Against the Prison Industrial Complex*. AK Press.

D'Angelo, Robin. 2018. *White Fragility: Why It's So Hard for White People to Talk about Racism.* Beacon Press.

Davis, Brandon. 2024. Chapter in 3 current volume.

Derenoncourt, Ellora. 2022. "Can You Move to Opportunity? Evidence from the Great Migration." *American Economic Review*, 112 (2): 369–408.
Desmond, Matthew. 2021. "Capitalism," pp. 165–87 in *The 1619 Project: A New Origin Story* edited by Nikole Hannah-Jones, Caitlin Roper, Ilana Silverman, and Jake Silverstein. One World.
Du Bois, W. E. B. 1903. *The Souls of Black Folk*. New York: Penguin.
Du Bois, W. E. B. 1935. *Black Reconstruction: An Essay toward a History of the Part which Black Folk Played in the Attempt to Reconstruct Democracy in America, 1860–1880*. Harcourt, Brace and Company.
Du Bois, W. E. B. 1948. "Race relations in the United States 1917–1947," *Phylon* (1940–1956), 9 (3): 234–47.
Dunivin, Zackary, Harry Yajoun Yan, Jelani Ince, and Fabio Rojas. 2022. "Black Lives Matter Protests Shift Public Discourse." *The Proceedings of the National Academy of Sciences*. 119 (10) e2117320119
Faulkenberry, T. Evan. 2016. "Poll Power: The Voter Education Project and the Financing of the Civil Rights Movement, 1961–1992." Dissertation. Department of History. The University of North Carolina at Chapel Hill.
Garrison,William L. 1973. *The Letters of William Lloyd Garrison*. Harvard University Press.
Go, Julian. 2020. "The Imperial Origins of American Policing: Militarization and Imperial Feedback in the Early 20th Century." *American Journal of Sociology* 2020 125:5, 1193–1254.
Guillebeau, Christopher.1999. "Affirmative Action in a Global Perspective: The Cases of South Africa and Brazil." *Sociological Spectrum*, 19:4, 443–65,
Harper, S., Lynch, J., Burris, S., and Davey Smith, G. Trends in the Black-White Life Expectancy Gap in the United States, 1983–2003. *JAMA*. 2007; 297(11): 1224–32. doi:10.1001/jama.297.11.1224
Hirschman, Albert O. 1970. *Exit, Voice, and Loyalty*. Harvard University Press.
Hoiles, R. C. 1942. "In his Own Words: R.C. Hoiles on WWII Japanese Internment." The Orange County Register. https://www.ocregister.com/2007/11/18/in-his-own-words-rc-hoiles-on-the-wwii-japanese-internment/
Hudson, Darrel L., Eli Puterman, Kirsten Bibbins-Domingo, Karen A. Matthews, Nancy E. Adler, Race. 2013. "Race, life course socioeconomic position, racial discrimination, depressive symptoms and self-rated health," *Social Science & Medicine* 97L7-14,
Hutt, William H. 1964. *The Economics of the Colour Bar*. London: The Institute for Economic Affairs.
Kendi, Ibram X. 2019. *How to be an Antiracist*. One World.
Lee, Taeku. 2002. *Mobilizing Public Opinion: Black Insurgency and Racial Attitudes in the Civil Rights Era*. The University of Chicago Press.
Levy, Jacob T. 2017. "Black Liberty Matters." *The Niskanen Center*. https://www.niskanencenter.org/black-liberty-matters/
Magness, Phillip. 2019. "Racial Determinism and Immigration in the Works of Ludwig von Mises: A Critique of Slobodian's Alt-Right Thesis." Social Science Research Network. https:// ssrn.com/ abstract= 3490 778.

Magness, Phillip. 2020a. "The Anti-discriminatory Tradition in Virginia School Public Choice Theory." *Public Choice* 183, 417–41.

Magness, Phillip. 2020b. "Does Classical Liberalism Need Intersectional Theory?" *Cato Unbound*. https://www.cato-unbound.org/2020/05/26/phillip-w-magness/does-classical-liberalism-need-intersectionality-theory/

Magness, Phillip. 2023. "Critical Race Theory in the Data: What the Statistics Show." *American Institute for Social Research* https://www.aier.org/article/critical-race-theory-in-data-what-the-statistics-show/

McCarthy, John D. and Mayer N. Zald. 1977. "Resource Mobilization and Social Movements: A Partial Theory." *American Journal of Sociology* 1977 82:6, 1212–1241.

Mill, John Stuart. 1869. *The Subjection of Women*. London: Longmans, Green, Reader, and Dyer.

Moore, W.L. and Bell, J.M. 2017. "The Right to Be Racist in College: Racist Speech, White Institutional Space, and the First Amendment." *Law & Policy*, 39: 99–120. https://doi.org/10.1111/lapo.12076

Morris, Aldon. 1983. *The Origins of the Civil Rights Movement*. Free Press.

Morris, Aldon. 2022. "Alternative View of Modernity: The Subaltern Speaks." *American Sociological Review* 87(1):1–16.

Mulligan, William and Maurice Eric, eds. 2013. *A Global History of Anti-Slavery Politics in the Nineteenth Century*. Palgrave.

NAACP. 2023. "Our History." Website of the National Association for the Advancement of Colored People. https://naacp.org/about/our-history

Noel, Hans. 2014. *Political Ideologies and Political Parties in America*. Cambridge University Press.

Quillian, L., Pager, D., Hexel, O., & Midtbøen, A. H. 2017. "Meta-analysis of field experiments shows no change in racial discrimination in hiring over time." *Proceedings of the National Academy of Sciences*, 114(41), 10870–15.

Ray, Victor. 2019. "A Theory of Racialized Organizations." *American Sociological Review*, 84(1), 26–53.

Ray, Victor. 2022. *On Critical Race Theory: Why it Matters and Why You Should Care*. Random House.

Ridgeway, C. L. 2014. "Why Status Matters for Inequality." *American Sociological Review*, 79(1), 1–16.

Rivera, L. A. 2012. "Hiring as Cultural Matching: The Case of Elite Professional Service Firms." *American Sociological Review*, 77(6), 999–1022.

Rojas, Fabio. 2007. *From Black Power to Black Studies: How a Radical Social Movement Became an Academic Discipline*. The Johns Hopkins University Press.

Rojas, Fabio. 2020. "Race," pp. 243–258 in *The Routledge Companion to Libertarianism* edited by Matt Zwolinski and Benjamin Ferguson. Routledge.

Rojas, Fabio. 2021. "Critical Race Theory." *Libertarianism.org*. https://www.libertarianism.org/topics/critical-race-theory#_ftn42

Rojas, Fabio. 2022. "Race." In *The Routledge Companion to Libertarianism*, edited by Matt Zwolinski and Benjamin Ferguson, 243–258. Routledge.

Rojas, Fabio. 2023. "The Black Reparations Project: A Handbook for Racial Justice," *Ethnic and Racial Studies*, DOI: 10.1080/01419870.2023.2279678

Sanghi, Siddhartha and Amy Smaldone. 2022. "The Evolution of the Racial Gap in U.S. Life Expectancy." The Federal Reserve Bank of St. Louis. https://www.stlouisfed.org/on-the-economy/2022/january/evolution-racial-gap-us-life expectancy#:~:text=Because%20of%20systemic%20differences%20in%20access%20to%20health,live%2075.3%20years%E2%80%943.5%20fewer%20years%20than%20white%20Americans

Seamster, L., & Ray, V. 2018. "Against Teleology in the Study of Race: Toward the Abolition of the Progress Paradigm." *Sociological Theory*, 36(4), 315–342.

Skrentny, J. D. 1998. "The Effect of the Cold War on African-American Civil Rights: America and the World Audience, 1945–1968." *Theory and Society*, 27(2), 237–285. http://www.jstor.org/stable/657868

Smith, Adam. 2005. *Lecture on Jurisprudence*. Liberty Fund Edition. http://dl.icdst.org/ pdfs/files/40620573fe42a9153911eda26f51be7b.pdf

Somin, Ilya. 2020. *Free to Move: Foot Voting, Migration, and Political Freedom*. Oxford University Press.

Tauber, Steven C. 1999. "The NAACP Legal Defense Fund and the U.S. Supreme Court's Racial Discrimination Decision Making." *Social Science Quarterly*, 80(2), 325–340. http://www.jstor.org/stable/42863903

US Census. 2020. "Poverty Rates for Blacks and Hispanics Reach Historic Lows in 2019." The United States Census Bureau. https://www.census.gov/library/stories/2020/09/poverty-rates-for-blacks-and-hispanics-reached-historic-lows-in-2019.html

US Census Bureau. 2022. Historical Income Tables: Households. https://www.census.gov/data/tables/time-series/demo/income-poverty/historical-income-households.html

Virdee, Satnam. 2019. "Racialized Capitalism: An Account of its Contested Origins and Consolidation." *Sociological Review* 67(1): 3–27.

NOTES

1. Readers who follow debates over critical race theory might be aware of classical liberal responses and critiques. The purpose of this chapter is to discuss how the sociological understanding of racial inequality and repression might be enriched by an exchange with classical liberalism. Thus, it might be a digression to review a debate occurring outside the traditional boundaries of sociology or critical race theory. For that reason, I will use this note to briefly summarize how classical liberals have responded to critical race theory and provide a few references. First, classical liberals tend to agree with critical race theorists that modern societies have very profound racial inequalities, but they disagree with critical race theorists' preferred policy solutions. One interesting example of this tendency is a debate that occurred in the now

defunct *Cato Unbound* journal. Political theorist Jacob Levy suggested that intersectional social theory, which is a theory closely aligned with critical race theory, has much to teach classical liberalism about the nature of racial inequity. He elaborated on a 2017 argument published by the Niskanen Center (Levy 2017). In contrast, economist and historian Phil Magness (2020b) argued that intersectionalism and related theories don't contribute much compared to existing work on racism. I argued (Rojas 2020) that it is deeply problematic that so many proponents of intersectionalism and critical race theory are quick to endorse socialist policies, which have a horrendous track record. Later, Magness (2023) has been critical of critical race theorists for implying that critics are engaged in a moral panic. I review the basics of critical race theory and its classical liberal critics in Rojas (2021).

Chapter 3

The Predatory States of America

Brandon Rudolph Davis

The existence of the predatory state and the inequality it produces requires a response. When societal inequalities grow so large as to threaten the fair operation of the political system, the political system should be used to ameliorate those inequalities (Tomasi 2012). Neutrality is tantamount to legitimizing the status quo and concealing its predacious machinations. Yet, all too often, when the state acts to reshape outcomes and behaviors, it is just as likely to exacerbate the problem as remedy it. Mass incarceration is an externality of a series of policy responses to increased crime rates and violence in urban minority communities. Moreover, state benevolence, like coercion, can also have negative effects on liberty. When governments act, there can be large gaps between intentions and outcomes. This is important because the more the government regulates, the less autonomy individuals have. Nevertheless, the principle of social justice requires more than just cursory acknowledgement and formal equality. It demands that people have access to the resources necessary to make their freedom valuable. A just society should be based on a fair system of mutual respect and cooperation, not social control, and coercion (Tomasi 2012).

In the liberal tradition, the legal system identifies and regulates cultural norms and laws. Nothing more clearly distinguishes a contract state from a predatory state than the rule of law. The rule of law protects the individual from others, the state, and from lesser forms of governance. All states use violence to enforce and maintain a standard of justice, but the contract state's use of violence is very different from the predatory state's application of the same power. The use of violence under the contract state presupposes the rule of law and formal equality. Within the contract state, the primary function of the government is to protect life and property, and the use of violence is legitimate only when based on an approved set of principles endorsed by the polis. This is how a just society manages the equitable distribution of justice (Tomasi 2012).

In the predatory state, there exist a distinct what, why, and how for the behavior of select social groups. What types of behavior are acceptable, why it's acceptable, and how it can be made unacceptable are essential to establishing and maintaining the two concurrent states. A predatory state is not just an institution, it's a political regime. Members of select social groups need only to believe that they will face higher levels of predation to alter their perceptions of what is possible and change their behavioral patterns, which inevitably aids in justifying their position within the predatory state.

The central problematic of the American criminal justice system is that crime and punishment are not directly related to criminal activity, and deviancy is not an earned status. Deviancy is a social construction, and crime and punishment are policy choices (Davis, B. 2021a, 591–615). The U.S. criminal justice system is a predacious institution, and it has been used with surgical precision to bifurcate the Americas polis. The Contract States of America are a constitutional, liberal democracy wherein the legal system not only establishes and respects individual rights, but also enforces transgressions of these rights. In the Predatory States of America, the use of violence is quotidian, and access to political rights, opportunities, and economic resources is significantly impaired if not completely cut off. I posit that conceptualizing the criminal justice system as part of the predatory state provides a vantage point for understanding how American social and political institutions have evolved to aid in the establishment and maintenance of both a contract and a predatory state. I will first examine the relationship between the predatory state and the criminal justice system and will then discuss how the distribution of justice occurs in the predatory state and how a predacious theoretical orientation fits within our understanding of criminal justice.

PREDATORY STATES AND CRIMINAL JUSTICE

Social identities are comprised of myths, stereotypes, belief systems, cultural characterizations, and popular images. They are generalized, subjective, and so much a part of our normal lives that we fail to see them (Tilly 2003). Moreover, identity formation is crucial to political membership. Political membership as a social construct is connected to one's social identity within the polis. Taken collectively, the members of the polis are called the people; individually, they are citizens in that they share in the power of the sovereign, and subjects as they are collectively under its authority. As members of the sovereign, they are bound to their fellow members, and as members of the state they are bound to the sovereign (Rousseau 1987). The concept of predatory state is rooted in the power and authority that the sovereign possesses over its subjects. Predation is the use of that power and authority to surveil and punish. Predation is not absolute, but it is a systemic, discreet, and effective means of social control that has been thoroughly ingrained within the liberal democratic state, making its manifestations seem commonplace (Davis, B. 2021b, 205–225). In the U.S., the predatory state is ubiquitous to the point of invisibility while at the same time operating openly through the criminal justice system.

The criminal justice system is such an effective state-making tool that for many citizens, their most frequent, visible, and direct contact with government is through local law enforcement, a state court, or a state prison, rather than through political or social institutions (Weaver and Lerman 2010, 817–833). Astonishingly, one-third of America's adult population has passed through the criminal justice system (Lerman and Weaver 2014a, 202–219), and some sixteen million U.S. residents have a criminal record (Brame et al. 2012, 21–27).

Mass incarceration is a policy choice. The growth of U.S. prison population was slow and methodical, the result of eleven presidential administrations and more than thirty congresses that exploited public fears of crime and racial tensions (Western 2006; Balko 2014). Therefore, crime and punishment are best understood as public choice problems. The systemic failures of the U.S. criminal justice system suggest the complicity of both prejudiced discriminators and unprejudiced discriminators. For example, if prosecutors are willing to bring charges in marginal and low-quality cases, it provides law enforcement with an incentive to make low-quality arrests, which I argue contributes to mass incarceration and the overrepresentation of racial minorities within the criminal justice system. Because the incentive structure within the criminal justice policy area only rewards punitive actions, punitive actions are repeated without question. Moreover, state actors—prosecutors, judges, and law enforcement—that engage in predatory behavior often face little to modest pushback and in some instances are encouraged to do so (DOJ 2015).

A public choice analysis as opposed to other critical theoretical positions is focused in part on the incentive structure and its effect on state actor decision making. For instance, Alabama and Mississippi are very similar. However, Mississippi has enacted policy changes that have significantly reduced its carceral footprint, whereas Alabama's Department of Corrections is on the verge of being taken over by the federal government due to massive overcrowding, violence, and inhumane conditions (McCann 2022; Hrynkiw 2023). From a public choice perspective, we can better understand why Alabama, facing a federal takeover and exorbitant (economic and humanitarian) costs, refuses to make any significant policy changes or release prisoners, even the elderly and infirmed (Hrynkiw 2023). The incentive structure surrounding criminal justice policy rewards punitivity to a point where it can obfuscate policy alternatives.

Applying a public choice approach helps us better understand the decision making of the individual, self-interested political actors behind these decisions. Governments, meaning politicians and bureaucrats, decide how crimes are policed, which laws are enforced, and when and with what severity to punish. Nevertheless, states and localities, not the federal government, are principally responsible for the criminal justice strategy and tactics utilized within their jurisdictions. Ultimately, decisions made at the state or local level determine the size of their correctional populations and their political choices have had serious implications for liberal democracy. States have the potential to be laboratories of both democracy and predation. With states' rights comes an equal, if not greater, obligation of a state's responsibilities.

Sociological research has found that the growth of the carceral state has been fueled by the incarceration of the poor and people of color (Western and Wildeman 2009, 221–242; Western and Muller 2013, 166–189; Pager, Western, and Sugie 2009, 195–213; Pattillo, Western, and Weiman 2004; Western and McClanahan 2000; Western, Lopoo, and McLanahan 2004, 21–45; Western 2006). Next to actual death, incarceration is one of the most severe punishments a society can impose. It is thought to serve one of three possible purposes: retribution, deterrence, or rehabilitation (Travis, Western, and Redburn 2014). Nevertheless, in every state, no matter the racial demographics, the incarceration rate for Blacks is higher than the rate for Whites (The Sentencing Project 2022b). At its height, the African American arrest rate was 1,460 per 100,000 (Western 2006). The drug-related arrest rate for Blacks was 4 times higher than for Whites, and Blacks were sent to prison for drugs offenses at 10 times the rate of Whites (NAACP 2016). These disparities exist even though Whites' reported drug use is five times larger (NAACP 2016). African American men born since the 1960s are more likely to have spent time in prison than have a bachelor's degree (Pettit 2012; Pettit and Western 2004, 151–169). Among prime-age (25–35) Black men, 15% of those who have not attended college and 33% of high school dropouts are incarcerated on an average day. The incarceration rate for Black male high school dropouts is an astonishing 35,000 per 100,000 (Travis, Western, and Redburn 2014). Moreover, mass incarceration has resulted in the disentrancement of 5.2 million Americans (Travis, Western, and Redburn 2014). Of which, the population is disproportionately young, Black, male, and poor. Over 5% of the adult Black population is disenfranchised (Travis, Western, and Redburn 2014; The Sentencing Project 2022b) and 1 in 19 voting-aged Blacks and over half a million Latino/a Americans are prohibited from voting (The Sentencing Project 2022b).

Since 2010, the number of incarcerated persons in the U.S. has steadily decreased from the 2008 all-time high of 2.3 million. In 2020, the Bureau of Justice Statistics (BJS) reported that there were 1.2 million people under the jurisdiction of state and federal correctional authorities and an additional 3.9 million individuals on community corrections (or probation and parole). The total U.S. correctional population, which includes every adult in custody (including pretrial detention), and on probation and parole, is over 5.5 million people (Bureau of Justice Statistics 2023). This is still a substantially larger population than any other nation and remains historically and comparatively unprecedented. Moreover, some 60% of America's correctional population are racial and ethnic minorities. The United States of America, the leader of the free world, incarcerates more of its residents *and* more of its racial and ethnic populations than any other nation.

Two national factors undoubtedly contributed to the decline in the U.S. prison population. First, since the 1990s there has been a continued and persistent decrease in the U.S. crime rate. Between 1993 and 2019 the Bureau of Justice Statistics (BJS) reported that the violent and property crime rates fell 74 and 71%, respectively (Criminal Victimization 2022). Scholars have offered various explanations as to why the U.S. crime rate fell so abruptly (Levitt 2004, 163–190). Nonetheless, the origins of the decline are still up for debate. Second, the forty year, 500% increase in the U.S. prison population created serious overcrowding issues in state prisons (The Sentencing Project 2022a). Consequently, state correctional expenditures have increased 347% (Urban Institute 2022). Criminal justice spending accounts for $1 of every $20 spent at the state level, $1 of every $5 spent at the county level, and $1 of every $6 spent at the municipal level (Auxier et al. 2020). Notwithstanding, reductions in crime rates and/or correctional costs and overcrowding were not on their own (or together) directly correlated with policy movement (Davis, B. 2023, 484–510). However, states did manage to make policy changes that reduced their correctional populations. Taking a public choice approach will help us better understand why some states made policy changes and others did not and why some states' policy changes were more effective than others.

Since 2010, forty-six states have made (or were forced to make) reductions in their prison populations, but the efficacy of these reforms and interventions has varied considerably. Nine states made considerable progress, reducing their prison populations between 30 and 43% (Ghandnoosh 2021, 1–5).[1] In twenty-five states, the reductions in population were less than 10%, while in twelve others, such reductions amounted to less than 5%, and in six, the reduction was between 0% and 1% (Ghandnoosh 2021, 1–5).[2] Prison admissions have fallen 32%, and the local jail population has decreased 26% (4.2 million). Lastly, the community corrections population (probation and parole) has decreased 22% (1.6 million), of which 97% are under the jurisdiction of state and local authorities (Probation and Parole Populations 2022; Jail Inmates 2022). The latter point is important because, if the alternative to incapacitation had been an increased reliance on community corrections, it would have effectively expanded state carceral footprints. Notwithstanding, numerous criminal justice policies have been associated with decarceration. However, the most successful state policy interventions and reforms focused on decreasing prison admissions through the reclassification of low-level felony drug and property crimes to misdemeanors, creating or expanding early release opportunities including making recalcifications retroactive, and decreasing prison readmissions of probationers and parolees for technical violations (Davis, B. 2023, 484–510).

The legal system is one part of the larger institution of social control and regime stability. However, it has a clear dual functionality. Its function within the predatory state is to make oppression and subjugation common practice through frequent and direct contact. The predatory state employs two distinct social control tactics to achieve this goal. The *front-loaded apparatuses* establish and maintain a steady state of conceptual incarceration, creating criminogenic conditions. The *back-loaded mechanisms* refer to the classed, gendered, racial, spatial, and generational concentration of policing tactics and the normalization of the disparate use of violence (Hawkins 2011, 3–48).

The predatory state utilizes violence toward a myriad of purposes. Violence is both a rational and effective means of reaching desired outcomes (Arendt 1970). It can be produced unilaterally, bilaterally, or multilaterally, and it can be used for both strategic and tactical purposes (Kalyvas 2006). Moreover, the use of violence increases with the extent of organizational specialization. The ability to employ violence is directly related to institutional size and capacity (Tilly 2003). Arguably, the criminal justice system has the largest social footprint of any U.S. institution, as indicated by the fact that its collective machinations have been termed “the carceral state.”

COMMUNITY AND NETWORK SPILLAGE

An institution with the size and capacity of the U.S. criminal justice system will undoubtedly produce some political spillage. The development of the American carceral state was a social phenomenon that has produced vast social problems, the negative effects of which, in some instances, can be identified with precision down to a street or city block. Yet these effects still produce significant community and network spillage. A large body of research has found that the racial, geographic, and spatial nature of predation produces adverse societal effects and can result in communal disengagement and de facto civic death. Surprisingly, research has found that criminality, per se, does not drive lower participation, but contact with the criminal justice system does (Weaver and Lerman 2010, 817–833).

Some scholars argue that lower participation rates in high-imprisonment communities are due to the diffusion of nontraditional beliefs (Hannerz 1969). These beliefs are thought to be shared through the process of cultural transmission and direct observation. Cultural transmission (or social learning) occurs when previously incarcerated individuals share their political opinions, beliefs, and attitudes with others in the social network. Research has found that living in neighborhoods with large community corrections populations has a politically demobilizing effect (Burch 2014), and that living in proximity to former inmates exposes neighbors to higher levels of apathy and perceptions of institutional discrimination (Abu-Jamal 1996, 42–47). Direct observation refers to the idea that living in proximity to former inmates increases the probability that neighbors will personally observe their neighbors having negative interactions with law enforcement and community corrections officers. Witnessing these negative interactions could have adverse interpretive effects on community members' perceptions of justice and their place within the polis.

Another line of inquiry focuses on group adaptations to social processes rather than on individual criminality. Social disorganization theories posit that some communities are unable to self-regulate due to the negative effects of incarceration, and as a result, some residents do not conform to formal and/or informal institutions of social control (Bursik Jr. and Grasmick 1999). Formal social networks include official affiliations such as political and organization memberships, while informal social networks include unofficial, non-biological kinship bonds and peer networks. Incarceration has been associated with familial destabilization and decreased community solidarity (Edin, Nelson, and Paranal 2001). The community loses the ability to enforce political and civic obligations, which contributes to lower levels of political participation.

Imprisonment damages social networks. Residents of high-imprisonment neighborhoods are less likely to join social and political organizations. Membership in local political and civic organizations trains citizens for political activity (Brady, Verba, and Schlozman 1995, 271–294). Research has found that trust and civic duty are learned from organizational involvement (Brehm and Rahn 1997, 999–1023). Imprisonment is also major source of social shame for the formerly incarcerated and their familial network, and social shame is correlated with decreased political and civic engagement (Austin 2004, 173–192).

By far, economic strain—on account of legal financial obligations, missed work, and attempts to maintain familial relationships—is the most reported source of stress related to incarceration (Johnson, R. 2009, 177–206).

Household poverty has been found to increase after family-member incarceration (Arditti, Lambert□Shute, and Joest 2003, 195–204). Over 50% of incarcerated fathers were the primary source of income for their family (Glaze and Maruschak 2008). Most often, women are left to expend the time, energy, and money necessary for maintaining the relationships. Even providing moral and emotional support through letters, phone calls, and visits is economically taxing. Resource (or economic) deprivation theory argues that imprisonment removes residents who contribute economically, forcing remaining members to cover the losses, depriving them of the time they would need to join organizations and develop civic skills (Verba, Schlozman, and Brady 1995). During incarceration, families must cover the costs of amenities, such as phone calls, food, and toiletries, which burdens impoverished families. Following release, 42% of men remain unemployed for up to one year (Visher, Debus-Sherrill, and Yahner 2011, 698–718). These men often reenter society burdened with large arrearages in child support, as well as parole and probation fines and fees that put additional economic stress on families. These legal and financial obligations also carry the additional threat of re-incarceration as a penalty for nonpayment (Katzenstein and Waller 2015, 638–656). Moreover, courts have upheld financial obligation laws that prevent the previously incarcerated from voting until their debt is paid in full (Meredith and Morse 2017, 309–338).

In addition, even short sentences in city or county jail are negatively associated with voter registration and turnout (Lerman and Weaver 2014b). Routine contact, such as being stopped, frisked, or pulled over by police, has been found to adversely affect political participation (Epp, Maynard-Moody, and Haider-Markel 2014). Research has also found that network contact has an adverse effect on governmental trust and feelings of civic duty (Davis, B. 2020, 909–924) and an adverse effect on individual well-being, which all correlate with political participation (Davis, B. 2021a, 591–615).

If the net effect of carceral contact is a reduction in participation, then select social groups are more likely to be excluded from democratic processes and from influencing political outcomes, creating inequalities of representation. This process undergirds the dual state. Moreover, it carries serious social and political implications for liberal democracy. For this reason, it is important to parse out which aspects of the criminal justice system are associated with the front- and back-loaded mechanisms of social control.

FRONT-LOADED APPARATUSES: PREDATORY POLICING AND ENFORCEMENT POLICIES

Police are the human embodiment of the state's monopoly on violence. The mere existence of police in a free society is a phenomenon worth contemplation. In liberal democracies, any concentration of power is viewed with skepticism, and as such, is curtailed by institutional checks and balances. Nevertheless, we are willing to invest street-level bureaucrats with the power to detain, arrest, invade privacy, and use lethal force. Policing is fundamentally about that legal order, but it is also a political profession, and as such, norms are partly responsible for law enforcement strategies. Policing or law enforcement strategies appear to lack epistemic and improvement norms, which are key to knowledge acquisition and production, and accountability.

One finds significant resistance within police departments to incorporating epistemic and improvement norms, arguably because to do so would increase accountability and create a public record of the predation meted out by police departments across the nation. In addition, idealized depictions of what is and is not "real police work," such as crime fighting and warrior policing, continue to shape the structure, operation, and culture of police departments. Policing has always been a dangerous job. And yet, it has become much safer since the 1970s, and that fact alone does not alleviate law enforcement's obligation to protect lives, including those of criminals. Police in the U.S. kill hundreds of unarmed suspects each year and maim countless others in situations where using a nonlethal response would not have put the officer's life in danger (Jones and Mendieta 2021).

A copious amount of research has confirmed that Blacks, Hispanics, and Native Americans are arrested at rates disproportionate relative to Whites. In addition, race has been found to play a more significant role in the policing of minor offenses (nonviolent crimes such as drug offenses) compared to arrests for violent crimes (e.g., murder, assault). This is despite self-reported similarities across race and ethnicity in committing minor offenses (Finkeldey and Demuth 2019, 1–25). Nevertheless, African Americans are 127% more likely, and Hispanics 60% more likely, to be arrested for drug offenses than are Whites. Overall, Blacks are 120% more likely, and Hispanics 38% more likely, than Whites to be arrested for drug distribution, and by age 29, Blacks are 247% more likely, and Hispanics 60% more likely, to have experienced an arrest than have Whites (Mitchell and Caudy 2017, 91–112). Disparities in drug distribution arrests between Blacks and Whites remained statistically significant when scholars controlled for neighborhood context (Mitchell and

Caudy 2017, 91–112). This data suggests that policing or law enforcement strategies are responsible for racial disparities in arrest rates.

Between 2004 and 2012, the New York Police Department (NYPD) made 4.6 million stops and frisked 2.4 million people (Ferrandino 2015, 209–229). 90% of all the NYPD stops were of non-whites and likewise 90% of these stops resulted in no summons being issued or arrests made (Mummolo 2018, 1–15). The NYPD disproportionately stopped non-whites, even though stops of Whites were more likely to yield contraband. In 2013, a federal judge ruled that the New York Police Department had been seriously abusing its stop-and-frisk authority (Ferrandino 2015, 209–229). The day after the court decision, the NYPD issued a memo reaffirming that all stops must be documented. The very next day, the number of stops declined drastically but the probability of recovering a weapon increased significantly (Mummolo 2018, 1–15). There followed a 90% decrease in stops; nevertheless, the New York City (NYC) crime rate continued to decline (White et al. 2016, 9–66).

A survey of individuals in NYC found that 71% of young people had been frisked. 91% reported threats and/or the use of physical force, 25% said the officer displayed a weapon, and 51% stated their mistreatment was based on their race (Fratello, Rengifo, and Trone 2013). Stop-and-Frisk is a highly aggressive and invasive policing strategy with serious constitutional implications for the Fourth Amendment. Nevertheless, the NYPD showed little to no curiosity about learning whether it was even effective or justifiable.

Preying on a subset of the NYC population and violating that group's constitutional rights was normal practice. Understanding policing as the front-loaded apparatuses of the predatory state, we can see how it makes oppression and subjugation common practice through frequent and direct contact. The negative externalities associated with policing are consistent with the goal of establishing and maintaining a steady state of conceptual incarceration and creating criminogenic conditions.

BACK-LOADED MECHANISMS: MISDEMEANOR ADJUDICATIONS AND SENTENCING

State courts handle over 90% of the nation's judicial business (George and Yoon 2017, 1887–1910). In 2019, there was an estimated grand total of 83.2 million incoming state cases. Of which, 78% consisted of traffic (42.2 million), civil (16.8 million), domestic relations (4.8 million), and juvenile cases (1.1 million). The remaining 22% were criminal cases (18.3 million). Of the criminal cases, 79% were misdemeanor cases (13.7 million) (Gibson et al. 2022). Natapoff (2018) was first to develop a national estimate of misdemeanor offenses (13 million in 2015) and Mayson and Stevenson

(2020) conducted the first multijurisdictional analysis of misdemeanor case processing. They found that the misdemeanor system disproportionately affects the poor and people of color, and that each jurisdiction relies on cash bail, which results in high rates of pretrial detention (Mayson and Stevenson 2020, 971–1044). This is important for two reasons. First, research has found that forgoing prosecution of nonviolent misdemeanor offenders is correlated with a 53% decrease in the probability of future offending (Agan, Doleac, and Harvey 2023, 1453–1505). Second, defendants from low-income zip codes are 15% more likely to be detained pretrial than defendants from wealthier zip codes (19% less likely) (Heaton, Mayson, and Stevenson 2017, 711–794). Pretrial detention increases the probability that a misdemeanant will plead guilty (25%), *irrespective of actual guilt*, and be sentenced to jail (43%) with a sentence twice the average term length (Heaton, Mayson, and Stevenson 2017, 711–794).

Misdemeanor convictions may also include large fines. Non-payment can result in a warrant for arrest and possibly jail time (Natapoff 2018). In the twenty-seven states with open arrest warrants, there are currently 5.7 million outstanding warrants, which do not include thousands of warrants held at local courthouses (Wagner et al. 2022). However, only 4% (240,000) of outstanding warrants involve violence, weapons, or sex crimes. Of the states with open records, Michigan has the most warrant cases (1.04 million), of which 1.7% are for violent offenses (Wagner et al. 2022).

Court dispositions of misdemeanors are woefully lacking. In New York State, since the late 1990s, over 40% of all misdemeanor dispositions have ended in some form of dismissal. Since 2010, over 50% of misdemeanor cases in New York State have ended in a dismissal, compared to under 20% ending in a conviction, of which the vast majority were conditional discharges (Kohler-Hausmann 2018), the U.S. Supreme Court has determined that misdemeanants who face fewer than six months in jail have no right to a jury trial, and that defendants who are not incarcerated have no right to legal counsel (Natapoff 2018). A National Association of Criminal Defense Lawyers (NACDL) (Boruchowitz et al. 2009) report found that the increased numbers of misdemeanor cases had placed a significant burden on courts and defense lawyers. The NACDL also found that even when there was a right to counsel, misdemeanants were often not informed or threatened with increased jail time to pressure defendants into waiving their right to counsel (Boruchowitz, Brink, and Dimino 2009).

In trial courts, defendants are at the mercy of the prosecutors—the most powerful and least accountable actors in the criminal justice system (Capers 2019, 1561–1610). Prosecutors have unfettered discretion, which despite its potential for abuse, is essential to the functioning of the system. Discretion gives prosecutors, even more than judges, immense control over the direction and outcome of criminal cases. They have sole discretion over seeking the death penalty. No other court official, including judges, juries, or any other individual or body, may initiate the process (Davis, A. J. 2007). Prosecutors wield this immense power alone. Other actors in the criminal justice system have little if any influence on the decisions of individual prosecutors (Wright 2017, 85–100).

Prosecutors initiate the criminal adjudication process, and the initial charging stage is the key moment in all prosecutions. The power to charge has increased over the years through the expansion of the criminal code and the length of sentences attached to criminal convictions. In addition, charges are not singular: any particular action may violate numerous criminal statutes. Prosecutorial charging decisions are central to their function and are effectively unreviewable (Wright, Levine, and Gold 2021). This is important because prosecutors are more likely to charge minority defendants than Whites with felonies (Davis, A. J. 2013, 821–851). Even when controlling for pre-charge case characteristics, prosecutors are still twice as likely to bring charges against a Black defendant (Davis, A. J. 2007), and Blacks are twice as likely as Whites to be charged with a crime carrying a mandatory minimum sentence (Rehavi and Starr 2014, 1320–1354). Starr and Rehavi (2014) found that after the U.S. Supreme Court made judicial mandatory sentencing guidelines optional, prosecutors' ability to control sentencing outcomes was adversely affected. As a result, there was a sharp and racially disparate increase in charges carrying mandatory minimum sentences (Starr and Rehavi 2013, 2–81). How prosecutors decide to adjudicate cases helps to reinforce policing tactics and normalizes the disparate application of violence.

Some legal scholars argue that prosecutorial powers and the impact they have on mass incarceration is overblown (Bellin 2019, 171–212; Bellin 2018, 835–857; Neal and Rick 2016, 1–41). Moreover, when a prosecutor decides to file charges, a suspect becomes a defendant, and defendants are arraigned in front of a judge. Once in court, judges control the proceedings. During pre-trial hearings, judges can discharge defendants or dismiss charges if they are not satisfied with the government's case. Post-arraignment and pre-trial, judges can grant motions to dismiss based on procedural irregularities, meritorious challenges to the validity of the charges, or constitutional rights violations, prosecutorial misconduct, etc. (Wright, Levine, and Gold 2021). Judges decide whether to accept or decline plea agreements. When a plea agreement is made, the court is tasked with determining if a factual basis exists for the guilty plea, and if the case were to be tried, would the government be able to prove every element of the crime beyond a reasonable doubt (Wright et al. 2021). Judges also empanel and instruct juries and rule on evidence. Prosecutors may recommend sentences, but judges decide on the sentence imposed, and they can depart from sentencing guidelines.

States adopted sentencing guidelines to increase uniformity in sentencing and decrease racial disparities (Tonry 2019, 1–34). Guidelines are recommendations based on the severity of the offense and the defendant's criminal history. These two factors intersect on a sentencing table and determine a sentencing range delineated by a minimum and maximum number of months of incarceration (Frase 2019, 79–135). Research has found that guidelines decreased the magnitude of racial disparities in sentencing (King and Light 2019, 365–437), and yet those disparities still persist (Painter-Davis and Ulmer 2020, 263–293). Blacks and Latinos remain more likely to be sentenced to prison, and for longer periods of time, than Whites and Asians. Blacks receive sentences 20% longer than Whites even when holding constant age, gender, and recommended sentence guideline lengths (Bushway and Piehl 2001, 733–764). An examination of 63,000 cases found that 57% of Blacks who had two prior convictions and had been given probation each time who were subsequently convicted of a third offense were sentenced to prison, compared to only 6% of similarly situated White offenders (Bell 2004).

Research on the sentencing of Latinos and Asians is underdeveloped relative to research on Black-White sentencing disparities (Johnson, B. D. and Betsinger 2009, 1045–1090; Steffensmeier and Demuth 2000, 705–729). Nevertheless, scholars have found that Latinos are sentenced at rates comparable to Blacks (Bales and Piquero 2012, 742–773; Demuth and Steffensmeier 2004, 994–1011). Latino defendants have the highest probability of receiving a harsh sentence (Steffensmeier and Demuth 2001, 145–178). 93% of Latinos sentenced under federal guidelines are incarcerated, compared to 85% of Blacks, 74% of Whites, and 71% of Asians (Walker, Spohn, and DeLone 2016). In state courts, 67% of Latinos sentenced for non-drug offenses are imprisoned, compared to 63% of Blacks and 46% of Whites. Latino drug offenders received the most punitive outcomes (Steffensmeier and Demuth 2000, 705–729). 87% of Latinos sentenced for drug offenses are imprisoned, compared to 70% of Blacks and 52% of Whites (Walker et al. 2016).

Asians receive the shortest sentences. Asians are 35% less likely than Whites, 37% less likely than Blacks, and 80% less likely than Hispanics to be sentenced to prison. Young White, Black, and Latino males have an 18, a 42, and a 106% greater probability of incarceration, respectively, than young Asian males (Johnson, B. D. and Betsinger 2009, 1045–1090). Scholars found no differences in the odds of incarceration for Asian and White drug offenders; however, Black and Hispanic drug offenders are over twice as likely as Asian drug offenders to be imprisoned (Walker et al. 2016).

Some scholars argue that judicial departures from sentencing guidelines are the primary reason racial disparities in sentencing persist (Albonetti 1997, 789–822; Kramer, John and Steffensmeir 1993, 357–376; Mustard 2001, 285–314). Park (2017) found evidence that racial disparities in sentencing are symptomatic of taste-based discrimination. Judges are required to consider sentencing guidelines, but they can depart from them and impose more lenient or more severe sentences. Subsequently, Blacks and Latinos are less likely than Whites to receive downward departures (Kramer, John H. and Ulmer 1996, 81–106; Ulmer 1997) or shorter sentences (Johnson, B. D., Ulmer, and Kramer 2008, 737–783; Kramer, John H. and Ulmer 2002, 897–932). For Blacks and Latinos, judicial departures are correlated with a greater probability of upward departures and longer sentences (Painter-Davis and Ulmer 2020, 263–293).

The sentencing disparities persist despite the guidelines and the discretion judges have in the courtroom. The discretionary power invested in judges and prosecutors is key to the functioning of a just legal system. But within the predatory state, this discretionary power is used to select and reinforce the disparate application of state violence.

CONCLUSION AND IMPLICATIONS

Under the predatory state, laws and institutions have emerged that aid in the establishment and maintenance of undeserved inequalities. Undeserved inequalities are those imposed by external forces, and which an individual cannot avoid or opt out of. If a person studies longer or practices more often, they can overcome some natural inequalities, but not all undeserved inequalities. Undeserved inequalities are structural or institutional disadvantages based on who a person is within the polis, and they inhibit the capacity of a group of people to exercise their rights and capitalize on opportunities. They are *not* the root cause of all inequalities, but they can pose significant impediments.

The most objectionable feature of the predatory state is its propensity toward obscurantism: rejecting well-substantiated new knowledge because the implications run contrary to the political ideology that justifies its existence. I do not deny that we must apply reason and prudence in accepting the conclusions drawn from the latest high-tech mathematical models. However, the reasons for the hesitancy must themselves be rational. I have little patience with those who oppose, for instance, the idea of systemic racism, simply because of the implications, and still less with those who regard it as unpatriotic or socialist to ask these questions at all.

The U.S. prison population has increased exponentially for over forty years and its expansion cannot be ascribed solely to higher levels of crime. Tragically, the burden of these negative outcomes is being borne disproportionately by the poor and by racial minorities. The executive branch and Congress created criminal justice polices with bad incentive structures that changed how American states and localities policed, sentenced, and incarcerated, and which in turn produced unfailingly negative outcomes for a subset of Americans. The growth of the predatory state has been slow and methodical, the result of policy choices of eleven presidential administrations, federal officials, and congressional legislators who exploited public fears of crime and declared wars on abstractions. Out of these abstractions, the predatory state was born. Acknowledging this will aid us in better understanding the American dual state.

The growth of mass incarceration is synonymous with the growth of government. And as the U.S. carceral footprint expands, so too does the reach of government into our everyday lives, which includes the criminalization of behaviors between consenting adults, albeit drugs use or sex work. Elizabeth Brown (2017; 2020; 2015) has reported extensively on U.S. law enforcement initiatives targeted at the horrendous practice of sex trafficking. Akin to the War on Drugs, lawmakers are using fear and inaccurate statistics (Kessler 2022) and federal dollars to incentivize local law enforcement to conduct sting operations around the country (Brown 2017). One such initiative, Operation Cross Country, involved agents from 55 FBI field offices, 74 federally led Human Trafficking Task Forces, and more than 400 federal, state, and local law-enforcement agencies (Brown 2017; FBI 2016). The first Cross Country operation resulted in the arrests of 21 teenagers (mostly 16- and 17-year-olds) for prostitution and 55 people the FBI described as pimps or traffickers. In addition, 175 adults were arrested for solicitation and 290 adults, mostly women, were arrested for prostitution. Operation Cross County II resulted in the arrest of 47 teenagers and 518 adults for prostitution, 73 adults for pimping, and 41 adults for unrelated charges. Between 2010 and 2015 over 10,000 people were arrested; nevertheless, only 1,800 of those arrestees were convicted of a crime.

Sex trafficking is abhorrent, and it must be sussed out wherever it exists. Notwithstanding, most of the arrests have been of adults engaging in consensual sex. Brown (2015) argues that " . . . even as the drug war's failures and costs become more apparent, the [U.S. has already began to repeat] the same mistakes when it comes to sex trafficking." The expansion of the carceral state has moved the government away for its narrower focus of protecting negative rights. As such the social control apparatus of the state has become ever more concerned with forcing people to behave according to the machinations of lawmakers and bureaucrats.

Central to the classical liberal tradition is the belief that liberty is freedom from coercion. And yet coercion is needed to facilitate human progress. It is necessary, for example, for the creation of social order. In that sense, classical liberalism is as much a philosophy as it is a form of social organization (Fawcett 2018). Within a liberal governmental order, members are free to choose their own path insomuch as they accept societal responsibilities and constraints. The disparities within the U.S. criminal justice system represent a failure of the liberal governmental order. Government failure is understood as the effect a set of institutional arrangements has on the social order. Evaluating institutional arrangements to understand which arrangements produce the most just social distribution is essentially an examination of governmental failure. For classical liberals, institutional arrangements should be arranged to protect the political rights of all members and respect them as autonomous self-authors. The standard should be a society in which all members are subject to the rule of law, have formal equality before the law, and have equal access to due process.

REFERENCES

Abu-Jamal, Mumia. 1996. "Live from Death Row." *Journal of Criminal Justice and Popular Culture* 4 (2): 42–47.

Agan, Amanda Y., Jennifer L. Doleac, and Anna Harvey. 2023. "Misdemeanor Prosecution." *Quarterly Journal of Economics* 138 (3): 1453–1505.

Albonetti, Celesta A. 1997. "Sentencing Under the Federal Sentencing Guidelines: Effects of Defendant Characteristics, Guilty Pleas, and Departures on Sentence Outcomes for Drug Offenses, 1991–1992." *Law and Society Review*: 789–822.

Arditti, Joyce A., Jennifer Lambert-Shute, and Karen Joest. 2003. "Saturday Morning at the Jail: Implications of Incarceration for Families and Children." *Family Relations* 52 (3): 195–204.

Arendt, Hannah. 1970. *On Violence*. New York: Harcourt, Brace & World.

Austin, Regina. 2004. "The Shame of It All: Stigma and the Political Disenfranchisement of Formerly Convicted and Incarcerated Persons." *Colum. Hum.Rts.L.Rev.* 36: 173–192.

Auxier, Richard C., Tracy Gordon, Nancy G. La Vigne, and Kim Rueben. 2020. "Criminal Justice Finance in the COVID-19 Recession and Beyond." Urban Wire. Urban Institute, accessed 10/31, 2022, https://www.urban.org/urban-wire/criminal-justice-finance-covid-19-recession-and-beyond.

Bales, William D. and Alex R. Piquero. 2012. "Racial/Ethnic Differentials in Sentencing to Incarceration." *Justice Quarterly* 29 (5): 742–773.

Balko, Radley. 2014. *Rise of the Warrior Cop: The Militarization of America's Police Forces*. New York, NY: PublicAffairs.

Bell, Derrick A. 2004. *Race, Racism, and American Law.* New York, NY: Aspen Publishers, 2004; 5th ed.

Bellin, Jeffrey. 2019. "The Power of Prosecutors." *NYUL Rev.* 94 (2): 171–212.

———. 2018. "Reassessing Prosecutorial Power through the Lens of Mass Incarceration." *Michigan Law Review* 116 (6): 835–857.

Boruchowitz, Robert C., Malia N. Brink, and Maureen Dimino. 2009. *Minor Crimes, Massive Waste: The Terrible Toll of America's Broken Misdemeanor Courts.* National Association of Criminal Defense Lawyers.

Brady, Henry E., Sidney Verba, and Kay Lehman Schlozman. 1995. "Beyond SES: A Resource Model of Political Participation." *American Political Science Review* 89 (02): 271–294.

Brame, R., M. G. Turner, R. Paternoster, and S. D. Bushway. 2012. "Cumulative Prevalence of Arrest from Ages 8 to 23 in a National Sample." *Pediatrics* 129 (1): 21–27.

Brehm, John and Wendy Rahn. 1997. "Individual-Level Evidence for the Causes and Consequences of Social Capital." *American Journal of Political Science*: 999–1023.

Brown, Elizabeth N. 2015. "The War on Sex Trafficking is the New War on Drugs." https://reason.com/., accessed November 18, 2022.

———. 2017. "American Sex Police." https://reason.com/., accessed November 18, 2022, https://reason.com/2017/03/14/american-sex-police/.

———. 2020. "Massage Parlor Panic." https://reason.com/., accessed November 18, 2022, https://reason.com/2020/02/02/massage-parlor-panic/.

Burch, Traci. 2014. "Mass Imprisonment and Political Participation: Evidence from North Carolina." *The Annals of the American Academy of Political and Social Science*.

Bureau of Justice Statistics. "Prisoners." Bureau of Justice Statistics. U.S. Department of Justice, Office of Justice Programs, accessed July 27, 2023, https://bjs.ojp.gov/.

Bursik Jr., Robert J. and Harold G. Grasmick. 1999. *Neighborhoods & Crime*. New York: Lexington Books.

Bushway, Shawn D. and Anne Morrison Piehl. 2001. "Judging Judicial Discretion: Legal Factors and Racial Discrimination in Sentencing." *Law and Society Review*: 733–764.

Capers, I. Bennett. 2019. "Against Prosecutors." *Cornell L.Rev.* 105 (6): 1561–1610.

Criminal Victimization. "Bureau of Justice Statistics." Bureau of Justice Statistics. U.S. Department of Justice, Office of Justice Programs, accessed October 24, 2022, https://bjs.ojp.gov/library/publications/list?series_filter=Criminal%20Victimization.

Davis, Angela J. 2007. *Arbitrary Justice: The Power of the American Prosecutor.* Oxford University Press.

———. 2013. "In Search of Racial Justice: The Role of the Prosecutor." *NYUJ Legis.& Pub.Pol'Y* 16 (3): 821–851.

Davis, Brandon. 2021a. "Feeling Politics: Carceral Contact, Well-being, and Participation." *Policy Studies Journal* 49 (2): 591–615.

———. 2021b. "Predation in State and Nation." *Race and Justice* 11 (2): 205–225.

———. 2023. "State Incarceration Policy in the US Federal System: Assessing Recent Approaches to Reducing Incarceration Rates." *Publius: The Journal of Federalism* 53 (3): 484–510.

———. 2020. "Testing Mechanisms: Carceral Contact and Political Participation." *Social Science Quarterly* 101 (2): 909–924.

Demuth, Stephen and Darrell Steffensmeier. 2004. "Ethnicity Effects on Sentence Outcomes in Large Urban Courts: Comparisons among White, Black, and Hispanic Defendants." *Social Science Quarterly* 85 (4): 994–1011.

DOJ. 2015. *Investigation of the Ferguson Police Department*. Washington, D.C.: U.S. Department of Justice.

Edin, Kathryn, Timothy Jon Nelson, and Rechelle Paranal. 2001. *Fatherhood and Incarceration as Potential Turning Points in the Criminal Careers of Unskilled Men.* Institute for Policy Research, Northwestern University Evanston, IL.

Epp, Charles R., Steven Maynard-Moody, and Donald P. Haider-Markel. 2014. *Pulled Over: How Police Stops Define Race and Citizenship*. Chicago, IL: University of Chicago Press.

Fawcett, Edmund. 2018. *Liberalism: The Life of an Idea*. Princeton, NJ: Princeton University Press.

FBI. 2016. "FBI Announces Results of Operation Cross Country X." www.fbi.gov., last modified October 17, accessed February 24, 2023, https://www.fbi.gov/news/press-releases/fbi-announces-results-of-operation-cross-country-x.

Ferrandino, Joseph. 2015. "Minority Threat Hypothesis and NYPD Stop and Frisk Policy." *Criminal Justice Review* 40 (2): 209–229.

Finkeldey, Jessica G. and Stephen Demuth. 2019. "Race/Ethnicity, Perceived Skin Color, and the Likelihood of Adult Arrest." *Race and Justice*: 1–25.

Frase, Richard S. 2019. "Forty Years of American Sentencing Guidelines: What Have We Learned?" *Crime and Justice* 48 (1): 79–135.

Fratello, Jennifer, Andrés F. Rengifo, and Jennifer Trone. 2013. "Coming of Age with Stop and Frisk: Experiences, Self-Perceptions, and Public Safety Implications." *New York: Vera Institute of Justice*.

George, Tracey E. and Albert H. Yoon. 2017. "Measuring Justice in State Courts: The Demographics of the State Judiciary." *Vand.L.Rev.* 70 (6): 1887–1910.

Ghandnoosh, Nazgol. 2021. *Can We Wait 60 Years to Cut the Prison Population in Half?* Washington, DC: The Sentencing Project.

Gibson, S., Harris, B., Waters, N., Genthon, K., Hamilton, M. and Robinson, D. "Csp Stat." Court Statistics Project., accessed December 2, 2022, www.courtstatistics.org.

Glaze, Lauren E. and Laura M. Maruschak. 2008. *Parents in Prison and their Minor Children.* US Department of Justice, Office of Justice Programs Washington, DC.

Hannerz, Ulf. 1969. *Soulside: Inquiries into Ghetto Culture and Community.* New York: Columbia University Press.

Hawkins, Darnell F. 2011. "Things Fall Apart: Revisiting Race and Ethnic Differences in Criminal Violence Amidst a Crime Drop." *Race and Justice* 1 (1): 3–48.

Heaton, Paul, Sandra Mayson, and Megan Stevenson. 2017. "The Downstream Consequences of Misdemeanor Pretrial Detention." *Stan.L.Rev.* 69 (3): 711–794.

Hrynkiw, Ivana. "Alabama Prisons Won't Release Elderly and Ailing: 'I Sure did Think I would Die in there.,'" last modified February 21, accessed February 27, 2023, https://www.al.com.

Jail Inmates. "Bureau of Justice Statistics." Bureau of Justice Statistics. U.S. Department of Justice, Office of Justice Programs, accessed October 24, 2022, https://bjs.ojp.gov/library/publications/list?series_filter=Jail%20Inmates.

Johnson, Brian D. and Sara Betsinger. 2009. "Punishing the 'Model Minority': Asian-American Criminal Sentencing Outcomes in Federal District Courts." *Criminology* 47 (4): 1045–1090.

Johnson, Brian D., Jeffery T. Ulmer, and John H. Kramer. 2008. "The Social Context of Guidelines Circumvention: The Case of Federal District Courts." *Criminology* 46 (3): 737–783.

Johnson, Rucker. 2009. "Ever-Increasing Levels of Parental Incarceration and the Consequences for Children." *Do Prisons Make Us Safer? The Benefits and Costs of the Prison Boom*: 177–206.

Jones, Ben and Eduardo Mendieta, eds. 2021. *The Ethics of Policing: New Perspectives on Law Enforcement*. NY: NYU Press.

Kalyvas, Stathis N. 2006. *The Logic of Violence in Civil War.* Cambridge Univ Press.

Katzenstein, Mary Fainsod and Maureen R. Waller. 2015. "Taxing the Poor: Incarceration, Poverty Governance, and the Seizure of Family Resources." *Perspectives on Politics* 13 (3): 638–656.

Kessler, Glenn. 2022. "Human Trafficking Statistics: Politicians Love them Though they Remain Imprecise." www.washingtonpost.com., last modified Jaunary 27, accessed February 24, 2023, https://www.washingtonpost.com/politics/2022/01/27/human-trafficking-statistics-politicians-love-them-though-they-remain-imprecise/.

King, Ryan D. and Michael T. Light. 2019. "Have Racial and Ethnic Disparities in Sentencing Declined?" *Crime and Justice* 48 (1): 365–437.

Kohler-Hausmann, Issa. 2018. *Misdemeanorland: Criminal Courts and Social Control in an Age of Broken Windows Policing.* Princeton University Press.

Kramer, John H. and Jeffery T. Ulmer. 2002. "Downward Departures for Serious Violent Offenders: Local Court '"corrections'" to Pennsylvania's Sentencing Guidelines." *Criminology* 40 (4): 897–932.

———. 1996. "Sentencing Disparity and Departures from Guidelines." *Justice Quarterly* 13 (1): 81–106.

Kramer, John and Darrell Steffensmeir. 1993. "Race and Imprisonment Decisions." *The Sociological Quarterly* 34 (2): 357–376.

Lerman, Amy E. and Vesla Weaver. 2014a. "Staying Out of Sight? Concentrated Policing and Local Political Action." *The Annals of the American Academy of Political and Social Science* 651 (1): 202–219.

Lerman, Amy E. and Vesla M. Weaver. 2014b. *Arresting Citizenship: The Democratic Consequences of American Crime Control.* Chicago: University of Chicago Press.

Levitt, Steven D. 2004. "Understanding Why Crime Fell in the 1990s: Four Factors that Explain the Decline and Six That Do Not." *Journal of Economic Perspectives* 18 (1): 163–190.

Mayson, Sandra G. and Megan T. Stevenson. 2020. "Misdemeanors by the Numbers." *BCL Rev.* 61 (3): 971–1044.

McCann, Sam. 2022. "What You Need to Know about the Alabama Prison Strike," last modified October 27, accessed February 27, 2023, https://www.vera.org/news/what-you-need-to-know-about-the-alabama-prison-strike.

Meredith, Marc, and Michael Morse. 2017. "Discretionary Disenfranchisement: The Case of Legal Financial Obligations." *The Journal of Legal Studies* 46 (2): 309–338.

Mitchell, Ojmarrh and Michael S. Caudy. 2017. "Race Differences in Drug Offending and Drug Distribution Arrests." *Crime & Delinquency* 63 (2): 91–112.

Mummolo, Jonathan. 2018. "Modern Police Tactics, Police-Citizen Interactions, and the Prospects for Reform." *The Journal of Politics* 80 (1): 1–15.

Mustard, David B. 2001. "Racial, Ethnic, and Gender Disparities in Sentencing: Evidence from the US Federal Courts." *The Journal of Law and Economics* 44 (1): 285–314.

NAACP. "Criminal Justice Fact Sheet." 2016. http://www.naacp.org/criminal-justice-fact-sheet/.

Natapoff, Alexandra. 2018. *Punishment without Crime: How our Massive Misdemeanor System Traps the Innocent and Makes America More Unequal*. New York, NY: Basic Books.

Neal, Derek and Armin Rick. 2016. "The Prison Boom and Sentencing Policy." *The Journal of Legal Studies* 45 (1): 1–41.

Pager, Devah, Bruce Western, and Naomi Sugie. 2009. "Sequencing Disadvantage: Barriers to Employment Facing Young Black and White Men with Criminal Records." *The Annals of the American Academy of Political and Social Science* 623 (1): 195–213.

Painter-Davis, Noah and Jeffery T. Ulmer. 2020. "Discretion and Disparity Under Sentencing Guidelines Revisited: The Interrelationship between Structured Sentencing Alternatives and Guideline Decision-Making." *Journal of Research in Crime and Delinquency* 57 (3): 263–293.

Park, Kyung H. 2017. "Do Judges have Tastes for Discrimination? Evidence from Criminal Courts." *Review of Economics and Statistics* 99 (5): 810–823.

Pattillo, Mary, Bruce Western, and David Weiman, eds. 2004. *Imprisoning America: The Social Effects of Mass Incarceration*. New York, NY: Russell Sage Foundation.

Pettit, Becky. 2012. *Invisible Men: Mass Incarceration and the Myth of Black Progress.* Russell Sage Foundation.

Pettit, Becky and Bruce Western. 2004. "Mass Imprisonment and the Life Course: Race and Class Inequality in US Incarceration." *American Sociological Review* 69 (2): 151–169.

Probation and Parole Populations. "Bureau of Justice Statistics." Bureau of Justice Statistics. U.S. Department of Justice, Office of Justice Programs, accessed October 24, 2022, https://bjs.ojp.gov.

Rehavi, M. Marit and Sonja B. Starr. 2014. "Racial Disparity in Federal Criminal Sentences." *Journal of Political Economy* 122 (6): 1320–1354.

Rousseau, Jean Jacques. 1987. *Basic Political Writings*. Translated by Donald A. Cress. Indianapolis: Hackett Publishing.

Starr, Sonja B. and M. Marit Rehavi. 2013. "Mandatory Sentencing and Racial Disparity: Assessing the Role of Prosecutors and the Effects of Booker." *Yale LJ* 123 (1): 2–81.

Steffensmeier, Darrell and Stephen Demuth. 2001. "Ethnicity and Judges' Sentencing Decisions: Hispanic-black-white Comparisons." *Criminology* 39 (1): 145–178.

———. 2000. "Ethnicity and Sentencing Outcomes in US Federal Courts: Who is Punished More Harshly?" *American Sociological Review*: 705–729.

The Sentencing Project. 2022a. "Growth in Mass Incarceration." The Sentencing Project, accessed October 24, 2022, https://www.sentencingproject.org/research/.

———. 2022b. "The Sentencing Project." The Sentencing Project. The Sentencing Project, accessed October 26, 2022, http://www.SentencingProject.org/.

Tilly, Charles. 2003. *The Politics of Collective Violence / Charles Tilly* Cambridge, U.K.; New York: Cambridge University Press, 2003.

Tomasi, John. 2012. *Free Market Fairness*. Princeton, NJ: Princeton University Press.

Tonry, Michael. 2019. "Fifty Years of American Sentencing Reform: Nine Lessons." *Crime and Justice* 48 (1): 1–34.

Travis, Jeremy, Bruce Western, and F. Stevens Redburn, eds. 2014. *The Growth of Incarceration in the United States: Exploring Causes and Consequences*. Washington D.C.: National Academies Press.

Ulmer, Jeffery T. 1997. *Social Worlds of Sentencing: Court Communities Under Sentencing Guidelines*. SUNY Press.

Urban Institute. "Criminal Justice Expenditures: Police, Corrections, and Courts." State and Local Backgrounders. Urban Institute, accessed October 31, 2022, https://www.urban.org/policy-centers/cross-center-initiatives/state-and-local-finance-initiative/state-and-local-backgrounders/criminal-justice-police-corrections-courts-expenditures.

Verba, Sidney, Kay Lehman Schlozman, and Henry Brady. 1995. *Voice and Equality: Civic Voluntarism in American Politics*. Vol. 4. Cambridge Univ Press.

Visher, Christy A., Sara A. Debus-Sherrill, and Jennifer Yahner. 2011. "Employment After Prison: A Longitudinal Study of Former Prisoners." *Justice Quarterly* 28 (5): 698–718.

Wagner, Mike, Doug Caruso, Daphne Chen, and John Futty. "Wanted: Suspects Run Free while Authorities Drown in Open Arrest Warrants." USA Today Network News. National Data & Investigations Team, last modified Nov. 21, accessed December 5, 2022, https://stories.usatodaynetwork.com/warrants/wanted-suspects-run-free-while-authorities-drown-in-open-arrest-warrants/.

Walker, Samuel, Cassia Spohn, and Miriam DeLone. 2016. *The Color of Justice: Race, Ethnicity, and Crime in America*. Cengage Learning.

Weaver, Vesla M. and Amy E. Lerman. 2010. "Political Consequences of the Carceral State." *American Political Science Review* 104 (04): 817–833.

Western, Bruce. 2006. *Punishment and Inequality in America / Bruce Western*. New York: Russell Sage, c2006.

Western, Bruce, Leonard Lopoo, and Sara McLanahan. 2004. "Incarceration and the Bonds among Parents in Fragile Families." *Imprisoning America: The Social Effects of Mass Incarceration*: 21–45.

Western, Bruce and Sara McClanahan. 2000. *Fathers Behind Bars: The Impact of Incarceration on Family Formation.* Princeton University.

Western, Bruce and Christopher Muller. 2013. "Mass Incarceration, Macrosociology, and the Poor." *The Annals of the American Academy of Political and Social Science* 647 (1): 166–189.

Western, Bruce and Christopher Wildeman. 2009. "The Black Family and Mass Incarceration." *The Annals of the American Academy of Political and Social Science* 621 (1): 221–242.

White, Michael D., Henry F. Fradella, Weston J. Morrow, and Doug Mellom. 2016. "Federal Civil Litigation as an Instrument of Police Reform: A Natural Experiment Exploring the Effects of the Floyd Ruling on Stop-and-Frisk Activities in New York City." *Ohio St.J.Crim.L.* 14: 9–66.

Wright, Ronald F. 2017. "Prosecutor Institutions and Incentives." *Criminology, Crim. just.L & Soc'Y* 18 (3): 85–100.

Wright, Ronald F., Kay L. Levine, and Russell M. Gold. 2021. *The Oxford Handbook of Prosecutors and Prosecution.* Oxford University Press.

NOTES

1. Arkansas, New Jersey, New York, Connecticut, Alabama, Rhode Island, Vermont, Hawaii, and California.

2. Conversely, during this same period, the prison populations increased in Montana, Idaho, Nebraska, and Kansas, peaking in 2019 (Ghandnoosh 2021).

Chapter 4

Classical Liberal Feminism and Gendered Labor Markets

Charlotta Stern

WHY CLASSICAL LIBERAL INSIGHTS ON GENDER AND LABOR MARKETS?

Most sociologists lean left. In surveys and voter-registration studies, the ratio of Democrats to Republicans in American sociology ranges between 59 to 1 and 19.5 to 1 (Klein and Stern 2009; see also Klein and Stern 2006; Duarte et al. 2014).[1] One survey reports more self-identified Marxists (25.5 percent) than self-identified Republicans (5.5 percent) in sociology (Gross and Simmons 2007), and another finds that more sociologists are comfortable with the prospect of working with a Communist colleague than a Republican or a hard-core Christian (Yancey 2011).[2]

More disputed is whether the near monopoly of the left is problematic. Most people would agree that ideological monopoly is a problem if the one-sidedness 1) creates a culture where ideological beliefs are treated as self-evidently true, 2) stunts theorizing and understanding by shunting research into certain ideas or topics, or 3) leads researchers to ignore inconvenient knowledge or plausible alternative explanations.

In this chapter, I argue that all three problems surface in the sociological study of gender differences in the labor market (henceforth sometimes referred to as gender sociology).[3] I also argue that the problems emanate from the particular definition of equality embraced by the left, and thus that the two are causally related to one another and greatly overlap.

HOW LEFT-FEMINIST IDEOLOGY AND CLASSICAL LIBERAL FEMINISM DIFFER

Before looking at each of these problems, I wish to compare the perspective that dominates sociological studies of gender differences in the labor market and the classical liberal alternative. To simplify, let's call the dominant sociological perspective "left-feminist." The left-feminists consists of a heterogeneous group of Marxist, socialist, critical, constructivist feminism, post-modern feminists (see, e.g., Tong 1989). In left-feminism, observable differences between men and women are the result of repression, discrimination, and/or patriarchal culture. Absent social constraints, humanity is assumed to be homogenous on a profound level, and men and women would be and act about the same way. A truly equal society, this thinking goes, is a society where couples "engage symmetrically in employment and caregiving" (Gornick & Meyers 2009, 4). Thus, inequality ends when there are virtually no differences between men and women in their care for children, choices of work, and labor market results (England 2010; Ridgeway and Correll 2004; Ridgeway 2009), or, in other words, there are "slim-outcome differences."

In envisioning such a society, left-feminism is bold, to say the least, since no society known to us shows such slim differences between men and women. It is also collectivist in that the end-goal of slim-outcome differences encompasses everyone. If women (and men) do not (yet) prefer, aspire, or choose the lifestyles defined as equal, they are unwilling victims of culture and oppression (examples of this argument include Charles and Grusky 2007; Ridgeway 2009; West and Zimmerman 1987). The victimhood stands in contrast to, among others, corporate men (and women), who strive to hold onto the power and privilege vested in patriarchy (England 2010).

In contrast, classical liberal feminism belongs firmly within the broader classical liberal tradition of individual rights, freedom of choice, and equality before the law. Classical liberal feminists share a belief in equal value of and equal rights for women and men but differ on what counts as equality. In classical liberal feminism, equality means that men and women have the same rights to pursue happiness in ways they see fit, assuming that they do not infringe on anyone else's right to do the same (Hoff Sommers 1994; Ingelhardt and Welzel 2005; McElroy 1982, 2002; Pinker 2002; Taylor 1992). It is an individualistic feminism favoring a society where women and men are free to express their different preferences, aspirations, and lifestyles. Classical liberal feminism is humble rather than bold; it does not presume that all individuals share the same goals. It is also stern, a feminism that strongly believes in reason and toleration, and presumes that individuals themselves are responsible for and best able to judge their pursuit of life goals.[4]

It seems common to describe the feminist movement as evolving from classical liberal feminism, often referred to as the first wave feminism, into the modern left-wing feminism, the third wave. Such descriptions seem to suggest that classical liberal feminism somehow is obsolete and a feminism of the past. Perhaps this is because the classical liberal definition of a feminist encompasses an ideology most people of the West agree upon; most Westerners think it is obvious that women and men should have equal rights. In that sense, we are all feminists. In Western societies, governments overall do grant nearly the same rights and obligations to both sexes, so feminism as a political struggle is not central to a classical liberal feminist.

While simplified, the depiction of two feminist ideologies highlights one indication of how the near monopoly of left-wing feminist ideology in gender sociology has created a situation where one definition of equality, slim-outcome differences, is the only definition discussed. In this view, an equal society is one in which women and men share parenting equally, strive equally for positions of status and power, and prefer occupations in a similar fashion. Had there been more ideological diversity in the field, I hypothesize, there would have been more discussion of the definition of equality itself, and more debate about whether it is reasonable to assume that all men and women share the goals of slim-outcome differences. For instance, under this presumption it would seem that a traditional lifestyle is incompatible with equality as well as with being a feminist. But with more ideological diversity, alternative definitions of equality such as free (formally unlimited) choice and movement, a classical liberal definition of equality, traditional lifestyles are not only acceptable but compatible with feminism (see also Winegard, Winegard, and Geary 2015).

A CULTURE WHERE IDEOLOGICAL BELIEFS ARE SEEN AS SELF-EVIDENTLY TRUE

On the surface, the sociology study of gender differences in the labor market seems heterogeneous; there is devaluation theory (England 2010), cognitive frame theory (Ridgeway 2009), structural theory (Risman 2004), and doing gender (West and Zimmerman 1987), to name a few. In fact, however, the ideology of slim-outcome differences limits scholars in the field to acknowledge only social constructivist theorizing.

This is despite the fact that evolutionary science continues to amass knowledge about how the reproductive differences between men and women have coevolved with corresponding hormonal, cognitive, and physiological differences between men and women (Baron-Cohen 2003; Campbell 2013; Pinker 2002). Examples of studies showing plausible biological differences, including hormone studies showing that "male" testosterone affects dominance, whereas "female" oxytocin affects social bonding (see studies cited in Croft et al. 2015). Similarly, as a result of such hormonal differences, competition studies show that men are more willing to compete than are women (Niederle and Vesterlund 2011). Men are also more inclined to take risks than are women (Byrnes, Miller, and Schaffer 2009). This willingness to compete and take risks often stems from over-confidence rather than actual competence (Niederle and Vesterlund 2011). Personality studies find that women are more agreeable, conscientious, extroverted, and neurotic than are men (Costa, Terracciano and McCrae 2001; Vianello et al. 2013; see also Feingold 1994). Intelligence studies show that men, on average, score higher on spatial ability and women, on average, score higher on verbal ability (Halpern 2012; Kimura 1999; see also special issue of *Mankind Quarterly* 2016; for Sweden see Madison 2016). There also seem to be fewer women in both the top and bottom of the IQ-distribution (Deary 2012; Flores-Mendoza et al. 2013; Johnson, Carothers and Deary 2008, Wai, Putallaz, and Makel 2012), suggesting that overall women are more "normal" than men.

Evolution may thus have shaped average differences in interests and preferences between men and women, differences that seem relevant to consider when trying to understand gender differences in the labor market. For example, occupational preference studies show that women are more likely to prefer occupations dealing with people, and men more likely to prefer occupations dealing with inanimate things, known as the systematizing-empathizing or people-things dimensions (Baron-Cohen 2003; Browne 2006; Gottfredson 1999; Holland 1959, 1997; Johnson et al. 2008). In sociology, preference theory stipulates that whereas men overall prefer a lifestyle centered on work and career, women prefer three different types of lifestyles: a minority of women prefer a lifestyle centered on the household, another minority of women prefer a lifestyle centered on work and career, while most women prefer a mixed lifestyle, balancing work and family life (Hakim 1995, 1998, 2002, 2008).

These differences between men and women in competitiveness, personality, IQ, and preferences are common findings in some parts of sociology and in neighboring fields. All of them are reported as stable results over time and contexts. Yet in sociological studies of labor market differences between men and women, they are ignored. Hypotheses about sex differences based on biological-difference ideas are rarely engaged (but see, e.g., Lueptow, Garovic-Szabo and Lueptow 2001; Udry 1995, 2000) and if they are, authors are often put under serious scrutiny and the results are ignored or doubted.[5]

Instead of acknowledging biological-differences ideas, scholars in the field write about gender differences in preferences as "essentialist ideology," which they say perpetuates erroneous stereotypes about natural male and female characteristics (Charles and Grusky 2007; England 2010). Explaining the essentialist ideology from their perspective, Charles and Grusky write:

> Although prevailing characterizations of male and female traits are complex and multifaceted, a core feature of such characterizations is that women are *presumed* to excel in personnel service, nurturance, and interpersonal interaction, and men are *presumed* to excel in interaction with things (rather than people) and in strenuous or physical labor. These *stereotypes about natural male and female characteristics* are disseminated and perpetuated through *popular culture and media*, through *social interaction* in which significant others (parents, peers, teachers) implicitly or explicitly support such interpretations, and through *micro-level cognitive processes* in which individuals pursue and remember evidence consistent with their preexisting stereotypes and ignore, discount, or forget evidence that undermines those stereotypes. (Charles and Grusky 2007, 333, italics added)

A careful examination of this quotation reveals how a seemingly multifaceted characterization is really just depicting one theme—that gender is socially constructed (highlighted by added italics). Charles and Grusky (2007) go on to argue that "essentialist" presumptions are internalized by employers, who practice "essentialist discrimination" and allocate men and women in accordance with them, and by workers, who aspire to occupations that satisfy "essentialist preferences" (ibid.). The concept "essentialist ideology" treats evolutionary differences as little more than cultural stereotypes. The left-feminist stance also shines through when Charles and Grusky (2004, 340) present the tradition of classical liberalism as a problem in reaching equality: " . . . the second revolution will face many obstacles, not the least of which is an entrenched tradition of classical liberalism that celebrates individual choice and thus supports and sustains those forms of inequality that can be represented as consistent with it." One fears to think of their alternative to the classical liberal tradition of celebrating choice.

In a related paper studying cross-national occupational sex segregation, Charles and Bradley (2009) discuss gendered preferences and claim to define it "in its broadest sense here, to encompass values socialized and internalized at the individual level, as well as the performative enactment of cultural scripts" (928). Yet "the broadest sense" includes only socially constructed mechanisms as underlying preferences. In a footnote following the definition, they do acknowledge that some social scientists have treated differences in preferences as in some sense genetic, citing Baron-Cohen's (2003) book *The Essential Difference.* The book presents research regarding how men's and women's brains are differently affected by hormones during development so that, on average, more women are "empathizers" whereas more men are "systemizers." But nothing more is mentioned in the article about this alternative explanation of preferences. A quick look into more recent studies of segregation suggest that slim-difference theorizing is still the norm in the field, and alternative explanations are not entertained (Thébaud and Charles 2018; Torre & Jacobs 2021; Humlum, Nandrup and Smith 2019).

A CONSTRUCTIVIST THEORY-MONOPOLY LIMITS THE QUALITY OF SCHOLARSHIP

As reviewed above, Charles and co-authors illustrate how sociologists studying labor market differences between men and women exclude all but socially constructed mechanisms from theorizing. Such neglect of well-established empirical findings and their potential impact on differences between men and women is unfortunate. Taking differences seriously could potentially yield new insights regarding male-female stratification. One could speculate that average differences between the sexes in terms of empathy or risk-taking affect choices in the labor market, choices that over time translate into average differences in career paths. Since sociologists are inherently interested in understanding mechanisms underlying social stratification, it seems damaging to expel such relevant and potent input.

Partly, of course, a focus on social constructivism in theorizing is a valid disciplinary choice in that sociology, as a discipline, deals with the social web of humans (see Horowitz, Yaworsky, and Kickham 2014). A sociologist myself, I am not suggesting that socialization and discrimination are unimportant social mechanisms. The radical changes of the last two hundred years have extended available roles, norms, identities, and choices for women (and men). In modern liberal democracies, women have rights to own property, vote in elections, and attend university. The pre-modern state-backed subjection of women to male rule is an equally clear illustration of how important female discrimination has been. As usual, classical liberals (feminist or not) frown upon government policies that infringe on individual rights!

Even so, theorizing that socialization and discrimination are the main, or even the sole, explanations for the remaining differences between men and women seems scientifically dubious given knowledge about evolutionary differences.[6] The slim-outcome difference definition of equality coupled with the lock-in of social constructivist theorizing locks in a culture of blank-slate scholarship (Pinker 2002), that is, scholarship that presumes the mind is free from innate traits, a *tabula rasa* shaped by experience or perception (Stern 2016).[7]

WHAT WOULD BE GAINED IF CLASSICAL LIBERAL EQUALITY WAS INCLUDED

In this section my aim is to give a few examples of how the domination of left-feminism limits what hypotheses are tested and what alternative explanations there could be for empirical findings. In what follows, gender equality in Sweden is used as a background to illustrate the limitation.

Sweden is often touted as one of the most gender-equal countries in the World (see, for instance, World Economic Forum 2015; UNDP Human Development Report 2015). Swedish culture is the most "feminine" culture in the world (Hofstede, Hofstede, and Minkov 2010). Typically, a feminine culture values social relations and quality of life. In a feminine culture, gender roles are more fleeting, with small differences between male and female roles.[8] Sweden is also the country with the most secular-rational citizens who state strong post-materialist values of self-expression, as seen in figure 4.1, which maps each country's location on two dimensions. On the vertical axis, the dimension called traditional versus secular-rational values indexes a number of questions relating to how important religion, traditional family

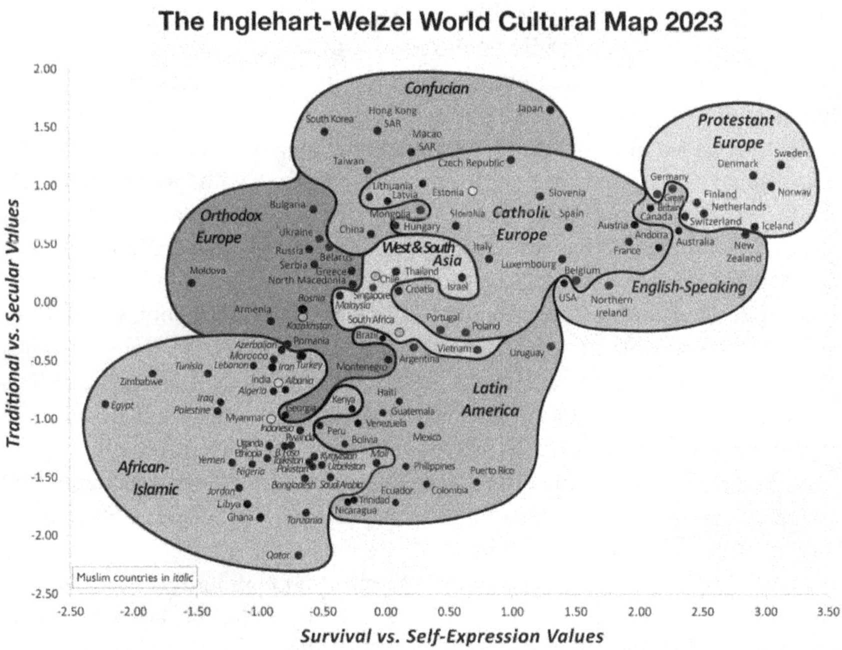

Figure 4.1. The Inglehart-Welzel World Cultural Map. World Values Survey 7 (2023). http://www.worldvaluessurvey.org/

values, and deference to authority, etc., are among people in a country. On the horizontal axis, the dimension called survival versus self-expression indexes a number of questions relating to the importance of economic and physical security, etc. Cultures ranking high on self-expression are high-trust cultures, with tolerance toward others, and high regard for individual freedom (Ingelhardt and Welzel 2005).

It should come as no surprise then that most Swedes hold gender-egalitarian attitudes (Jakobsson and Kotsadam 2010), and are positive toward gender equality at home (Bernhardt, Noack, and Lyngstad, 2008).

In 1974, Sweden became the first country to implement state-supported parental leave. Swedish parents can freely share 12 months of paid parental leave (Duvander, Ferrarini, and Thalberg 2005). Sweden has tax-funded and heavily subsidized preschools available to all children over one year of age, and Swedish children are on average enrolled in pre-school by the time they are 1.5 years old (Duvander 2006). These state-supported family policies have often been credited for Sweden's success in combining a (relatively) high fertility rate with high female labor force participation rates (Duvander et al. 2005; Sjöberg 2004).

Swedish men and women participate in the labor market to almost the same extent (90 percent of males and 85 percent of females; SCB 2022). Less than five percent of women are homemakers (ibid.). As in most wealthy Western countries, Swedish women outperform men in school grades and in educational achievement (SCB 2022).

Still, when making choices in the educational system, women tend to choose educational fields that lead to occupations dealing with people, and men tend to choose educational fields leading to occupations dealing with things (Statistics Sweden 2014; see also Gottfredson 1999). The pattern has been quite stable since the 1970s (Jonsson 2004). The result is a gender-segregated labor market (Kumlin 2010; Halldén 2014), and, as it turns out, up until the 1990s, Swedish women and men were more segregated into different occupations than women and men in the United States, Germany, Portugal, and Italy (Charles and Grusky 2004; Blackburn, Jarman and Brooks 2000). Today, Sweden is a mid-level segregated country, partly because of changes in the Swedish labor market, and partly because some Eastern European countries and some Southern European countries have more-segregated labor markets than they did in the end of the 1990s (Halldén 2014).

In Sweden, traditional gender-role socialization and anti-female discrimination have withered; sex segregation in the labor market has not. One of the most influential attempts to understand the stability in Sweden and world-wide is Charles and Grusky's (2004) book *Occupational Ghettos*. To understand the "failure of egalitarianism" (Charles and Grusky 2007, 329; see also Charles 2008; Charles and Bradley 2009; Charles and Grusky 2004) an explanation is put forth based on the co-existence of "liberal egalitarian values" with an "essentialist ideology." According to their theory, segregation of women and men into different occupations persists in Sweden because:

> Normative mandates for self-expression and the associated celebration of individual choice encourage sex segregation because males and females draw upon different cultural schemas and different social resources as they seek to realize and express their true "selves," and because they anticipate that others will hold them accountable to established gender scripts (Charles and Bradley 2009, p. 929).

It is fair to say that the Swedish state has both encouraged and enforced dual-earner/dual-care families (or slim-outcome-difference feminism) in both policy and ideology.[9] In spite of this, it also seems that Swedish culture tolerates and even supports the individual's freedom to choose lifestyles relatively free from traditional values, so that men and women are empowered to explore choices that express their interests and preferences to an exceptional degree compared to other countries.[10] If social context matters for outcomes, it makes little sense to explain Sweden's occupational segregation as merely a product of "essentialist ideology." Such an explanation would seem to lack an answer to how such "essentialist ideology" is sustained when traditionalist norms are eroded and government policy militates against outcome differences.

Continuing to view occupational segregation as a strong sign of inequality only makes sense if one holds a slim-difference view of equality. Had there been room for more a classical liberal understanding of equality, the stability of occupational segregation in the Swedish context would perhaps have been open to alternative hypotheses informed by evolutionary-based preference differences between men and women. Including classical liberal intuitions would open up new avenues of research and push knowledge further. A classical liberal understanding of equality would also question whether a labor market characterized by slim-outcome-difference, called "full integration" and "complete equality" in Charles and Grusky's terminology, is a desirable social state, especially if it is achieved by government coercion.

OTHER EXAMPLES OF UNTESTED HYPOTHESIS AND UNDEREXPLORED ALTERNATIVE EXPLANATIONS

To summarize, for the most part gender sociologists assume that absent structural and cultural constraints such as glass ceilings and "essentialist" attitudes about household labor, there would be slim-outcome differences between men and women (i.e., a left-feminist version of equality). Seldom is it seriously discussed whether the slim-difference assumption is a reasonable expectation.

The purpose of the following section is to outline some examples of untested hypotheses and underexplored explanations to give some concrete examples of potential knowledge lost due to missing explorations into differences between men and women informed by evolutionary science. Explorations of such differences, in combination with social variables, would get us closer to discerning how much of the success gap is driven by differences between women and men and how much is driven by differential treatment of women and men. For instance, occupational positions that yield high incomes and power tend to be stressful, competitive, and demanding. A difference-informed sociology would explore whether fewer women than men find such positions attractive (Pinker 2009). Perhaps fewer women feel they would thrive in a competitive climate, or be willing to tolerate the stress and acrimony of being a boss, and prefer to take up occupations that are more collaborative, etc. All of these are testable hypotheses that, as far as I know, have remained untested in sociological studies of labor market difference between women and men.

I hypothesize that such difference-informed theorizing is rare because it would challenge the slim-difference outcome hypothesis and open up the possible conclusion that fewer women aspire to and compete for recognition and status in the workplace.

Similarly, very few studies investigate the potential impact of differences between men and women in productivity on work-life success. Wages and promotions are partially determined by productivity, broadly defined. We rarely measure such differences in on-the-job productivity directly because it is hard to measure. However, one area where productivity can be measured is in academic publishing. Studies of academic publishing tend to find average differences between men and women in publishing, differences that used to be large (Cole and Zuckerman 1984; Long 1992) but are declining (Xie and Shauman 1998). One source of the mean difference in publishing is that top producers are more likely to be male (Cole and Zuckerman 1984, Long 1992).

Productivity differences between men and women have also been found in matched employer-employee data from Denmark, where women on average are found to be less productive than men (Gallen 2015). Gallen finds that mothers are paid much lower wages than men, but according to her findings, mothers' estimated productivity gap completely explains their pay gap (Gallen 2015, 1).

Large-scale studies in sociology and economics where productivity is estimated with more easily observed approximations, such as tenure, work-place experience, education, and on-the-job training, show that differences in productivity explain part of the male-female wage gap.[11] The wage gap, however, is never "fully explained." The never-fully-explained part can be interpreted as cultural discrimination against women (England 1992; 2010) or unmeasured productivity differences (Becker 1985), or a combination of the two. In cultural explanations, wage gaps between mothers and fathers are theorized as due to stereotypes of mothers being less committed to work, and fathers as serious breadwinners. The latter explanation is found in studies of "daddy bonuses" (Hodges and Budig 2010) and "motherhood penalties" (Correll, Benard, and Paik 2007; see also Budig and England 2001; Anderson, Binder, and Krause 2003). In contrast, Becker (1985) theorized that mothers, on average, may be less productive because they use more of their energy caring for children.[12]

It seems likely that both productivity and cultural explanations have merit, and therefore the small amount of attention aimed at exploring differences between men and women in productivity is unfortunate. After all, men and women behave very differently in their division of time between household and labor markets. Returning to the Swedish context, for instance, we find that the opportunities to share parental leave time equally among parents has had a small but increasing effect on parental choice. On average, women take 75 percent of the parental leave. When they return to work, women with small children work part-time (Statistics Sweden 2012). Swedish women do more household work than their spouses (ibid.). On average, we also find that Swedish women are absent from work about twice as much due to sickness than are men (Statistics Sweden 2012), and stay home from work to take care of sick children more often than fathers (Eriksson 2011). On average, women, especially mothers with small children, may very well be or be seen as less productive at work. Given their larger responsibilities for childcare, it would be astonishing if they were not.

A DIFFERENCE-INFORMED EXPLANATION OF LABOR MARKET SUCCESS

Asking questions informed by potential differences could further our understanding of the persistence of differences between men and women in the labor market. Interestingly, a difference-informed alternative has been available in sociology at least since the 1990s. In a number of articles and books, Catherine Hakim has put forth a preference theory that calls the slim-outcome-difference ideology into question. Hakim has discussed persistent differences in lifestyle preferences among women and men in their career and family orientation (briefly introduced above and outlined in Hakim 1995; 1998; 2002; 2008). With a title of "Five Feminist Myths about Women's

Employment" published in 1995 in *British Journal of Sociology*, Hakim is clearly trying to engage gender scholars. Her impact in *Gender & Society* is more than meager, her work on preference differences has been cited twice in the journal.[13] It is hard to know the reason why there is so little impact, but one speculation is that gender sociologists refuse to engage Hakim's work because her theorizing is difference-informed.

THE INTOLERANCE TOWARD A DIFFERENCE-INFORMED FEMINIST IDEOLOGY

Gender sociology's insistence on a "proper" lifestyle choice fosters a culture of intolerance toward alternative lifestyle choices that may appeal to some men and women—such as a traditional lifestyle with a male breadwinner and a female caretaker. We should all share the slim-outcome difference lifestyle, according to gender sociology. But even in Sweden one will find a minority of families that prefer a traditional lifestyle for religious, conservative, or green values, although they are certainly fewer than in other cultures, and probably[14] more stigmatized. In Swedish families in general, women take most of the responsibility for the household and parenting when their children are small. About half of Swedish mothers utilize the entire state-subsidized parental leave period, except the weeks earmarked for the father of the child (Eriksson 2016). More women also work part-time while the children are small.[15] From a left-feminist perspective, these choices are nefarious because they reproduce differences between women and men. If families continue on this path, the slim-outcome difference will remain distant. From a classical liberal standpoint, these choices are less problematic. What a truly feminist society would look like is unknown, and the goal is not to cohere on a particular lifestyle but to allow all women (and men) to pursue their own path in life.

CONCLUSION

The left-feminists' domination of gender sociology has resulted in a strong norm to explain differences between men and women only in terms of culture, broadly defined, and to ignore or gloss over biological or preference explanations, and hence to interpret differences in outcome as resulting from socialization into gender roles or to discrimination of various sorts. As a result, the field is impoverished. It excludes alternative ideas about equality, and therefore shuns from its imagination the complexity of human life. Humans are social and cultural beings, to be sure, but also biological creatures.

Now, one can question whether differences in preferences between the average man and the average woman are significant enough to cause the differences observed in the labor market. Many gender sociologists would doubt that. There are examples of situations where small differences in preferences can produce large results, with Schelling's (1978) segregation dynamics and tipping points as a relevant example. I hypothesize that small differences between men and women in preferences, coupled with reproductive differences, will continue to impact labor market success and occupational choice.

One could argue that the taboos and blindness are means used by gender sociology scholars to undermine what they conceive to be the prevailing essentialist ideology. Ignoring differences is a way to provide an alternative constructivist interpretation to help erode our patriarchal past. Thus, gender sociologists feel the need to exaggerate the near sameness of men and women, to free men and women from the sex stereotypical shackles of the past. Questioning the status quo and critically examining conventional beliefs is indeed in line with the scientific approach. Ignoring potentially relevant knowledge, however, is not. The difference between scholars and activists after all is that scholars should embrace the scientific norm of pursuing truth, broadly speaking.

Lastly, scientists always choose perspectives and theoretical lenses in studying society, and such perspectives and lenses are always colored by the scientist's ideological stance (see Myrdal 1969; Weber 1949). Gender sociology, then, it might be argued, has chosen the lens of social constructivism to study gender relations; social constructivism is a valid theoretical perspective and it is a perspective well suited for challenging notions of individual behavior free from social constraints. But constructivists risk overstating the causal force of social constraints, in ways analogous to how rationalists overstate free choice. Indeed, in gender sociology this risk is no mere possibility; rather, it has reached a point where scholars overstate the extent to which women (and men) are ruled by socialization in making their choices. In social science, theories should be used to make sense of reality, but they also need to respond to and be kept in check by empirical reality. Holding on to an oversimplified theory of gender is damaging and will continue to hurt the long-standing reputation of sociology. Part of the solution would be including a more varied ideological framework, where classical liberal ideas would be one route ahead.

REFERENCES

Anderson, Deborah, Binder, Melissa, and Kate Krause. 2003. "The Motherhood Wage Penalty Revisited: Experience, Heterogeneity, Work Effort, and Work-Schedule Flexibility." *Industrial and Labor Relations Review*, 56 (2): 273–94.

Baron-Cohen, Simon. 2003. *The Essential Difference. The Truth about the Male and Female Brain*. New York, NY: Basic Books.

Becker, Gary S. 1985. "Human Capital, Effort, and the Sexual Division of Labor." *Journal of Labor Economics,* 3 (1, Part 2): S33–58. https://doi.org/10.1086/298075.

Berggren, Niclas, Jordahl, Henrik, and Charlotta Stern. 2009. "The Political Opinions of Swedish Social Scientists." *Finnish Economic Papers,* 22 (2): 75–88.

Bernhardt, Eva, Noack, Turid, and Torskild H. Lyngstad. 2008. "Shared Housework in Norway and Sweden: Advancing the Gender Revolution." *Journal of European Social Policy,* 18: 275–88.

Blackburn, Robert M., Jarman, Jennifer, and Bradley Brookes. 2000. "The Puzzle of Gender Segregation and Inequality: A Cross-National Analysis." *European Sociological Review,* 16: 119–35.

Browne, Kingsley. R. 2006. "Evolved Sex Differences and Occupational Segregation." *Journal of Organizational Behavior,* 27 (2): 143–62.

Budig, Michelle J. and Paula England. 2001. "The Wage Penalty for Motherhood." *American Sociological Review*, 66 (2), 204–25.

Byrnes, James P., Miller, David C., and William D. Schaffer. 2009. "Gender Differences in Risk-Taking: A meta-analysis." *Psychological Bulletin,* 125: 367–83.

Campbell, Anne. 2013. *A Mind of Her Own. The Evolutionary Psychology of Women.* 2nd edition. Cambridge, UK: Oxford University Press.

Caplan, Bryan. 2022. *Don't Be a Feminist: Essays on Genuine Justice*. Independently published.

Charles, Maria. 2008. "Culture and Inequality: Identity, Ideology, and Difference in 'Postascriptive Society.'" *The ANNALS of the American Academy of Political and Social Science,* 619 (1): 41–58. https://doi.org/10.1177/0002716208319824.

Charles, Maria and Karen Bradley. 2009. "Indulging Our Gendered Selves? Sex Segregation by Field of Study in 44 Countries." *American Journal of Sociology,* 114 (4): 924–76.

Charles, Maria and David B. Grusky. 2004. *Occupational Ghettos. The Worldwide Segregation of Women and Men*. Stanford, CA: Stanford University Press.

Charles, Maria and David B. Grusky. 2007. "Egalitarianism and Gender Inequality." pp. 327–42 in Grusky D. B. & S. Szelényi (eds.) *The Inequality Reader: Contemporary and Foundational Readings in Race, Class, and Gender*. Boulder, CO: Westview Press.

Cole, Jonathan R. and Harriet Zuckerman. 1984. "The Productivity Puzzle: Persistence and Change in Patterns of Publication of Men and Women Scientists." *Advances in Motivation and Achievement,* 2: 217–58.

Correll, Shelley, Benard, Stephen, and In Paik. 2007. "Getting a Job: Is There a Motherhood Penalty?" *American Journal of Sociology,* 112 (5): 1297–339.

Costa, Paul.T., Terracciano, Antonio, and Robert R. McCrae. 2001. "Gender Differences in Personality Traits Across Cultures: Robust and Surprising Findings." *Journal of Personality and Social Psychology,* 81: 322–31; see also http://www.ncbi.nlm.nih.gov/pmc/articles/PMC2031866/).

Crawford, Jarret T., and Lee J. Jussim, eds. 2018. *The Politics of Social Psychology: Frontiers of Social Psychology*. New York, NY; London: Routledge.

Croft, Alyssa, Schmader, Toni, and Katharina Block. 2015. "An Underexamined Inequality: Cultural and Psychological Barriers to Men's Engagement with Communal Roles." *Personality and Social Psychology Review,* 19 (4): 343–70.

Deary, Ian J. 2012. "Intelligence." *Annual Review of Psychology,* 63 (1): 453–82. https://doi.org/10.1146/annurev-psych-120710-100353.

Duarte, José L., Crawford, Jarret T., Stern, Charlotta, Haidt, Jonathan, Jussim, Lee and Philip E. Tetlock. 2014. "Political diversity will improve social psychological science." *Behavioral and Brain Sciences*, 38.

Duvander, Ann-Zofie. 2006. "När är det dags för dagis? En studie om vid vilken ålder barn börjar på förskola och föräldrars åsikt om detta." (When is it Time for Pre-School? A Study of at what age children start pre-school and parental views about it). *Working paper: Institutet för Framtidsstudier*. 2006: 2. Stockholm.

Duvander, Ann-Zofie, Tommy Ferrarini, and Sara Thalberg. 2005. "Swedish Parental Leave and Gender Equality." 2005: 11. Institutet för framtidsstudier.

England, Paula. 1992. *Comparable Worth*. New York: Aldine De Gruyter.

England, Paula. 2010. "The Gender Revolution. Uneven and Stalled." *Gender & Society*, 24 (2): 149–66.

Eriksson, Helen. 2011. "The Gendering Effects of Sweden's Gender-Neutral Care Leave Policy." *Population Review,* 50 (1). https://doi.org/10.1353/prv.2011.a433541.

Feingold, Alan. 1994. "Gender Differences in Personality: A meta-analysis." *Psychological Bulletin,* 116 (3): 429–56.

Flores-Mendoza, Carmen, Widaman, Keith F., Rindermann, Heiner, Primi, Ricardo, Mansur-Alves, Marcela, and Carla Couto Pena. 2013. "Cognitive Sex Differences in Reasoning Tasks: Evidence from Brazilian Samples of Educational Settings." *Intelligence,* 41: 70–84.

Gallen, Yana. 2015. "The Gender Productivity Gap." https://yanagallen.com/Gallen_Yana_JMP.pdf.

Gornick, Janet C. and Marcia Meyers. 2009. *Gender Equality: Transforming Family Division of Labor*. London: Verso Books.

Gottfredson, Linda S. 1999. "The Nature and Nurture of Vocational Interests." In M. L. Savickas & A. R. Spokane (Eds.), *Vocational Interests: Their Meaning, Measurement, and Use in Counseling*. Davies-Black Publishing.

Gross, Neil and Solon Simmons. 2007. "The Social and Political Views of American Professors." Working paper presented at the *Harvard University Symposium on Professors and Their Politics*, Cambridge, MA, October 6, 2007.

Hakim, Catherine. 1995. "Five Feminist Myths about Women's Employment." *British Journal of Sociology*: 429–55.

Hakim, Catherine. 1998. "Developing a Sociology for the Twenty-First Century: Preference Theory." *The British Journal of Sociology,* 49 (1): 137–43. https://doi.org/10.2307/591267.

Hakim, Catherine. 2000. *Work-Lifestyle Choices in the 21st Century: Preference Theory*. Oxford: Oxford University Press.

Hakim, Catherine. 2002. "Lifestyle Preferences as Determinants of Women's Differentiated Labor Market Careers." *Work and Occupations,* 29 (4): 428–59.

Hakim, Catherine. 2008. "Diversity in Tastes, Values, and Preferences: Comment on Jonung and Ståhlberg." *Econ Journal Watch,* 5 (2): 204–18.

Halldén, Karin. 2014. "Könssegregering efter yrke på den svenska arbetsmarknaden år 2000–2010." [Gender Segregation after Occupation in the Swedish Labor Market during 2000–2010]. In Kunze, A. & Thorburn, K. (eds). *Yrke, karriär och lön—kvinnors och mäns olika villkor på den svenska arbetsmarknaden*. SOU 2014:81. Stockholm: Fritzes.

Halpern, Diane F. 2012. *Sex Differences in Cognitive Abilities*. (4th ed.) New York, NY: Psychology Press.

Hodges, Melissa and Michelle Budig. 2010. "Who Gets the Daddy Bonus? Organizational Hegemonic Masculinity and the Impact of Fatherhood on Earnings." *Gender & Society,* 24: 717–45.

Hoff Sommers, Christina. 1995. *Who Stole Feminism? How Women Have Betrayed Women*. New York: Simon & Schuster.

Hofstede, Geert H., Hofstede, Gert Jan, and Michael Minkov. 2010. *Cultures and Organizations: Software of the Mind*. New York, NY: McGraw Hill.

Holland, John. L. 1959. "A Theory of Occupational Choice." *Journal of Counseling Psychology,* 6: 35–45.

Holland, John. L. 1997. *Making Vocational Choices: A Theory of Vocational Personalities and Work Environments*. 3rd ed. Odessa, FL: Psychological Assessment Resources, Inc.

Horowitz, Mark, Yaworsky, William, and Kenneth Kickham. 2014. "Whither the Blank Slate? A Report on the Reception of Evolutionary Biological Ideas among Sociological Theorists." *Sociological Spectrum,* 34 (6): 489–509.

Humlum, Maria K., Nandrup, Anne B., and Nina Smith. 2019. "Closing or reproducing the gender gap? Parental transmission, social norms and education choice." *Journal of Population Economics*, 32: 455–500.

Inglehart, Ronald and Christian Welzel. 2005. *Modernization, Cultural Change, and Democracy. The Human Development Sequence*. Oxford: Cambridge University Press.

Jakobsson, Niklas and Andreas Kotsadam. 2010. "Do Attitudes Toward Gender Equality Really Differ Between Norway and Sweden?" *Journal of European Social Policy,* 20 (2): 142–59.

Johnson, John A. 2008. "Preferences Underlying Women's Choices in Academic Economics." *Econ. Journal Watch,* 5 (2): 209–26.

Jurik, Nancy C., and Cynthia Siemsen. 2009. "'Doing Gender' as Canon or Agenda: A Symposium on West and Zimmerman." *Gender and Society,* 23 (1): 72–75.

Johnson, Wendy, Carothers, Andrew, and Ian J. Deary. 2008. "Sex Differences in Variability in General Intelligence. A New Look at the Old Question." *Perspectives on Psychological Science,* 3 (6): 518–31.

Jonsson, Jan O. 2004. "Könssegregeringen inom utbildningssystemet: Förändringar och förklaringar." [Gender segregation within the Educational System: Changes and Explanations]. In Löfström (ed.), *Den könsuppdelade arbetsmarknaden*, 2004:43, bilaga 6, pp. 339–66. Stockholm: Fritzes.

Kimura, Doreen. 1999. *Sex and Cognition*. Cambridge, MA: MIT Press.

Klein, Daniel B. and Charlotta Stern. 2006. "Sociology and Classical Liberalism." *The Independent Review. A Journal of Political Economy,* XI (1): 37–52.

Klein, Daniel B. and Charlotta Stern. 2009. "By the Numbers: The Ideological Profile of Professors." In R. Maranto, R. E. Redding, & F. M. Hess(eds). *The Politically Correct University.*Washington DC: The AEI Press.

Klein, Daniel B. and Charlotta Stern. 2009. "Groupthink in Academia. Majoritarian Departmental Politics and the Professional Pyramid." *The Independent Review. A journal of Political Economy,* 13 (4): 586–600.

Kumlin, Johanna. 2010. "Har kvinnor och män blivit mer jämnt fördelade över yrken, organisationer och arbetsplatser i Sverige under perioden 1990–2003?" [Have women and men become more evenly divided over occupations, organizations, and workplaces in Sweden during the period 1990–2003] *Arbetsrapport. Institutet för Framtidsstudier*. 2010:8.

Long, J. Scott. 1992. "Measures of Sex Differences in Scientific Productivity." *Social Forces,* 7(1): 159–78.

Lueptow, Lloyd, Garovic-Szabo, Lori, and Margaret B. Lueptow. 2001. "Social Change and the Persistence of Sex Typing: 1974–1997." *Social Forces,* 80(1): 1–36.

Madison, Guy. 2016. "Sex Differences in Adult Intelligence in Sweden." *Mankind Quarterly,* 57 (1): 9–24.

Mankind Quarterly. (2016) Special Issue on Sex Differences in Intelligence, 57 (1).

Marini, Margaret M. and Mary C. Brinton. 1984. "Sex Typing in Occupational Socializations." In B. F. Reskin (ed.), *Sex Segregation in the Workplace: Trends, Explanations, Remedies*. Washington, DC: National Academy Press.

Martin, Chris C. 2016. "How ideology has hindered sociological insight." *The American Sociologist,* 47 (1): 115–30.

Meyersson Milgrom, Eva M., Trond Petersen, and Vemund Snartland. 2001. "Equal Pay for Equal Work? Evidence from Sweden and a Comparison with Norway and the U.S." *The Scandinavian Journal of Economics,* 103 (4): 559–83. https://doi.org/10.1111/1467-9442.00260.

McElroy, Wendy. 1982. *Freedom, Feminism, and the State*. Washington, DC: Cato Institute.

McElroy, Wendy. 2002. *Liberty for Women: Freedom and Feminism in the Twenty-First Century*. Chicago: Ivan R. Dee.

Moro, Andrea. 2009. "Statistical Discrimination." In S. N. Durlauf & L. E. Blume (eds.), *The New Palgrave Dictionary of Economics*. Online Edition. Palgrave Macmillan. Accessed 29 February 2016. http://www.dictionaryofeconomics.com/article?id=pde2009_S000544

Myrdal, Gunnar. 1969. *Objectivity in Social Research*. New York: Pantheon Books.

Niederle, Muriel, and Lise Vesterlund. 2011. "Gender and Competition." *Annual Review of Economics,* 3 (1): 601–30. https://doi.org/10.1146/annurev-economics-111809-125122.

Pinker, Steven. 2002. *The Blank Slate. The Modern Denial of Human Nature*. New York: Penguin Books.

Pinker, Susan. 2009. *The Sexual Paradox: Men, Women, and the Real Gender Gap*. New York: Scribner.

Ridgeway, Cecilia L. and Shelley J. Correll. 2004. "Unpacking the Gender System: A Theoretical Perspective on Gender Beliefs and Social Relations." *Gender & Society,* 18 (4): 510–33.

Ridgeway, Cecilia. L. 2009. "Framed Before We Know It. How Gender Shapes Social Relations." *Gender & Society,* 23 (2): 145–60.

Risman, Barbara J. 2004. "Gender as Social Structure: Theory Wrestling with Activism." *Gender & Society,* 18 (4): 429–50.

SCB. 2022. "Women and Men in Sweden 2022."

Schelling, Thomas C. 1978. *Micromotives and Macrobehavior*. New York: Norton.

Sjöberg, Ola. 2004. "The Role of Family Policy Institutions in Explaining Gender-Role Attitudes: A Comparative Multilevel Analysis of Thirteen Industrialized Countries." *Journal of European Social Policy,* 14 (2): 107–23. https://doi.org/10.1177/0958928704042003.

Stern, Charlotta. 2016. "Undoing Insularity: A Small Study of Gender Sociology's Big Problem." *Econ. Journal Watch,* 13 (3): 452–66.

Taylor, Joan Kennedy. 1992. *Reclaiming the Mainstream: Individualist Feminism Reconsidered*. Amherst, NY: Prometheus Books.

Thébaud, Sarah and Maria Charles. 2018. "Segregation, Stereotypes, and STEM." *Social Sciences,* 7 (7): 111.

Tong, Rosemarie. 1989. *Feminist Thought. A Comprehensive Introduction*. London: Routledge.

Torre, Margarita and Jerry A. Jacobs. 2021. "The Gender Mobility Paradox: Gender Segregation and Women's Mobility Across Gender-Type Boundaries, 1970–2018." *Gender & Society,* 35 (6): 853–83.

Udry, J. Richard. 1995. "Sociology and Biology: What Biology Do Sociologists Need to Know?" *Social Forces,* 73 (4): 1267–78.

Udry, J. Richard. 2000. "Biological Limits of Gender Construction." *American Sociological Review,* 65 (3): 443–57.

UNDP Human Development Report. 2015. *Work for Human Development*. Downloaded at: http://hdr.undp.org/sites/default/files/2015_human_development_report.pdf

Vianello, Michelangelo, Schnabel, Konrad, Sriram, N., and Brian Nosek. 2013. "Gender Differences in Explicit and Implicit Personality Traits." *Personality and Individual Differences,* 55: 994–99.

Weber, M. 1904 [1949]. "'Objectivity' in Social Science and Social Policy," p. 50–112 in *The Methodology of Social Sciences*. Translated and edited by E. Shils & H. Finch. Glencoe, Illinois: Free Press.

West, Candace, and Don H. Zimmerman. 1987. "Doing Gender." *Gender & Society*, 1 (2): 125–51. https://doi.org/10.1177/0891243287001002002.

Xie, Yu and Kimberelee. A. Shauman. 1998. "Sex differences in research productivity revisited: New evidence about an old puzzle." *American Sociological Review*, 63: 847–70.

Yancey, George. 2011. *Compromising Scholarship. Religious and Political Bias in American Higher Education*. Waco, TX: Baylor University Press.

Wai, Jonathan. Putallaz, Martha, and Matthew C. Makel. 2012. "Studying Intellectual Outliers: Are there sex differences, and are the smart getting smarter?" *Current Directions in Psychological Science*, 21 (6): 382–90.

Winegard, Benjamin M., Winegard Bo M., and Robert. O. Deaner. 2014. "Misrepresentations of Evolutionary Psychology in Sex and Gender Textbooks." *Evolutionary Psychology: An International Journal of Evolutionary Approaches to Psychology and Behavior*, 12: 474–507.

Winegard, Bo M., Winegard, Benjamin M., and David C. Geary. 2015. "Too Paranoid to See Progress: Social Psychology is Probably Liberal, but it Doesn't Believe in Progress," *Behavioral & Brain Sciences*.

West, Candace and Don H. Zimmerman. 1987. "Doing Gender," *Gender and Society*, 1: 125–51.

World Economic Forum 2015. *The Global Gender Gap Report*. Geneva, Switzerland: World Economic Forum. Downloaded at: http://reports.weforum.org/global-gender-gap-report-2015/the-global-gender-gap-index-results-in-2015/

NOTES

1. This chapter is a slightly rewritten version of a previously studied essay in *The Politics of Social Psychology*, edited by Jarret T. Crawford and Lee Jussim (Crawford and Jussim 2018). I am grateful to Rowland and Littlefield for permission to republish the chapter. I also want to thank Fabio Rojas and Bill Glod for their insightful feedback on the present version.

2. The left-wing character is also true of Sweden, where the largest political party among academic sociologists is the former Communist party (Berggren, Jordahl, & Stern, 2009). Sweden has a proportional political system and in 2009 Swedish politics had eight political parties. In the electorate the Social Democratic Party and the Moderate Party (right liberal) are the largest parties overall. The Left Party (the former Communist party) is one of the smallest parties.

3. The focus of the chapter is the sociological study of gender differences in the labor market, and I use the term "gender sociology" to make reading a bit easier and to distinguish the field from general stratification research which also studies gender stratification. Gender sociology is more specialized, and, idealtypically, scholars in the field are gender-studics scholars, sociologists specialized in gender topics. Typically, scholars who read and publish in *Gender and Society*, a top-journal in the field of women's studies and in sociology overall (Jurik & Siemsen, 2009).

4. The idealtypical presentation of the feminist ideologies is reminiscent of the stereotypical depiction of the difference between economics and sociology; "economics is all about how people make choices; sociology is all about how people have no choice." A related criticism of left-wing feminism's insistence on social constructivism is thus that it presents us with an over-socialized view of women being pushed by culture (whereas men with power seem to be able to practice "rational choice" in their suppression of women).

5. The hostility of sociologists toward biology and evolutionary principles is not unique to the field of labor markets and gender; about half doubt that evolutionary factors affect gender difference (see Horowitz, Yaworsky & Kickham 2014 and the references therein). See also Winegard, Winegard, & Deaner (2014) on how evolutionary psychology is misrepresented in sex and gender textbooks.

6. Personally, I also find it quite demeaning toward women (and men). I also find that the portrayal of modern societies as oppressive to women is so widespread that young women (and men) grow up thinking that their situation in the labor market is marked by unfairness and hostility. Such portrayal fosters an attitude among women that they need ever more government intervention to even the odds. I also think the portrayal has had the unintended consequence of making feminism unpopular, to the extent that books are written to discourage from the identity (Caplan 2022).

7. Studies also find that few sociology textbooks present sociobiology and the few that do, present the field as reductionist and genetic determinism (Machalek and Martin 2004, cited in Horowitz et al. 2014). Surveys of sociologists' views on evolutionary theory find the most common perception to be "I am open to considering evolutionary ideas but I am not sure that much of human social behavior and organization can be explained by evolutionary processes" (49 percent of survey respondents, reported in Horowitz et al. 2014). Forty-one percent agree or strongly agree with the view that sociologists have allowed ideology to blind them to the major significance of evolutionary biological processes in shaping human social behavior and organization (ibid.). Overall, Horowitz et al. (2014) conclude "that sociological theorists are most inclined to reject evolutionary reasoning when it is employed to explain behavioral differences between women and men" (ibid., 499). Describing oneself as a feminist theorist or a radical is correlated with a rejection of evolutionary theory (Horowitz et al. 2014).

8. In contrast, a masculine culture values competitiveness, assertiveness, and material well-being., whereas masculine cultures hold more strictly divided gender roles with larger differences between male and female roles (ibid.).

9. From an ideological point of view it is interesting to note that Statistics Sweden defines gender equality as "women and men have equal power to shape society and their own lives. This implies the same opportunities, rights and obligations in all spheres of life." (SCB, 2014, 2) The definition touches both the classical liberal and the left-wing feminist vision. Statistics Sweden then goes on to state that "the quantitative aspect (of gender equality) implies *an equal distribution of women and men in all areas of society*, such as education, work, recreation and positions of power. If a group comprises more than 60 percent women, it is women-dominated. If men make up more than 60 percent of a group it is men-dominated. Qualitative gender equality

implies that the knowledge, experiences and values of both women and men are given equal weight and are used to enrich and direct all spheres of society." (SCB, 2014, p.2, italics added).

10. The choice in a self-expressive culture would mean choosing what one deems a meaningful occupation, not necessarily an occupation that gives the highest monetary rewards.

11. Occupational segregation also explains part of the wage gap (Meyersson et al. 2001).

12. Sociologists also theorize gender gaps as due to statistical discrimination (see Moro 2009).

13. A SSCI search yields that Hakim (1995) is cited 145 times, 24 times in Women's studies (a collection of journals categorized by SSCI), zero times in *Gender & Society* (a major journal of the field). Hakim (1998) is cited 70 times, 8 times in Women's studies, and zero times in *Gender & Society*. Hakim (2002) is cited 138 times, 13 times in Women's studies, 2 times in *Gender & Society*.

14. I write probably, although I find Swedes to be intolerant toward traditional lifestyles. However, I am not knowledgeable of data with questions about "conservative lifestyle" values; it seems most value studies are interested in "modern lifestyle" values such as attitudes toward working mothers, divorce, homosexuality, etc.

15. The glass is actually half-full, because in the other half of Swedish families parents share parental leave—although it is not exactly equally divided between woman and man, it is clear that many Swedish fathers take active care of their children when small (ibid.). The nurturing father being a strong norm in Sweden is not surprising, given the world's most feminine culture!

Chapter 5

Toward a Classical Liberal Sociological Theory of Health Care

Lauren Hall

Sociology of health and medical sociology as fields have helped move the understanding of health and illness past the biomedical model that treats the body like a machine.[1] In the process, they have helped develop a more holistic understanding of the way in which non-biological processes and the social environment broadly contribute not only to health and disease states but also to how we understand the very nature of health and disease. Sociologists have contributed to our understanding of medicalization (Conrad 2005, 2007; Conrad and Leiter 2004), health disparities (Williams 1997), medical paternalism (Buchanan 1978), medical dominance (Abbott 2014) and social construction of illness (Brown 1995), among other important areas.”

Despite these advances, sociology as a discipline remains suspicious of one set of tools that could inform these and other issues within the context of medicine and healthcare. Classical liberalism, a pluralistic set of approaches devoted to understanding human freedom, provides a toolbox that could be used effectively by sociologists and the social sciences generally to identify problems and solutions to a range of complex sociological health phenomena. While classical liberal thought sometimes seems most relevant to economic and political theory, ideas developed by classical liberals pervade such disparate areas as economics, urban studies, global development (Acemoglu 2013), criminal justice (Balko 2021), and many others. As such, classical liberal principles are relevant to a whole host of issues that are also relevant to sociologists. Classical liberalism—particularly the subdiscipline of Austrian economics—like sociology, emphasizes the ways individuals operate in their social contexts and the complexity involved in living in a social order. Nowhere is this more true than in the medical and health care context, where individual decisions are framed and formed by broader structures including professional associations, hospital and provider culture, liability concerns, regulations, reimbursement structures, religious and cultural beliefs, and the media.

At the same time, because classical liberalism—as a toolbox and a set of normative commitments—and sociology—as a discipline—approach complex social phenomena from disparate perspectives, both can benefit from the pairing. Sociology tends to emphasize the power of social phenomena, while classical liberalism has, until recently, emphasized the power of the state. But classical liberals are paying increasing attention to the ways non-state social power is wielded while sociologists are paying increasing attention to the way state power molds and forms informal social pressures and power. This overlap is particularly true in the case of medicine, and medical sociologists and anthropologies are increasingly active in areas that would traditionally be the focus of policy and economics scholars, to the benefit of both. Even if sociologists reject the substantive normative commitments that ground classical liberalism broadly, they can still benefit from the toolbox that classical liberal scholars have developed over the years, a toolbox developed in large part to analyze and assess government and other kinds of coercive power.

In what follows, I will lay out some ways in which I see classical liberal principles and approaches as contributing to sociological conversations surrounding two primary issues: medicalization (and, by extension, medical dominance) and health disparities. These are both areas that have deep roots in the sociological literature and to which sociologists have made the primary contributions to our understanding of these phenomena. At the same time, I will argue that classical liberal principles and approaches can deepen our sociological understanding of medicalization and health disparities and assist us in setting agendas for future research and reform moving forward. I end the chapter with a discussion of the way in which classical liberal principles and approaches can help medical and healthcare sociologists ask a greater range of research questions, particularly with reference to the possibilities for health care reform.

MEDICALIZATION: MARKETS, CIVIL SOCIETY, INNOVATION, AND EQUITY

Sociologists have transformed our understanding of the complex way in which human conditions become (and un-become) disease states (Conrad 2007; Friedson 1970; Zola 1972). Medicalization of alcoholism shifted our understanding of that phenomenon from one of vice to one of medical condition, treatable via various interventions, including pharmaceutical interventions. On the other hand, the de-medicalization of homosexuality moved that phenomenon from a mental illness to a normalized variation of human sexuality. Medicalization is, in turn, tightly linked to the concept of medical professional dominance, though recent sociological research has sought to decouple these concepts as the impact of third-party payers, media and marketing, and other shifts have challenged traditional medical dominance in health care fields (Conrad 2005; Furedi 2006). Medical dominance, or the way in which the medical profession claims ownership over various human phenomena and therefore exerts control over how a phenomenon is understood, is crucial to our understanding of how birth, for example, was medicalized throughout the twentieth century (Hall 2019; Wertz and Wertz 1977). While modern scholars recognize that medical dominance may not be the sole cause of medicalization, medicalization and the dominance of the medical professions were and continue to be important and connected themes in the framing and structuring of the modern health care system.

While there are a range of classical liberal principles that relate to the problem of medical dominance and the related phenomenon of medicalization, in what follows I focus on four primary ones since they provide the clearest connection between the way classical liberals, particularly those from the Austrian tradition, understand the problem of medicalization and medical dominance. These principles are *regulatory capture*, *competition*, *entrepreneurial discovery*, and *dispersed knowledge*. These four ideas are inter-related and can help scholars organize a broader theory of competition and monopoly, out of which medical dominance and, to some degree, medicalization, stems. Obviously sociologists are aware of these phenomena, whether they call them by these names or not. But clear labeling may help future scholars clarify their own research agendas as well as the causal connections and direction of causality between state action and various social phenomena that is often unclear (Davis 2006).

As sociologist Paul Starr points out in *The Social Transformation of American Medicine*, the structure of American healthcare was largely dictated by a series of conflicts over power and status that played out throughout the twentieth century (though beginning much earlier). On Starr's reading, physicians used their greater social status and access to political power to mold the structure of American healthcare to be both physician- and procedure-centric. Classical liberal economists recognize this phenomenon as *regulatory capture*, or the way in which the public institutions created to regulate a specific set of interests or industry soon end up controlled by and directed by the interests or industry being regulated (Dal Bó 2006). Theresa Morris discusses a similar process when exploring the role physicians play in shaping the rules regarding liability in many states, highlighting the paradox of physicians pushing for increased protections from liability at the same time that medical errors and patient morbidity and mortality are rising (Morris 2013). Using the lens of regulatory capture can help highlight these phenomena and clarify the ways in which state power is often wielded to protect precisely those whose power it is meant to limit and control.

One primary effect of regulatory capture is that it is frequently used to limit *competition* from other providers. While non-classical liberals often view competition as a negative aspect of market systems (Brown 2015), classical liberals defend competition not because it involves ruthless conflict, but instead because competition facilitates the discovery of new kinds of knowledge and the best way to use that knowledge to assist others (Kirzner 1997). The misunderstanding of competition as inherently destructive or zero-sum as opposed to a non-zero sum discovery process is a major misunderstanding of classical liberal theory, perhaps facilitated by depictions like those in Ayn Rand, where competition is the hallmark of masculine and patriarchal strongmen like Rand's character Hank Reardon. Whatever the cause, the misunderstanding of why competition is important has made it harder for sociologists to recognize how crucial markets and the competition they engender is for preserving spaces where, for example, marginalized communities might provide alternatives to existing power structures.

The importance of competition hinges on the notion of *entrepreneurial discovery*, or the way in which entrepreneurs (understood broadly as those seeking opportunities to fulfill unmet needs) seek new problems to solve, either as part of a market-based system or a civil-social system characterized by mutual-aid or philanthropy. On this understanding, entrepreneurs seek out new ways to help people, either for profit or on humanitarian grounds (or both), and as part of this process they also seek out new information about people's desires, needs, and concerns. The entrepreneurial model is not primarily motivated by the act of competing itself, but is instead motivated by knowledge seeking as a way to identify gaps in the current system of needs-provision and ways in which the entrepreneur can fill them.

At the same time, competition is necessary for an entrepreneurial system to function, since any entrepreneur will be unable to put his or her newly discovered knowledge to use if there is no way to bring that knowledge to bear on the problems faced by her neighbors or community. This requires that the entrepreneur's solutions "compete" with other potential solutions in some kind of market, whether that be an economic market or the market of ideas. Such competition is not, however, zero sum, since the addition of knowledge frequently improves existing solutions while also filling needs that are otherwise unmet. Thus the ability of entrepreneurs to collect and use knowledge to solve problems hinges on the availability of room in the current system for their solutions to be made available. The history of midwifery bears this process out, albeit in reverse. In what follows I use the tradition of grand midwifery in Black communities in the South as a case study, but there are many more in the medical literature we could choose from to illustrate the point.

As physicians sought to consolidate control over the provision of medical care in the late 1800s and early 1900s, physicians sought to limit competition with midwives, who were particularly popular with women of color and recent immigrants, via a combination of state laws and regulations that expressly forbade midwives from practicing their art without physician oversight. Many scholars have described the way black midwives were licensed out of existence in the South throughout the early part of the twentieth century (Logan and Clark 2013; Luke 2018), through a combination of professional capture of midwifery by nursing and the legal subservience of nursing under physician control. An important undercurrent in these accounts that is rarely made explicit is that the loss of diverse providers was not merely the loss of providers who looked like their patients, which is of limited use on its own, but was in fact the loss of providers with intimate *local and dispersed knowledge* of their clients and whose style of practice was uniquely able to assess the needs of their clients and adapt their care to those needs.

Black midwives, unlike white physicians, typically provided most of their care in the home itself and the care they provided extended far beyond traditional medical interventions. The decentralized location of midwifery proved crucial to its positive outcomes, given that caregivers that operate in the home are much better able than those in hospitals to assess idiosyncratic needs such as food insecurity, domestic violence, mental illness, the general state of a client's support system, presence or absence of neighbors and close relatives, and other variables deeply relevant to medical outcomes. All these factors are crucial in a provider's ability to provide the kind of care and facilitate access to resources that can help save maternal and infant lives. Yet physicians in hospitals lack this local knowledge precisely because they remove patients from their contexts and bring them into a standardized environment where patients are, by necessity, reduced to their constituent component parts (Lindheim 1981). Grand midwife Onnie Lee Logan discusses the way in which grand midwives, unlike their white physician counterparts who also attended births, would come into an expecting woman's home, assess the needs of the expecting mother, her existing children and the other adults in the home, and then create an action plan for birth that might include doing laundry, making meals, sewing new clothes for the baby, collaboration with neighbors to provide childcare, or consulting the local physician (Logan and Clark 2013).

Classical liberal thinkers like Friedrich Hayek (1945) and Kirzner (1997) emphasize precisely this kind of local knowledge in their arguments against central planning. Hayek in particular argues that it is not merely that central planners are less efficient than entrepreneurs at gathering such local knowledge, but in fact that there is *no way* for a central planner to have access to all the relevant knowledge needed to make centralized decisions. Hayek's primary example is prices, but in the health care context one can easily see a parallel in those who make medical decisions absent any knowledge of a person's lifestyle, support network, existing responsibilities, and so on. Competition, as opposed to central planning, creates a system that empowers entrepreneurs, in the broadest possible sense, to be alert to the needs of others and then able to act to fulfill those needs.

Anti-competitive measures such as licensing (Anderson et al. 2020; Hamowy 1979), certificate of need (CON) laws (Conover and Bailey 2020), and other kinds of restrictions on practice serve not just to increase the costs entrepreneurs face in solving people's problems—whether those costs are prosecution or fines or simply expensive education or the costs of fulfilling regulatory requirements—but also serve to destroy access to the local and usually non-aggregate *dispersed knowledge* about clients and their needs. The loss of that local knowledge means not just less personalized care, but also care that lacks the ability to adapt itself to the needs of its client base, leaving serious gaps in care, gaps that are at the center of concerns about racial disparities in health. A major tragedy of the elimination of grand midwives was that the loss of these entrepreneurs meant that black women in the South were left at the whim of a largely white and male medical establishment that rarely had black maternal health, dignity, or autonomy at its core, to say the least (Washington 2008). Concerns about Black women being coerced and their concerns dismissed by a largely white medical profession continue today (Hoffman et al. 2016; McMillan Cottom n.d.). A more concrete understanding of the role dispersed knowledge plays in health outcomes would help sociologists and policy makers clarify why diverse providers are so important; it's not merely a question of matching the race of a provider to the patient. Diverse providers are more likely (but not guaranteed) to have access to unique, local, and dispersed knowledge about their clients that is directly relevant to patient care, sometimes because their practice patterns are themselves different from the norm, but sometimes because their own experiences as members of minoritized communities informs their practice patterns (or both, as in the case of black doulas and midwives). In fact, one critique of white-dominated conversations about health disparities in maternity care involves the rejection of the assumption that white medical knowledge is superior to the local and dispersed knowledge of black women themselves (Scott et al. n.d.).

The importance of dispersed knowledge links to another classical liberal principle with active relevance for sociologists. Classical liberals focus on individuals and individual preferences in part because they see the individual as a primary source of agency, but also because individuals are likely to have the best understanding of their unique goals, talents, and preferences. The classical liberal emphasis on the individual relates directly to sociological concerns about standardization in medicine. As many sociologists have pointed out, medicine tends to treat the norm and struggles to address the needs of those on the margins. Medicalization as a process encourages standardization, because it facilitates fitting patients into a standard box that can be placed under scientific control via the reductionist methods of the scientific method, effectively reducing patients to the sum of their medical parts. Standardization works well in the case of something relatively discrete like a surgery, but as sociologists point out, even after a discrete event like a surgery, social and individual characteristics play a crucial role in medical outcomes because they bear on ability to follow post-operative procedures, consistently take prescribed medications, or be safe from abuse or coercion in the home, as just a few examples (Kaufman 2006, 2015). Standardization is therefore limited in its ability to provide high quality health care, even in the context of a hospital. As some sociologists have pointed out, standardization of care is sometimes even less about assuring quality of care than it is about the hospital context itself and the need to shield providers and the hospital from liability (Morris 2013).

There therefore remains a tight link between respect for individuals, encouragement of competition and the entrepreneurial discovery that follows from competition, and the provision of holistic healthcare that resists standardization and provides care for those with non-normative needs and preferences. My own work, for example, has unearthed anecdotal evidence that the restrictive licensing requirements for midwives in New York State prevent women of color from serving their communities as birth workers, despite their interest in doing so. In interviews with women of color who are interested in birth work in the Bronx, some report that they are forced to practice in other states or to primarily serve white women in home births because the current constellation of regulations makes midwifery education expensive, keeps Medicaid reimbursements for midwifery care artificially low, and restricts access to birth centers and other locations where apartment-dwellers might feel more comfortable giving birth. The result is a serious dearth of midwives of color; those that do exist tend to treat largely white populations (Hall 2019). Understanding the way regulatory capture works to limit competition and therefore limit health care entrepreneurs from serving their own communities might be an area where sociologists could make even more progress than they already have.

HEALTH DISPARITIES: VULNERABLE POPULATIONS, MONOPOLIES, AND REGRESSIVE EFFECTS

The principles of regulatory capture, competition, dispersed knowledge, and entrepreneurial discovery directly impact questions of disparities in care, a major area of interest for sociologists like David Williams (Williams 1997, 2012; Williams et al. 1997; Williams, Lawrence, and Davis 2019; Williams and Cooper 2019; Williams and Rucker 2000). Health disparities took on increasing relevance post-2020 when the combination of the death of George Floyd and the disparate effects of COVID on communities of color encouraged greater attention to the vulnerability of these communities both within the medical system and outside it.

That regulatory capture creates medical monopolies and eliminates competition connects directly to sociological concerns over medical domination, defined broadly as the way medical professionals like physicians claim hierarchical authority over other kinds of healthcare providers (Friedson 1970). This medical dominance, in turn, has repercussions for racial disparities in health, not only because medical providers tend to be, on average, white and male, but also because in many instances of racial disparities, the disparities result, not from too little medical care, but from the wrong kind of health care in the first place. Sociologists have emphasized concerns about lack of high-quality food and lack of consistent primary and preventive care while the medical and reimbursement structures incentivize instead specialized and often invasive care after preventable problems become acute. In both maternity care and end-of-life care, researchers find that black patients, for example, often lack access to less acute forms of healthcare that can prevent them from needing acute care later on. Lack of access to high-quality prenatal care, for example, is one predictor of pre-term birth (Gadson, Akpovi, and Mehta 2017)). Similarly, black Americans are much less likely to know that palliative care exists and that access to such care can keep them comfortable at home with family—even extending their lifespan compared to acute care—rather than hospitalized at the end of life (Drisdom 2013; Enguidanos et al. 2011; Mor, Papandonatos, and Miller 2005). Other research suggests that moving the location of care back to the home can prevent crises and improve outcomes across a range of conditions (Dodge et al. 2019; Goldfeld et al. 2019; Health 1998).

Troublingly, the modern medical context in the United States is characterized by increasing consolidation as single hospital systems that employ an increasing number of primary care providers combine with reimbursement systems that prioritize procedures over high-quality communication. The more healthcare consolidates into a hospital-centric and increasingly corporatized and centralized system and the more interested parties like the American Medical Association and the American Hospital Association continue to shape the structure of health care regulations and licensing, the ability of people with diverse and complex needs to have their voices heard and access providers capable of working with those needs will be limited. Consolidation emerges to manage costs, create liability buffers and navigate (and shape) regulation, not to improve quality of or access to care.

As in most cases, the effects of this consolidation and monopolization are likely to be regressive, since those with higher incomes are able to pay out of pocket to access the providers they can't access through normal channels (Hall and Horwitz 2021). These regressive effects will hit vulnerable and minority communities hardest precisely because they are more likely to lack the mobility and resources to remove themselves from a medically dominant system the way others can.[2] The consolidated landscape means that healthcare entrepreneurs like midwives face an increasingly difficult fight to make space to access the decentralized knowledge that makes them so effective. The causal pathway between regulation, consolidation, and poor patient outcomes has downstream negative impacts on our standard bioethical commitments, commitments that are increasingly difficult to uphold in a modern corporatized, consolidated, and heavily regulated healthcare industry where individual patients and providers have very little power to withdraw even consent (Hall 2019).

Regulatory capture and the monopolistic dominance that results contributes to coercion and domination in the medical field, including abuse and coercion in hospital settings; racial disparities in care; cooperation between medical providers and the criminal justice system (criminalization of mental health, addiction, parenting, etc.) precisely because patients no longer have a way to exit coercive hospital environments. In a true market, a patient could leave a coercive provider, at least most of the time. In the consolidated medical environment of today, patients frequently have little choice of providers, either because their insurance does not cover alternative providers or because geographically there is only one provider in their area, sometimes the result of certificate of need laws and other regulations that intentionally limit the supply of providers to benefit those already practicing (Stratmann et al., 2020). Anecdotal evidence finds concerning reports of coercion and abuse in hospital maternity wards. Birth and death compound this vulnerability, since birthing and dying people are often time- and mobility-limited, making exit, even where alternatives exist, difficult. Such vulnerability to coercion combines with sociological concerns about iatrogenic harm, compounding concerns about the role domination plays in undermining consent, nonmaleficence, justice, and other foundational ethical commitments in the medical context.

THE FUTURE OF HEALTH CARE POLICY: AGENDA SETTING

One area where sociology scholars could benefit from classical liberal perspectives is in the area of agenda setting and reform. To take one example, David Williams's contributions to the fields of health sociology, public health, and race and medicine have been formative in the way those disciplines think about problems like racial disparities in health and inequity broadly. Yet even a scholar of Williams's stature may develop blind spots when it comes to proposing solutions. These blind spots could be reduced or eliminated via a combination of sociological and classical liberal perspectives. In what follows I focus on Williams's work in large part because his scholarship is so broad and important, but the benefits of incorporating classical liberal principles extend beyond issues relating to race and medicine.

In a recent article, Williams and his co-author Lisa Cooper (2019) argue for a series of practical solutions to reduce racial inequities in health. In each section, the authors argue for more government oversight and more government funding to alleviate existing inequities. While many of these proposals for reform seem commonsensical, a broader question lies beneath precisely the need for reform they point to: if these reforms are so obvious, why haven't they been implemented? The answer to that question comes, in part, from classical liberal and other analyses of the way in which interest groups influence policymaking, as well as work on the perverse incentives built into the very model of healthcare that we must accept as our starting point (Hall 2019; Hall and Horwitz 2021).

Williams and Cooper, for example, correctly point out that "only 3% of America's health care expenditure is on prevention," but later in the same section they argue in favor of Sanders's Medicare-For-All Act as one example of a powerful way to ensure greater access. But the authors do not mention—or may not be aware of—the perverse incentives built into the structure of Medicare itself, incentives that prioritize procedures and prevent access to exactly the kind of high-quality preventive care for which they advocate (Hall 2019; Hall and Horwitz 2021; Kaufman 2015).

Similarly, in their discussion of the need to address patients' social risk factors, Williams and Cooper do not discuss the ways in which hospitals compete directly with supportive social services and the role consolidation plays in reducing options for marginalized communities (Hall and Horwitz 2021; Kaufman 2015). Many of the programs the authors tout as particularly promising due to their combination of medical, social, legal, and other supports are particularly difficult to instantiate in our current model, given the structures of Medicare and Medicaid and their prioritization of medical professionals and procedures, though the authors seem unaware of these broader regulatory barriers (Williams and Cooper 2019:11).

Finally, in their discussion of increasing the diversity of medical providers, they do not mention the way regulations like Certificate of Need laws and stringent licensing laws limit providers of color who are less likely to be able to afford to navigate the regulatory process (see Hall 2019). Such regulations interact with payment models in ways that directly undermine recruitment of diverse providers. Black midwives and doulas in many states have pointed out that Medicaid reimbursement rates are typically too low for them to focus their practices on Medicaid recipients alone, forcing them to take more affluent clients to offset the losses of low Medicaid payments. Black healthcare providers are more likely to carry significant student loan debt, making it harder financially for them to treat low-income clients, compounding the regressive effects on both diverse clients and diverse providers (Hall 2019; Hall and Horwitz 2021).

In all of these cases, reducing the regulatory burden in clear and strategic ways could facilitate greater levels of healthy competition, a greater diversity of providers, and greater access for diverse individuals with a range of unique needs and preferences. None of this requires that we jettison government regulation altogether. Instead, sociologists and classical liberal scholars from a range of disciplines, as well as policy makers and policy analysts, could work together to identify the ways in which the regulatory process is and will be shaped by powerful interest groups whose goals frequently differ from the needs of health consumers and the most marginalized populations.

Despite these apparent differences in focus, there are clear areas of concordance between the sociological and classical liberal approaches, as we can also see in Williams's work. One interesting part of the Williams and Cooper piece focuses on how to build political will for reforms to help reduce disparities in care and outcomes. The authors note that the "most widely used framing strategies do not work because the dominant racial framing blocks this alternative viewpoint" (Williams and Cooper 2019:14). They point out that various approaches to diversity, including viewing it as a strength and framing inequities "as reflecting white privilege or as structurally driven," are largely unsuccessful in mobilizing support for policies that would reduce disparities in health.

On the other hand, successful strategies include those that focus on "widely shared American values (like ingenuity and enhancing opportunity for all) and that linked communities in a sense of shared fate. Specific [successful] frames identified included emphasizing opportunity for all, highlighting effective solutions and innovation, and making salient the interdependence of all communities, stressing preventing community problems before they occurred, and emphasizing fairness" (Williams and Cooper 2019:15). Whatever one thinks of these frames, emphasizing shared values is an important way to get people onto the same page. Many, though not all, of these shared values are those supported by classical liberal principles, including commitments to fair and transparent competition and equal opportunity. Framing health disparities as the result, in part, of collusion between corporations and government to reduce competition could create more widespread mobilization among populations who would traditionally not care about racial disparities in health at all. At the very least, such a frame might create a nonzero sum problem out of what is often characterized as a zero-sum tradeoff, with those with access to high-quality healthcare being asked to make sacrifices for access for others. The reform reality, however, is much more nonzero sum: by eliminating misguided and protectionist regulations, we can create a higher quality and more just healthcare landscape for all Americans.

Another area of overlap can be seen when Williams supports enlisting local stakeholders as "agents of change to seek solutions to local problems. As Williams and Cooper point out, "[r]esearch has found that those most knowledgeable about social factors are often the least politically active" (Williams and Cooper 2019:16). This suggests, first, that political actors will often lack critical insights and information about the communities they claim to serve, a standard classical liberal insight (Hayek 1945), but one also supported by much of the sociological literature. Both the sociological and classical liberal perspectives tend to support bottom-up or grassroots initiatives precisely because initiatives that form at this level will have crucial knowledge that higher levels of decision-makers often lack. Healthcare in particular tends to be extremely preference-sensitive, meaning that local and idiosyncratic knowledge and preferences will play a very important role in outcomes (Hall 2019).

While the landscape for healthcare reform is certainly complex, a combination of insights from classical liberalism and sociology provides a comprehensive agenda for reform. The solution is not, unsurprisingly, more centralized control, but in fact greater pluralism in the provision of healthcare in order to access this dispersed local knowledge and facilitate healthcare entrepreneurs in serving their community's unique needs. Whether such providers are midwives of color or urban mutual aid organizations (Domínguez et al. 2020; Halley 2021), the increasing standardization of the provision of medical care and the centralization of that care in clinics increasingly owned by a single hospital system and paid for by an increasingly small number of third-party payers signals that we are crowding out these providers and limiting the competition they could foster.

While there may be a tendency to view some models as beneficial—midwives and doulas of color—while viewing other models with suspicion—Evangelical Christian insurance, for example—scholars should resist this tendency precisely because the epistemological problem pointed out by classical liberals like Hayek remains: communities will have unique healthcare needs and our ability to access those needs as outsiders will always be limited. Respect for pluralism in healthcare means, from a classical liberal perspective, respecting a variety of pluralistic options, even if we may disagree with the principles that animate such options or the means they choose to achieve their goals. Some obvious caveats exist, most notably the limitations laid out in the classical liberal commitment to limiting force and fraud. A pluralistic healthcare environment does not require that policymakers reject all concerns over safety, efficacy, and harm, but instead that policymakers may want to flip the current model where the state uses double standards for medical and non-medical providers and instead move to a model where state regulators perhaps wait for harm to manifest before regulating and even facilitate (if not provide) resources for pluralistic models that show significant promise. Creating such pluralism requires at its foundation a classical liberal toleration of a range of healthcare options, despite surface level disagreements.

Further reform options are suggested by another classical liberal principle that dovetails with sociological research, that of spontaneous or emergent orders. One might ask not how government could reform from the top down, but rather how would people solve their own health care problems if they were free to do so? The answer can be found in a range of bottom-up movements in provision of healthcare that range from reform movements to resistance movements. Movements like grey market home birth midwives operating in Alabama and Georgia (Grant n.d.), the creation of groups like Black Mamas Matter that support black birth workers (Aghajanian 2015), mutual aid approaches like "comfort care homes" that provide cost-free locations to care for terminally ill patients outside hospitals and formal outpatient hospices (Halley 2021), and more diverse mutual aid healthcare movements (Birdsong 2020) all aim to decentralize, pluralize, and demonopolize healthcare by creating competitive alternatives to the current consolidated system, whether such movements are animated by market principles or operate outside markets in the worlds of philanthropy or mutual aid. Such movements are also likely to better address the social determinants of health by linking people to community supports, reducing isolation, and addressing pressing social needs that contribute to poor health outcomes, including poverty, familial instability, and lack of stable housing.

These movements generally share in common a focus on polycentricity—meaning that they are non-hierarchical and typically have multiple locations of decision-making—and flexibility, and while some focus on resistance and the most vulnerable among us, other polycentric shifts are happening in the middle and upper classes as well, as evidenced by the growth of concierge care, which provides more flexible and individualistic care than can be provided in the current third-party payer system (Gustke 2012). I call this approach an "ecosystem approach" to healthcare reform. In the past, I have used the phrase "healthcare watershed" to describe how upstream regulations affected patient experiences downstream, but I also became convinced during that research that, much like ecologists learned in the early stages of the environmental movement, diverse healthcare ecosystems are better able to sustain crises and provide a greater host of niches that meet the unique needs of an array of diverse human beings. A diverse ecosystem of providers and locations of care is better able to sustain shocks than a consolidated and monopolistic system that focuses on a medical model at the expense of other kinds of health care. The COVID-19 pandemic provided merely one example of how a single shock can easily overwhelm a consolidated, centralized, and standardized healthcare system. Lessons from classical liberal thinkers (broadly construed) like Elinor Ostrom (McGinnis 2018; Ostrom 2015) find that network systems can provide better solutions to idiosyncratic healthcare problems, with the important caveat that the innovators who create such systems must be able to operate without excessive governmental interference and oversight.

As with any area of public policy, there are, of course, tradeoffs. The more diverse a healthcare ecosystem, the argument goes, the more time-consuming it will be for clients to find information on the quality of providers. The heuristic of "big academic hospital = quality" seems a reasonable one for people without medical training. At the same time, given the data on medical errors, cascades of intervention, and iatrogenic harm in hospital settings, it might behoove us to be more circumspect about precisely which heuristics we trust in the medical setting (Makary and Daniel 2016). Despite the expansive medical research of the negative side-effects and harms caused by excessive regulation, the alternative to a highly regulated healthcare system is often framed as a kind of "anarchy" of choice, where patients will be beset by quacks and alternative providers offering substandard or dangerous medical care.

Fortunately, the real world offers counter examples to these fears. One can envision a range of ways of diversifying the healthcare ecosystem that does not require people to simply put their trust in whatever provider advertises the loudest. Experiments like the "Birth Bundle" at the Minnesota Birth Center or the D.C. Birth Center find maternal fetal specialists working directly with midwives to triage care in an appropriate and safe manner to prevent escalation while providing patients a range of providers and locations of care for birth (Fairman 2010). Similarly, the very nature of palliative care as a discipline involves providing a diverse ecosystem of providers, ranging from physicians and nurse practitioners to social workers to hospice workers and volunteers with minimal medical training, in a bid to provide a diverse ecosystem for the dying and to maximize the chances that providers will access idiosyncratic and localized knowledge of how this particular patient can and would like to die (Zitter 2017). These programs are similar to those advocated for by Williams and other sociologists. However, regulatory limitations and the structure of third-party payers, largely dictated the federal government, threaten to prevent the diversification of the healthcare ecosystem.

This then, may be the last classical liberal lesson to offer the sociological community as both explore possibilities for reform. While much attention is paid in economics to various kinds of "market failures," very little attention is paid to *government failures*, or areas where government policies both fail to provide adequate results and sometimes even harm the very people they claim to be helping. The procedure- and medical-dominance of Medicare discussed by Paul Starr is merely one example. Sociologists like Theresa Morris have highlighted the counterproductivity of calls for tort reform in a world where medical errors are distressingly common (Morris 2013). In both cases, classical liberals and sociologists can look at the unintended consequences of government activity in the healthcare space and start asking the question "who are we crowding out with these initiatives?" If one goal of healthcare reform, as I've argued here, is a more diverse healthcare ecosystem, are there ways to structure government policies like health insurance to support such an ecosystem? Or are the lessons around regulatory capture and lobbying that we've learned over the past century indicative that the problem will be pervasive and that other alternatives to government-funded healthcare should be investigated? Alternatives exist, ranging from mutual aid and "third way" models to the growth of innovative concierge medicine practices that are moving out of the high-income space and seeking to provide alternatives for lower-income individuals and families. Whatever the answer, the combination of classical liberal principles and sociological insights provides us with a unique set of questions to ask about future reforms and a powerful set of research questions moving forward.

REFERENCES

Abbott, Andrew. 2014. *The System of Professions: An Essay on the Division of Expert Labor*. University of Chicago Press.

Acemoglu, Daron. 2013. *Why Nations Fail*. Main edition. London: Profile Books.

Aghajanian, Liana. 2015. "Los Angeles Midwives Aim to End Racial Disparities at Birth." *Aljazeera America*, September 5.

Anderson, D. Mark, Ryan Brown, Kerwin Kofi Charles, and Daniel I. Rees. 2020. "Occupational Licensing and Maternal Health: Evidence from Early Midwifery Laws." *Journal of Political Economy* 128(11):4337–83. doi: 10.1086/710555.

Balko, Radley. 2021. *Rise of the Warrior Cop: The Militarization of America's Police Forces*. 1st edition. PublicAffairs.

Birdsong, Mia. 2020. *How We Show Up: Reclaiming Family, Friendship, and Community*. New York: Hachette Go.

Brown, Phil. 1995. "Naming and Framing: The Social Construction of Diagnosis and Illness." *Journal of Health and Social Behavior* 34–52. doi: 10.2307/2626956.

Brown, Wendy. 2015. *Undoing the Demos: Neoliberalism's Stealth Revolution*. 1st edition. New York: Zone Books.

Buchanan, Allen. 1978. "Medical Paternalism." *Philosophy & Public Affairs* 7(4):370–90.

Conover, Christopher J., and James Bailey. 2020. "Certificate of Need Laws: A Systematic Review and Cost-Effectiveness Analysis." *BMC Health Services Research* 20. doi: 10.1186/s12913-020-05563-1.

Conrad, Peter. 2005. "The Shifting Engines of Medicalization." *Journal of Health and Social Behavior* 46(1): 3–14.

Conrad, Peter. 2007. *The Medicalization of Society: On the Transformation of Human Conditions into Treatable Disorders*. Baltimore: Johns Hopkins University Press.

Conrad, Peter, and Valerie Leiter. 2004. "Medicalization, Markets and Consumers." *Journal of Health and Social Behavior* 45: 158–76.

Dal Bó, Ernesto. 2006. "Regulatory Capture: A Review." *Oxford Review of Economic Policy* 22(2):203–25. doi: 10.1093/oxrep/grj013.

Davis, Joseph E. 2006. "How Medicalization Lost Its Way." *Society* 43(6): 51–56. doi: 10.1007/BF02698486.

Dodge, Kenneth A., W. Benjamin Goodman, Yu Bai, Karen O'Donnell, and Robert A. Murphy. 2019. "Effect of a Community Agency-Administered Nurse Home Visitation Program on Program Use and Maternal and Infant Health Outcomes: A Randomized Clinical Trial." *JAMA Network Open* 2(11):e1914522. doi: 10.1001/jamanetworkopen.2019.14522.

Domínguez, Daniela G., Dellanira García, David A. Martínez, and Belinda Hernandez-Arriaga. 2020. "Leveraging the Power of Mutual Aid, Coalitions, Leadership, and Advocacy during COVID-19." *American Psychologist* 75: 909–18. doi: 10.1037/amp0000693.

Drisdom, Sheronda. 2013. "Barriers to Using Palliative Care: Insight Into African American Culture." *Clinical Journal of Oncology Nursing* 17(4): 376–80. doi: 10.1188/13.CJON.376-380.

Enguidanos, Susan, Alexis Coulourides Kogan, Karl Lorenz, and George Taylor. 2011. "Use of Role Model Stories to Overcome Barriers to Hospice Among African Americans." *Journal of Palliative Medicine* 14(2): 161–68. doi: 10.1089/jpm.2010.0380.

Fairman, Julie. 2010. "'Go to Ruth's House': The Social Activism of Ruth Lubic and the Family Health and Birth Center." *Nursing History Review: Official Journal of the American Association for the History of Nursing* 18: 118–29.

Freidson, E. 1970. "Profession of Medicine: A Study of the Sociology of Applied Knowlege." Dodd, Mead & Company.

Furedi, Frank. 2006. "The End of Professional Dominance." *Society* 43(6): 14–18. doi: 10.1007/BF02698479.

Gadson, Alexis, Eloho Akpovi, and Pooja K. Mehta. 2017. "Exploring the Social Determinants of Racial/Ethnic Disparities in Prenatal Care Utilization and Maternal Outcome." *Seminars in Perinatology* 41(5): 308–17. doi: 10.1053/j.semperi.2017.04.008.

Goldfeld, Sharon, Anna Price, Charlene Smith, Tracey Bruce, Hannah Bryson, Fiona Mensah, Francesca Orsini, Lisa Gold, Harriet Hiscock, Lara Bishop, Ashlee Smith, Susan Perlen, and Lynn Kemp. 2019. "Nurse Home Visiting for Families Experiencing Adversity: A Randomized Trial." *Pediatrics* 143(1). doi: 10.1542/peds.2018-1206.

Grant, Rebecca. n.d. "The Rebel Midwives Of Alabama." *The Huffington Post*. Retrieved January 25, 2019 (https://highlinc.huffingtonpost.com/articles/en/alabama-midwives/).

Gustke, Constance. 2012. "Concierge Medicine: Not Just for the Rich, Anymore." Retrieved February 10, 2018 (https://www.cnbc.com/id/100314847).

Hall, Lauren K. 2019. *The Medicalization of Birth and Death*. 1st edition. Baltimore: Johns Hopkins University Press.

Hall, Lauren K., and Steven Horwitz. 2021. *Midwifery Licensing: Medicalization of Birth and Special Interests*. Mercatus Center.

Halley, Catherine. 2021. "Community Care in the AIDS Crisis." *JSTOR Daily*. Retrieved September 16, 2022 (https://daily.jstor.org/community-care-in-the-aids-crisis/).

Hamowy, R. 1979. "The Early Development of Medical Licensing Laws in the United States, 1875–1900." *The Journal of Libertarian Studies* 3(1): 73–119.

Hayek, F. A. 1945. "The Use of Knowledge in Society." *The American Economic Review* 4(35): 519–30.

Health, Council on Child and Adolescent. 1998. "The Role of Home-Visitation Programs in Improving Health Outcomes for Children and Families." *Pediatrics* 101(3): 486–89. doi: 10.1542/peds.101.3.486.

Hoffman, Kelly M., Sophie Trawalter, Jordan R. Axt, and M. Norman Oliver. 2016. "Racial Bias in Pain Assessment and Treatment Recommendations, and False Beliefs About Biological Differences Between Blacks and Whites." *Proceedings of the National Academy of Sciences* 113(16): 4296–4301. doi: 10.1073/pnas.1516047113.

Kaufman, Sharon R. 2006. *And a Time to Die: How American Hospitals Shape the End of Life*. Chicago: University of Chicago Press.

Kaufman, Sharon R. 2015. *Ordinary Medicine: Extraordinary Treatments, Longer Lives, and Where to Draw the Line*. Durham, NC: Duke University Press.

Kirzner, Israel M. 1997. "Entrepreneurial Discovery and the Competitive Market Process: An Austrian Approach." *Journal of Economic Literature* 35(1): 60–85.

Lindheim, Roslyn. 1981. "Birthing Centers and Hospices: Reclaiming Birth and Death." *Annual Review of Public Health* 2: 1–29. doi: https://doi.org/10.1146/annurev.pu.02.050181.000245.

Logan, Onnie Lee, and Katherine Clark. 2013. *Motherwit: An Alabama Midwife's Story*. San Francisco, CA: Untreed Reads Publishing.

Luke, Jenny M. 2018. *Delivered by Midwives: African American Midwifery in the Twentieth-Century South*. Jackson: University Press of Mississippi.

Makary, Martin A., and Michael Daniel. 2016. "Medical Error—The Third Leading Cause of Death in the US." *BMJ* i2139. doi: 10.1136/bmj.i2139.

McGinnis, Michael. 2018. "Commons, Institutional Diversity, and Polycentric Governance in US Health Policy." Pp. 279–307 in *Elinor Ostrom and the Bloomington School of Political Economy*. Vol. 4: Policy Applications and Extensions, edited by M. McGinnis and Cole, Daniel. Lexington Books.

McMillan Cottom, Tressie. n.d. "Why Are Pregnant Black Women Viewed as Incompetent?" *Time*.

Mor, Vincent, George Papandonatos, and Susan C. Miller. 2005. "End-of-Life Hospitalization for African American and Non-Latino White Nursing Home Residents: Variation by Race and a Facility's Racial Composition." *Journal of Palliative Medicine* 8(1):58–68. doi: 10.1089/jpm.2005.8.58.

Morris, Theresa. 2013. *Cut It Out: The C-Section Epidemic in America*. New York, NY: New York University Press.

Ostrom, Elinor. 2015. *Governing the Commons: The Evolution of Institutions for Collective Action*. Reissue edition. Cambridge, United Kingdom: Cambridge University Press.

Scott, Karen, Stephanie Bray, Ifeyinwa Asiodu, and Monica McLemore. n.d. "An Inconvenient Truth: You Have No Answer That Black Women Don't Already Possess." *Black Women Birthing Justice*. Retrieved January 25, 2019 (http://www.blackwomenbirthingjustice.org/single-post/2018/10/31/An-inconvenient-truth-You-have-no-answer-that-Black-women-don%E2%80%99t-already-possess).

Starr, Paul. 2017. *The Social Transformation of American Medicine*. New York: Basic Books.

Stratmann, Thomas, Matthew Baker and Elise Amez-Dros. 2020. "Public Health in Rural States: The Case against Certificate-of-Need Laws." *Mercatus Center*. Retrieved November 13, 2020 (https://www.mercatus.org/publications/healthcare/public-health-rural-states-case-against-certificate-need-laws-0).

Washington, Harriet. 2008. *Medical Apartheid: The Dark History of Medical Experimentation on Black Americans from Colonial Times to the Present*. New York, NY: Anchor Books.

Wertz, Richard W., and Dorothy C. Wertz. 1977. *Lying-In: A History of Childbirth in America*. New York: Free Press.

Williams, D. R. 1997. "Race and Health: Basic Questions, Emerging Directions." *Annals of Epidemiology* 7(5): 322–33.

Williams, David R. 2012. "Miles to Go Before We Sleep: Racial Inequities in Health." *Journal of Health and Social Behavior* 53(3): 279–95. doi: 10.1177/0022146512455804.

Williams, David R., and Lisa A. Cooper. 2019. "Reducing Racial Inequities in Health: Using What We Already Know to Take Action." *International Journal of Environmental Research and Public Health* 16(4): 606. doi: 10.3390/ijerph16040606.

Williams, David R., Jourdyn A. Lawrence, and Brigette A. Davis. 2019. "Racism and Health: Evidence and Needed Research." *Annual Review of Public Health* 40(1): 105–25. doi: 10.1146/annurev-publhealth-040218-043750.

Williams, David R., and Toni D. Rucker. 2000. "Understanding and Addressing Racial Disparities in Health Care." *Health Care Financing Review* 21(4): 75–90.

Williams, David R., Yan Yu, James S. Jackson, and Norman B. Anderson. 1997. "Racial Differences in Physical and Mental Health: Socio-Economic Status, Stress and Discrimination." *Journal of Health Psychology* 2(3): 335–51. doi: 10.1177/135910539700200305.

Zitter, Jessica Nutik. 2017. *Extreme Measures: Finding a Better Path to the End of Life*. New York: Avery.

Zola, Irving Kenneth. 1972. "Medicine as an Institution of Social Control." *The Sociological Review* 20(4): 487–504. doi: 10.1111/j.1467-954X.1972.tb00220.x.

NOTES

1. I would like to thank all the workshop participants for this volume for their incisive and supportive comments. I would also like to thank the Institute for Humane Studies and the Mercatus Center for their support of my research on healthcare, going back to 2015. Finally, I would like to thank Steve Horwitz, whose mentorship over the years helped me develop my Austrian sensibilities while encouraging me to build bridges with other disciplines and approaches. May his memory be a blessing.

2. We see clear evidence of this in data from the CDC during COVID that found that white women were more than twice as likely as women of color to flee NYC during the height of the COVID-19 outbreak to give birth more safely upstate. Black and Hispanic women, presumably because they lacked access to remote work that would allow them mobility as well as resources to move, were more likely to give birth in overwhelmed NYC hospitals, hospitals that were requiring a range of intrusive and harmful practices such as separation of mothers and babies, and separation of mothers from support persons like partners and doulas.

Chapter 6

Contending for Freedom

How Classical Liberal Social Science Informs Social Movement Studies

Mikayla Novak

The reception of social movement phenomena in classical liberal thought, and vice versa, is puzzling. The historical trajectory of liberalism has been undeniably shaped by articulation and advocacy for extending rights and freedoms to ever more people, and in ways which resemble social movement activity as commonly recognized today. At the very least, it can be said that prominent liberal thinkers through the ages—such as Locke, Voltaire, Smith, Wollstonecraft, Cobden, Mill, and Douglass—have influenced both scholarly and popular perceptions of freedom. However, it is also clear that numerous social movement activists explicitly embraced liberal principles and rhetoric when pressing claims to be freed from oppression of all stripes, and to enjoy liberties to associate with others culturally, economically, politically, and socially. Consider, for example, the liberal influences underlying the words and deeds of abolition, suffrage, racial equality, and low tax movements, to name a few. Despite all of this, modern liberal thought appears to be dominated by a neglect, and in some cases outright objection, toward movement activism and the sense of contentiousness it brings to socio-political order.

Certain academic specialists of social movement studies, a sub-strand of research within sociology, have recognized the significance of pro-liberty argumentation by movement leaders and other key activists. The freedom to live inclusively and productively in society has served as a mainstay method for social movements to frame rights claims, and minorities have creatively and passionately identified the imperfectabilities of majorities in living up to the ethical and normative standards of rules and systems rationalized in liberalism's name (e.g., Clark 1989; Powell 2000; Sandefur 2018). Even so, it is argued here that the extent to which classical liberal ideas have inspired movement mobilization and organization have been underappreciated within the sociological canon. This lack of appreciation may be regarded as an example of a broader issue concerning the neglectful, if not hostile, reception toward liberalism within modern sociology (Klein and Stern 2006).

My core proposition for this chapter is that the intellectual estrangement between classical liberal and social movement theories is unwarranted. Scholarly proponents of liberalism and social movement studies have developed a similar range of concepts and analytical propositions largely independently of one another. Although this had led in some measure to the separable development of language and insularity with regard to disciplinary networks, this does not preclude opportunities for productive intellectual exchange and mutual learning between liberal strands of political economy and social theory and the important sociological sub-discipline of social movement studies. An example of this is in the domain of entrepreneurship, a topic of mutual interest both to liberal thinkers and social movement scholars. Specifically, it is identified that social movement participants carry out entrepreneurial activities such as generating pro-liberty frames, organizing collective participation in protests and other key movement activities, and playing a role in generating institutional changes. Additional opportunities for mutual understanding between liberals and sociologists may arise through in-depth inquiries into the nature of movement leadership and organizational self-governance, both crucial variables in attempting to understand how activists sustain their contentious activities in uncertain, and often repressive, environments. Finally, there is an opportunity for both streams of scholarship to come together on questions raised by the Virginia school of political economy: how rules internally govern social movements; and how activism is implicated in the development and revision of societal-level rules that govern all people within a polity.

I argue that liberals can legitimately study social movements and, in so doing, learn more about processes pertaining to the society in which they live. Sociologists can, similarly, realize valuable learnings about society by better understanding how liberal intellectual contributions can explain social movement processes and outcomes. In saying this, the opportunity for the mutual learning I describe seem, to date, to have largely been left untouched by both liberals and sociologists. This trend is possibly owing to some long-lasting impressions, indeed stereotypes, that liberals and sociologists attribute to one another in respect of social movements. A range of prominent liberals over the past century have connected the likes of activism and protest with the risk of societal disorder. Conversely, liberal consternation surrounding social movements has been labelled by sociologists as *apologia* for hegemonic privilege that works to frustrate the achievement of new rights claims. This positioning of social movements as a mutual focal point of tension between classical liberals and sociologists will surely be difficult to displace, for there is some element of truth behind some of the claims made by both parties of each other. At the very least, to be open to academic conversation about social movements, and their determinants and consequences, is posited as a necessary minimal condition to help reduce epistemic and normative animosities between classical liberals and sociologists.

Before proceeding any further, some definitional effort is in order. To better understand the nature and consequences of societal change, and how individuals and groups cope with the typically disruptive element of change, many researchers turn to the study of social movements. But what are they? I recently described *social movements* as sustained collective engagements by multiple participants, typically involving counter-hegemonic or extra-institutional activities, which aim at effecting change within society (Novak 2021a, p. 3). Movement participants engage in a struggle to amend and reform the structures and flows pertaining to human behaviors, interests, practices, and values. Conceptually, social movements are also viewed as one of many elements mediating between the effects of individual agency and collective structure upon changes to society's institutions and practices. A key aspect of support for, and, certainly, opposition against, movements is their preparedness to use alternative, non-traditional, and often unconventional methods to fulfill their objectives. Indeed, social movements are frequently involved in the organization, and propagation, of extra-institutional tactics and challenges to power incumbencies—for example, in the form of protests, rallies, strikes, boycotts, and so on—to raise public attention and mobilize support for, and effect change in the direction of, their cause (Sharp 1973; Tilly 2008).

The study of social movements represents a mainstay of sociological inquiry, and interest in movement participation, tactics, and outcomes is present in other social scientific disciplines. Explanations of movement characteristics and activities are also represented in alternative traditions of thought, including Marxism, post-modernism, and critical studies. Whereas intellectual engagement with social movements amongst specialists of economics and rational choice theory exists (e.g., Opp 1989; Chong 1991; Lichbach 1995), I argue that opportunities remain to productively integrate the study of social movements with broader categories of classical liberal inquiry. *Classical liberalism* is broadly defined in this chapter as a set of ideological and philosophical dispositions emphasizing the primacy of individual liberty, freedom of association in economic and social contexts, toleration of alternative beliefs, perspectives, and worldviews, and constrained governmental activity in accordance with the rule of law.

This chapter advances a case for understanding social movement activities by applying the key postulates of classical liberal social science. The structure of the chapter is as follows. Section 2 outlines the major conceptual and methodological commitments of liberalism, as it is represented in its contemporary guise by the Austrian, Bloomington, and Virginia schools, and applies those themes to phenomena of social movement participation, activity, and impact. In doing so, I highlight a range of theoretical congruencies with key ideas in social movement studies, such as the entrepreneurial character of movement conduct (Austrian school), the self-governing capacities of movement organizations and networks (Bloomington school) as well as the contribution of social movements in challenging political and other sources of domination and oppression (Virginia school). In Section 3, I describe the key elements of largely normative tensions between the proponents of classical liberal social science and social movement studies. These tensions mainly concern the application of power dynamics in, and, relatedly, the appropriateness of extra-institutional, and often disruptive, tactics to, influence economic, political, and social outcomes. Whilst this characterization of the tension between the studies of liberalism and social movements is admittedly non-exhaustive, it is argued that the tensions identified in this chapter also point to a potential focal opportunity for future dialogue. Section 4 concludes the chapter.

CLASSICAL LIBERAL SOCIAL SCIENCE AND SOCIAL MOVEMENT THEORY: TOWARD CONSILIENCE

Classical liberal scholarship is noted for its dynamic and variegated character, reflecting both its intellectual durability and flexibility in the face of cultural, economic, political, and social transformations spanning centuries. A consequence of this is differing scholarly interpretations of the priority and relevance given to certain dimensions of liberty, and debates over their most appropriate means of realization in actually existing societies. In its contemporary form it is arguable that liberalism is closely associated with certain strands of heterodox political economy, all of which share with sociology a critique of the ontological and methodological presumptions of static, equilibrium-oriented neoclassical economics (e.g., Boettke 1997). These strands are known as the Austrian (with Ludwig von Mises and Friedrich Hayek as figureheads), Bloomington (Elinor and Vincent Ostrom), and Virginia (James M. Buchanan) schools.

Whereas these schools of thought are known to overlap conceptually and analytically (Boettke and Snow 2014), they each bring distinctive insights toward an understanding of human action. Austrians recognize the subjectivity of individual action, and the creative, entrepreneurial aspects of such action in dynamic and uncertain environments (Boettke and Coyne 2015). Proponents of the Bloomington school emphasize the coordinative capacities of heterogeneous individuals in bringing forth emergent systems of governance, including social norms that facilitate collective action (Lemke and Tarko 2020). Finally, the Virginia school considers the possibilities of non-market decision making amongst a variety of actors spanning domains of human activity, including political conduct within a regulated sphere of constitutional (and related) rules and procedures (Wagner 2018; Congleton et al. 2019).

In keeping with the interdisciplinary orientation of modern classical liberalism, in recent decades there has been a growing cross-fertilization of ideas between the noted strands of heterodox political economy and economic sociology. These contributions, referred to here as "classical liberal social science," stress the significance of the cultural and social contexts of action that are navigated by people, as they freely associate with one another in their pursuit of shared objectives (e.g., Chamlee-Wright and Storr 2015; Langrill and Storr 2015; Storr and John 2020). Referring favorably to the liberal sociological perspectives of key luminaries such as Adam Smith, Max Weber, Alfred Schütz, and Peter Berger, classical liberal social science explores the potentialities of securing individual freedom within broader epistemic and institutional avenues for societal learning, meaning, and coordination. Ultimately, the value of this approach is in the appreciation of liberalism as an inherently social theory, inviting explorations as to how individuals are to live more freely in diverse and challenging environments of human association and interaction.

AUSTRIAN LIBERAL POLITICAL ECONOMY, AND THE CASE OF MOVEMENT ENTREPRENEURSHIP

The main elements of classical liberal social science can be used to comprehend social movement activities in various ways. One way to proceed is through the identification of Austrian-style entrepreneurial impulses amongst movement participants, including on the part of leading activists or figureheads who are crucially involved in such processes as the articulation and framing of movement causes, organization of resources, development of tactics, negotiations with allies, and even counter-movements and other adversaries, and so on. These personalities are interchangeably described in literature as either "extra-institutional," "moral," or "norm" entrepreneurs (e.g., King and Soule 2007; Ellickson 2001; Staggenborg 2013). American Civil Rights movement leader Martin Luther King is commonly nominated as an example of such an entrepreneur, given his ability to persuasively situate the struggle for racial anti-discrimination within historical and theological contexts (Williams 1995; Selby 2008).

Paul DiMaggio (1988) has presented another relevant form of entrepreneurship, labelled "institutional entrepreneurship," which refers to the efforts of certain actors to leverage material resources, and manipulate cultural-social meanings, to change existing institutions or generate new ones. This strand of entrepreneurship may especially apply to social movements that have the effect of introducing transformative changes which persist over time. It is in respect of entrepreneurial action, and the contentious novelties that such social movement operation propounds in cultural, economic, and other contexts, in turn inviting crossover opportunities for research for both liberal and social movement theorists.

The extent of entrepreneurship displayed by social movement participants is not limited to the novel generation and application of tactical postures against political and other targets. Activists also have the capacity to organize social movement affairs with resourceful others and, within this, mobilize the support of potentially significant numbers of people to their cause. Of significance here is the contribution of McCarthy and Zald (1973, 1977), who specifically refer to "movement entrepreneurs" whom establish organizational vehicles to advance movement objectives. In order to sustain social movement organizations, McCarthy and Zald identify the utilization of skills on the part of entrepreneurs to interrelatedly accumulate finances and resources, and to attract the attention of media outlets, politicians, and the general public alike.

Acknowledgment of collective dimensions underpinning social movements is encapsulated by McCarthy and Zald's insight that entrepreneurs need to induce involvements from a variety of potential movement constituencies. These include beneficiary groups, who come to subjectively believe that they may directly gain advantages should the movement win concessions from their opponents, as well as those sets of persons who conscientiously embroil themselves in the movement but, at best, indirectly gain a "warm inner glow" of sharing values with the movement. The task of any given movement entrepreneur to actively cultivate constituencies is further incentivized by competition among social movement organizations for funds and supporters (Stern 1999). Building upon these earlier contributions have been a range of "critical mass" or "threshold" models that indicate that the willingness of a given individual to participate in a social movement event, such as a protest, is contingent upon evidence that a sufficient number of other people are involved (e.g., Granovetter 1978). It is not out of the question that movement entrepreneurs would play a crucial role in publicly articulating the purported strength of the movement cause so as to solicit greater participation.

The entrepreneurial element of social movement literature bears resemblance to an earlier tradition in sociology, and aspects of political economy, which recognize patterns of leadership behavior amongst prominent activists. From the political economy standpoint, the figures of Max Weber, Joseph Schumpeter, and Friedrich von Wieser are held as exemplars of early twentieth-century Continental European sensibilities regarding the place of leadership in persuading a mass of followers within society to advance socio-political change (Kolev 2019). Dissatisfied with the lack of agentic impulses in prominent movement theories—such as the macro-historical "opportunity structure" contributions of Tilly, Tarrow, and McAdam—Morris and Staggenborg (2004, p. 171) remind us that "[l]eaders are critical to social movements: they inspire commitment, mobilize resources, create and recognize opportunities, devise strategies, frame demands, and influence outcomes." It is far from coincidental that the terms "entrepreneur" and "leader" are frequently used interchangeably or are interpreted as being synonymous with one another—as is the case, for example, the identification of norm entrepreneur Martin Luther King as America's Civil Rights movement leader.

Heterodox political economy literature yields differing insights into the character of entrepreneurship which essentially equate with the distinctions between moderate and radical social movements in sociological literature (Haines 1984; Fitzgerald and Rogers 2000; Robnett et al. 2015). First, entrepreneurship may assume "Schumpeterian" disruptive qualities as a result of introducing novelties in societal practices with the effect of inducing structural change (Schumpeter [1934] 1961). Arguably the most apt instantiation of the Schumpeterian impulse motivating social movements to work against incumbent regimes and systems is that of the revolutionary movement—such as those participants of the 1789 French Revolution who succeeded in displacing the monarchical *ancien régime*, or, more recently, the successful protestors of the late 1980s and early 1990s in Eastern Europe and Central Asia who replaced communist with democratic governments.

Second, movement entrepreneurs may consist of a "Kirznerian" alertness element insofar as they perceive economic, cultural, political, and other opportunities to effect change largely within the given contexts of society (Lavoie 1991). It is anecdotally observed that a range of social movements—say, female suffrage movement of the nineteenth and twentieth centuries, or American Civil Rights movement of the twentieth century—did not seek totalizing changes to existing socio-political arrangements, but, rather, aimed for the extension of rights within them. For any given movement, even those seeking modest degrees of change, their mobilization prowess may be disincentivized by arguments for the status quo by oppositional counter-movement groups, including those arguments framing movement agitation for change as acts of deviance that aim to disrupt social order (Becker 1963).

Movement entrepreneurialism, as is the case for conceivably every other facet of movement activity, is conducted under risky, if not uncertain, circumstances. The inherent contingency of entrepreneurship in this context is conditioned by assessments as to the success, or failure, of movement advocacy for certain societal changes. Movements may fail to draw in popular support, compromising their ability to procure sufficient resources (including activist time and commitment) needed to successfully prosecute a case for change. The dynamic between movement participants and political actors for societal influence cannot be ignored here. Law enforcement bodies, whether acting on behalf of authoritarian or democratic political regimes, may raise the effective costs of displaying public contention on the part of activists, as well as arrest, harass, or surveil movement leaders and their supporters (Earl 2011; Coyne and Hall 2018). Another possibility that cannot be discounted is the capacity of political actors, including bureaucracy and military personnel, to manipulate movement activists in order to fulfill state goals (Marx 1979)—one example of this is the strategic effort of the Egyptian military to co-opt the Arab Spring movement to displace the Muslim Brotherhood-led government (Holdo 2019). Whilst not every effort by public authorities to quell movement protests succeeds (e.g., Opp 1998), maneuvers by military and police that happen to nullify social movement effectiveness are likely to have long-lasting ramifications for civil, personal, and political liberties.

Another hallmark of a classical liberal perspective of social movements is its acknowledgment of unanticipated consequences flowing from protests and other movement activities (Smith [1776] 1999; Merton 1936). An example of this is how successful social movement activities—say, in respect of a given cause, or partaken in a locality—fosters an *ex-post* emulation of strategies and tactics by the purveyors of other causes, a process presumably scarcely imagined by participants in the originating movements (Meyer and Whittier 1994). Several researchers suggest that anti-slavery and anti-racism movements in the U.S. and elsewhere served as a template for other movements to articulate humanistic and pro-liberty claims, and to pursue counter-hegemonic tactics to persuasive effect (for discussions about the connections between abolitionist and early feminist movements, see, for example, Rosenthal et al. 1985; and Pierson 2003). Movement entrepreneurship can draw upon, and learn from, contentious precedents in the process of constructing their own, contemporaneous demands for societal change, providing a potential avenue for liberal rights claims to be applied toward a burgeoning array of issues and concerns (Welzel 2013).

BLOOMINGTON LIBERAL POLITICAL ECONOMY, AND THE CASE OF MOVEMENT SELF-GOVERNANCE

The Bloomington school contribution to social movement theory lies in its referral to the endogenous creation and maintenance of decision rules, encompassing how a movement is to be constituted as well as how protests, and other tactics, are to be planned. The methods social movements use to sustain collective action, through persuasive narrative framing, identity construction and cultural work, and emotional bonding amongst movement participants, are other notable applications of social movement theory interpretable through a Bloomington framework (Novak 2021c). By way of an example, studies point to efforts by the low-tax U.S. Tea Party movement to build a collective identity amongst supporters, and to rationalize their strategic and tactical choices through a framing of rights that rhetorically merge liberty and justice themes (van Dyke and Meyer 2014; Heaney and Rojas 2015). In applying the ideas of Elinor and Vincent Ostrom to the study of social movements, one finds a counteracting response to Mancur Olson's (1965) hypothesis that movement-based collective action threatens to be unviable owing to the mass abstention from, or reneging commitments to, movement participation and support. Social movements, it is argued, present a good case for how people can resolve issues and sustain multi-person commitments in interaction with, but also beyond, the boundaries of market and state.

Refuting stereotypes of entrepreneurship as soloistic efforts for change by charismatic or talented individuals, classical liberal social science in the Bloomington sense recognizes that entrepreneurial processes are conducted in broader societal contexts that necessitate collaboration and support from others. Indeed, social movement environments are characterized by divergent, and subjective, preferences regarding preferred states of the world, and strategic and tactical means of achieving desired changes, as well as decentralized capabilities, knowledge, and resources amongst activist participants and movement supporters. In practice, numerous (but not all) social movements aspire to maintain decentered, if not "leaderless," networks of activists, and often in alliance with supporter groups. It is suggested that such movement configurations allow for deliberative decision-making amongst participants, as well as provide logistical flexibilities, that may not otherwise be afforded to individuals loosely affiliated with hierarchical social movement organizations (Levine 2019; Shantz 2020). Social movement scholars have turned their attention toward decision-making processes within anarchistic movements (Williams 2017; Shantz 2020). Polletta (2002) chronicles a range of participatory activities jointly undertaken within various American social movements, such as the Civil Rights and women's liberation movements, during the twentieth century, whilst Kinna et al. (2019) offers a Bloomington-style analysis of decision-making and rule formation within the Occupy Wall Street movement. These modes of social movement organizing appear to correspond with the Ostrom's normative concerns to uphold vibrant, and diverse, associational forms of life, which, in turn, serve the purpose of promoting emergent self-governance capacities amongst people (V. Ostrom 1997).

Another important contribution of the Bloomington school is the attention it has drawn to the existence of a range of common goods, which are shared by large numbers of people but is also vulnerable to overuse and similar other forms of exploitation (E. Ostrom 1990). An array of modern social movements, particularly of an anti-capitalist persuasion, have embraced the language of the commons in their efforts to oppose the specification of property rights to the likes of natural and environmental resources, cultural and digital artifacts, other works subject to intellectual property regulations, and urban amenities (Kashwan et al. 2021; Troncoso 2015; Wall 2017). Activists have explicated the term "commoning" to refer to processes wherein social movement participants collaborate in defining and managing goods to be commonly, rather than privately, provisioned. There are plentiful opportunities for classical liberal scholars to critically investigate the attributes and impacts of such attempts by movements to contentiously delineate non-state *and* non-market sites of interaction. In other words, the Bloomington school offers an approach to inquiry that formally recognizes social movement activity as the intersection of voluntary and collective action.

VIRGINIA LIBERAL POLITICAL ECONOMY AND THE CASE OF MOVEMENT ENTANGLEMENT

The Virginia school perspective of political economy, especially the public choice approach to political theory and analysis, also offers a range of insights of potential value for social movement scholars. Arguably the most relevant application of public choice to theories of social movements involves the feasibility of large-scale collective action as a means of expressing political demands, as canonically articulated by Olson, beyond the confines of voting during general elections or referendum events. Olson's arguments continue to influence academic debate, but the public choice element of Virginia political economy has matured over the years to accommodate non-instrumental patterns of collective action (Brennan 2008; van Winden 2007) and the entangled nature of political interactions (Wagner 1993, 2016). These expressive, or arguably "non-rational," dimensions of collective action appear to align reasonably well with an identifiable "cultural turn" in social movement theory, from the "new social movement" theories (e.g., Habermas 1981; Melucci 1985) through to the incorporation of emotions in movement activism (Goodwin et al. 2001; Jasper 2011). To an extent I have already engaged with the affective dimension of social movements; thus I seek to explore further the entangled dimension of activist engagements.

Historical and contemporary experiences both attest to the proclivity of social movement participants communicating and negotiating with diverse actors within society to effect desired changes. Consistent with the reality of the state as constituted by an ecology of organizations and bodies, movement activists and their supporters are observed to opportunistically engage with, and strategically arbitrage between, legislative, administrative, judicial branches, and even other levels, of government to gain political concessions (Novak 2021a). A relatively recent example of this has been the multi-faceted tactics deployed by movements promoting marriage equality of gay and lesbian couples. In the U.S. context various movement pressures—in the form of protests, referenda initiatives, legal challenges, and so on—contributed to the gradual diffusion of legal reforms across certain state jurisdictions from the early 2000s (e.g., Cole 2016; Eskridge and Riano 2020). This process, as spurred on by movement advocacy and agitation against the status quo, eventually culminated in the Supreme Court's 2015 decision in the *Obergefell v. Hodges* case to legalize same-sex marriage on a nation-wide basis.

Part of the growth in social movement studies is also attributed to investigations over the extent to which social movements challenge, and contestably engage with, other non-state actors. Studies have addressed interactivity between movement participants and corporations (Soule 2012), media outlets (Gamson and Wolfsfeld 1993), and the associations, interest groups, and non-government organizations within civil society (Diani 2015). An interesting example in this regard is the use of proprietary social media platforms by social movement participants to network with supporters and allies, mobilize protest actions, and to frame arguments against authoritarian political regimes (e.g., Lee et al. 2017; Enikolopov et al. 2020; c.f., Munger et al. 2019). For sociologists these seemingly disparate ideas have been assimilated into an overarching construct of "field theory" (Fligstein and McAdam 2012), with the involvement of movement participants into differing fields of activity—each with their own cultural, economic, political, and social competences, resources, and status positions—bringing about tensions but also the occasional opportunities to realize mutual gains from exchange among diverse actors.

The nature of entanglements involving social movements is potentially complex, reflecting in part the likelihood for extensive overlaps across economic, political, and social tactics and targeted groups. In the case of the American Civil Rights movement, for example, participants engaged in actions with profound economic effects such as consumer boycotts and sit-ins, politically petitioned different levels of government, and worked locally, regionally, and nationally to raise the socio-cultural costs of discrimination. Different tactics were often in effect at the same time, and sometimes even in a similar location, say in certain jurisdictions of the American South (Morris 1984). All in all, it is considered that social movement entanglements represent part of the broader feature of liberal-democratic processes wherein differing individuals and groups play a role in revealing problems, express the intensity with which those problems are being felt, as well as draw political and social attention to them (Novak 2021c).

CLASSICAL LIBERAL SOCIAL MOVEMENT THEORY? ONGOING TENSIONS AND CHALLENGES

It should be unsurprising to state that the academic study of social movements is characterized by contention. Whereas the purpose of this chapter is to articulate a case for the productive study of social movements using the intellectual affordances of classical liberalism, I appreciate that this contribution potentially adds to the contentious quality of movement scholarship. Broadly speaking, the perspectives of classical liberalism and sociology are commonly viewed as being in a state of tension with one another—with competing interpretations about the features and implications of social movements posing as a focal point for tensions between the two bodies of thought. In seeking to construct bridges of dialogue and understanding between liberalism and sociology, there is a need to squarely address the tensions as they are illuminated by discussions about social movements.

THE LIBERALS' "SOCIETAL DISORDER" CRITIQUE

Liberals have long submitted that societal conditions conducive to peace and prosperity are those which correspond with facilitation of mutually beneficial reciprocities, including voluntary economic and extra-economic exchanges, amongst intimates and non-intimates alike. The achievement of societal order is predicated upon an intersecting range of crucial formal and informal institutions and practices—such as the preservation of life, sufficiently protective security of one's own, justly acquired properties, political conduct in accordance with the rule of law, and observance of informal norms promoting dignity, mutual respect, and trust. Classical liberal thought is noted for its trenchant critiques of the multiple manifestations of illiberalism that are perceived to threaten, or have led, to departures from societal order. For several influential figures of modern liberalism, social movement activities were occasionally identified as being embroiled in a range of mutually inclusive concerns that I shall henceforth label as the "*societal disorder*" argument.

It is supposed that the liberals' social disorder objection against social movements manifests itself in several interdependent mechanisms or processes. In this chapter, I focus upon two mechanisms. The first refers to the societal losses stemming from rent-seeking activities, entailing the use of scarce resources in lobbying and petitioning for fiscal, legal, and regulatory advantages provided by government (Tullock 1967; Hillman and Long 2019). Social movement participants and their allies may not operate merely within the domain of institutionalized, "insider" politics to attain policy ratification for their specific causes—say, in the form of submissions presented through official inquiries—but may seek to exert political pressures by engaging in public protests and other disruptive activities, all of which absorb time, labor, and other resources. Classical liberal social science literature highlights two key problems associated with rent seeking. One is that rent-seeking is likely to flout basic notions of equality, justice, and liberty in the conduct of public governance, consequent to departures from the impartial and like-for-like treatment of individuals by government (Hayek 1960; Buchanan and Congleton 1998). The other is the prospect that rent-seeking activities risk promoting cultural and political dynamics to the effect that groups increasingly bargain, and contest for, advantages coercively secured through the political process rather than through voluntaristic persuasion and trades, with long-term costs to economic prosperity and social cohesion.

The second, and last, manifestation of the liberals' societal disorder objection I raise is that of the application of violence. By raising their voices in the public square, and thrusting their bodies toward barricades and their opponents, social movement participants are commonly perceived as a highly disruptive, if not destabilizing, societal force, challenging various forms of authority and the beliefs, mores, institutions, and practices underpinning them (Novak 2021a). Of concern to many classical liberals is the probability that movements tend to violence, entailing the harming of life and destruction of property, as participants intolerantly seek an end-state utopic vision of their preferred state of the world (Popper [1945] 2013). Violence may be a deliberately chosen strategic stance against typically demonized and reviled opposition, or may arise as the (intended or unintended) consequence of provocations by governments and other actors. Shaffer (1975) indicates that the strains and frustrations of state coercion may induce a counterresponse by the coerced public, which could spill over into violence. Aside from empirical doubts as to the effectiveness of violent tactical ploys as compared with non-violent strategies (Chenoweth and Stephan 2011; Feinberg et al. 2020), violence may be said to feed into broader anxieties, which are not felt merely amongst liberals, about the potentially substantial damages posed by disorder for widespread social cooperation.

Interspersed in contemporary classical liberal literature are statements pointing to social movements as a crucible of economic, political, and social problems. Several liberals decried the influence of labor movements (together with formal trade union organizations and working-class, laborist political parties) in disrupting production, stoking price inflationary pressures, and suppressing labor market competition (e.g., Hutt 1964; Hayek 1972). In his treatise, *Human Action*, the Austrian economist Ludwig von Mises ([1949] 2007) not only associated labor movement activism with societal disturbance but with a distortion of labor and factor markets, the economic damages of which are entrenched by political acceptance of union agendas to centralize wages determination and restrict labor market entries. James Buchanan enunciated withering critiques of violent student protestors, and the concessions granted to them, on American campuses during the 1960s and 1970s. He partly attributed the concessions to violence to publicly funded university frameworks with lax governance and inconsistent rule-enforcement mechanisms (Buchanan and Devletoglou 1970). More recently, a number of classical liberals have censured the rent-seeking proclivities of a range of environmental activists harboring anti-capitalist sympathies (e.g., Lal 2006).

Whilst it is true that collective actors, such as social movements, may organize in ways that subvert liberal political institutions, the rent-seeking construct may become over-generalized as an "all-weather" critique of conceivably any political interaction with legislators and bureaucrats. Putting aside the subjectivist insight that individuals may *themselves* not perceive their rent-seeking activities to be loss-inducing (Makovi 2015), it is conceivable that resources may be expended, under certain circumstances, in the political pursuit of causes that *extend* human liberties. Over the past few decades, a variety of social movements, and allied associations and interest groups, have successfully lobbied governments to diminish local, regional, and national tax burdens, as well as ease regulatory and legal obstacles in a range of areas (Burg 2004; King 2010; Warburg 2017). There are also examples of identity-based movements persuading legislative and judicial branches of government to eliminate discriminatory barriers to property, work, services provision, and free association (Novak 2016). Although liberalization efforts do imply the expending of resources, their normative value ultimately rests in their subsequent reallocation (and growth in the overall quantum) of economic and social resources in morally appealing ways. For example, liberalization is conducive to interactivity on the part of a greater number of participants in voluntaristic exchanges, including on the part of marginalized, subaltern communities previously oppressed by restrictive laws and policies. As noted, certain social movements have been implicated in the promotions of freedom described here.

A totemic commitment of classical liberalism is its emphasis upon peace, implying a preference for nonviolent tactical choices when signaling disagreement and dissent against multiple sources of overbearing authority. Several arguments have been raised in favor of the presumptive liberal case for nonviolence, on analytical and normative grounds. Destruction and theft of property imposes a range of costs upon victims, including opportunity costs foregone in replacing damaged or stolen goods. Resorting to violence when expressing demands for societal change is also considered to reduce the likelihood of agreement-making and coordination, particularly if violence is countered by additional violent acts. Another reason in favor of liberalism's nonviolence presumption is that—reflecting the entangled complexion of economic, political, and other relationships, and the dispersed character of property ownership and use—it is oftentimes difficult for social movement participants to accurately, and justly, identify their targets.

Non-violence does not nullify the prospect of contentious displays by social movements that may be inconvenient, or even disruptive to some degree, but which are, nevertheless, consistent with basic liberal tenets such as freedom of assembly and expression. The hermeneutical philosopher Gary Madison (1998) refers to this argument as the "self-limitation" proviso of social movement action. Specifically, movement participants have the freedom to vigorously partake in efforts to advance their change objectives, but not in an unrestrained and violent manner disrespecting the life, property, and equal liberty of others. This proviso includes the freedom of opponents to subscribe to views contrary to those held by movement activists, and even for activists to change their minds and abstain from contentious activities as they see fit. I argue that the self-limiting tactical tilt is also likely to engender efficacious social movement practice, especially regarding the need to employ discursive and other novelties in *persuading*, rather than *coercing*, people over the case for societal change (Novak 2021a). It is generically posited that persuading, through voluntaristic means, a positive mindset conducive to change is more likely to be culturally, politically, and sociologically enduring than the constant application of costly force, the latter likely arousing public enmity toward the enforced change and the identifiable political carriers of such change (Shaffer op. cit.). All in all, the liberal stance is advanced on the ground of avoiding the multiple, and significant, costs surrounding violent extremism.

THE SOCIOLOGISTS' "HEGEMONIC DEFENSE" CRITIQUE

It is true that an impression can be gleaned from academic and popular writings that a number of liberal thinkers have harbored negative sentiments toward social movements and their activist stances in their quest to propel change. This has been taken in some quarters, especially in sociology, that the critique of movements as rent-seekers, and disruptors more generally, serves as a mask allegedly concealing an underlying liberal preferment to maintain power and privileges—presumably advantaging wealthy elites and their political sponsors at the expense of the public. Similarly, there are aspersions to the effect that liberalism is antithetical to democratic political processes (Bonefeld 2017; Irving 2020; c.f., Novak 2021c). Effectively I am referring to a "*hegemonic defense*" argument, located particularly within critical sociology, to the effect that criticisms of social movements stand as a rationalization of power and privilege structures, and the manifold inequalities resulting from those.

Much of the critique surrounding classical liberal perspectives on power has been directed to Buchanan's (1987) unanimity voting rule as the standard for registering agreements on the structure of rules for governing society. Critics argue that this contractarian theory entrenches a status quo bias given that proposals to amend, or overturn, rules are subject to effective veto by any dissenting individual (Udehn 1996; Melenovsky 2019), although others note the unanimity rule is properly construed as a normative-ideal standard against which actually existing proposals for rule adjustment may be compared (Meadowcroft 2014). The contractarianism of Buchanan serves additional purposes that are assumed to be supported by sociologists—including that political processes not override the concerns and interests of minorities, and that the choice element in political decision-making be respected (e.g., Thrasher 2019; Magness 2020; Vanberg 2020).

The critical focus upon the contractarian element of liberal thought overlooks a processual, and open-ended, perspective of liberal-democratic processes, which seems more amenable to the formal inclusion of social movement involvements. Generations of liberals, such as John Stuart Mill, Frank Knight, and Buchanan himself, outlined the importance of democracy in facilitating discussions amongst diverse individuals about matters of public opinion. Arguably one of the more robust defenses for liberal democracy was articulated by Don Lavoie, an influential figure in classical liberal social science involved in the reconciliation between economic sociology and liberal political economy. Also inspired by Hayekian themes, Lavoie states that "[d]emocracy is not a quality of the conscious will of a representative organization that has been legitimated by the public, but a quality of the discursive process of the distributed wills of the public itself" (Lavoie 1993, p. 111). Social movements may be conceived as important collective actors in this open-ended liberal-democratic process, helping to reveal economic, political, and social problems, expressing the intensity with which those problems are being experienced, and discursively framing potential solutions.

The fundamentally sociological orientation of classical liberal social science also lends itself to recognizing the structural, and oft-informal, dimensions of power that ramify throughout societies. Sometimes referred to as "thick libertarianism," this dimension of intellectual inquiry explores the ways in which the exercise of freedoms is facilitated, or otherwise curtailed, by not only legal codes and formal institutions but by a constellation of beliefs, norms, and values that are interwoven into shared meanings and understandings attributed to social behavior and conduct. The liberal appreciation of the cultural and sociological attributes of freedom, and of power that constrains creative agency, opens intellectual space for considering those social movements that operate outside formal political channels, and partake in efforts to transform cultural precepts. The relevance of this discussion for social movement studies is that liberals recognize that the domain of movement activism need not be restricted to bargaining for favorable political exchanges with the likes of legislators and bureaucrats. This is unsurprising given the longstanding classical liberal analytical and normative emphasis upon the rich ecology of human interactions within civil society. Consistent with this, recognition of a thick libertarian orientation to social scientific study bears some resemblances with decades-long investigations, as referred to previously in this chapter, concerning the operations and effects of culturally oriented "new" social movements.

An example of social movement involvement in the development of thick libertarianism is the contribution of feminist movements in not only articulating the moral case against patriarchy, but constructing alternative, non-state systems of organization and support to address gendered abuse and discrimination (e.g., Johnson 2013). Of broader significance from the social movement standpoint is that the value, and outcomes, of intersectional voluntary and collective action cannot necessarily be known in advance—even to activists who engage in plans within their circumstances of time and place—but, nevertheless, governance systems ordered on liberal principles allow movement participants to engage in conjoint strategic and tactical discoveries to effectuate varying kinds of anti-hegemonic change. The first-wave feminists, including protestors for suffrage, could scarcely have imagined how succeeding generations would freely build upon their originating example to contend for gender equality in cultural, economic, political, social, and other domains.

CONCLUSION

As highlighted by its interpretation of social movement activities and their effects, classical liberal social science is posited to contribute to contemporary sociological thought in several ways. It provides for sophisticated conceptions of individualism and human agency, contextualized by the operation of culture, norms, and formal institutions. Whereas the nature and implications of engagements between movement participants *qua* citizens with the state are of significant concern to liberals, the classical liberal social science approach can illuminate the full extent of interactivity among gain-seeking and meaning-making individuals amongst non-state domains of activity. Consistent with its emphasis upon normative individualism, classical liberal social science also contributes to sociology a relational framework of freedom, wherein individuals and groups agree to work together in a struggle for enhanced liberties across multiple dimensions. Freedom is, indeed, something we do together, and the social movement example highlights how people associate voluntarily to pursue a host of collective action possibilities, including challenging founts of civil, corporate, and public power.

I propose that there are opportunities for both classical liberals and social movement scholars to use social movements as an intellectual focal point to better understand the perspectives of the counterparty. But this (dare one say it) contention underplays the common ground already, but by and large mutually exclusively, laid out by both liberals and sociologists with an interest in social movement activities. As indicated in this chapter, both strands of inquiry have articulated theories and analytical frames to study entrepreneurial action, and about leadership qualities often attributed to prominent movement figures. In response to the notion that collective action is, somehow, infeasible, both Bloomington political economy and social movement studies have indicated how sharing experiences and ideas, and using frames and narratives to engender group solidarity, have sustained social movements oftentimes in the face of incredible resistance from political actors and a variety of groups who wish to frustrate societal change. Finally, in this chapter I identified how both academics specializing in Virginia political economy and social movements have brought into prominence the interaction between social movements and varied individuals and groups across a variety of domains and fields. The potentially productive engagement between liberal and sociological studies is not restricted to the preceding suggestions. There appears ample scope for sociologists to offer insights of value to liberal thinkers on topics such as the social dimensions of non-economic entrepreneurship, socio-political alertness in different cultural and institutional contexts, ethnographic and other examinations of deliberative procedures undertaken by activists, social network analyses of movement structures, and how structural contexts shape activist perceptions in respect to the feasibility of differing tactics for political change.

It is important to appreciate that not all social movements are explicitly liberal in their ideological orientation, or are functionally liberal with respect to their impacts upon a range of societal outcomes. Added to this is the qualifier that movement participants may subscribe to a diversity of beliefs, some of them non-liberal in character. Although there are very real concerns about rent-seeking and political favoritism garnered by activists, and the occasionally violent tactics used by social movement participants that may harm life and property, not all social movements should be tarred with the same brush of negativity or dismissal. This is because some important movements, and key figures therein, have operated in ways that have effectively expanded the possibilities for people to lead freer lives. Whilst it is conceptually and empirically necessary to separate liberal wheat from non-liberal chaff, so to speak, classical liberal social science illuminates the reality of pro-liberty social movements. In daring to dream of a freer future, and being prepared to partake in risky collective actions, a range of social movements have, under certain circumstances, helped to close the distinction between liberal theory and reality, and belief and practice.

REFERENCES

Becker, Howard S. 1963. *Outsiders: Studies in the Sociology of Deviance*, Free Press, New York.

Boettke, Peter J. 1997. "Where Did Economics Go Wrong? Modern Economics as a Flight from Reality." *Critical Review: A Journal of Politics and Society* 11, no. 1, pp. 11–64.

Boettke, Peter J. and Coyne, Christopher J. 2015. *The Oxford Handbook of Austrian Economics*, Oxford University Press, New York.

Boettke, Peter J. and Snow, Nicholas A. 2014. "Political Economy and the Science of Association: A Suggested Reconstruction of Public Choice through the Alliance of the Vienna, Virginia, and Bloomington Schools of Political Economy." *Review of Austrian Economics* 27, no. 1, pp. 97–110.

Bonefeld, Werner. 2017. *The Strong State and the Free Economy*, Rowman & Littlefield, London.

Brennan, Geoffrey. 2008. "Psychological Dimensions in Voter Choice." *Public Choice* 137, nos. 3/4, pp. 475–489.

Buchanan, James M. 1987. "The Constitution of Economic Policy." *American Economic Review* 77, no. 3, pp. 243–250.

Buchanan, James M. and Congleton, Roger D. 1998. *Politics by Principle, Not Interest: Towards Nondiscriminatory Democracy*, Cambridge University Press, New York.

Buchanan, James M. and Devletoglou, Nicos E. 1970. *Academia in Anarchy: An Economic Diagnosis*, Basic Books, New York.

Burg, David. F. 2004. *A World History of Tax Rebellions: An Encyclopedia of Tax Rebels, Revolts, and Riots from Antiquity to the Present.* Routledge, New York.

Chamlee-Wright, Emelie and Storr, Virgil H. 2015. "Social Economy as an Extension of the Austrian Research Program," in Peter J. Boettke & Christopher J. Coyne (eds.), *The Oxford Handbook of Austrian Economics*, Oxford University Press, New York, pp. 247–271.

Chenoweth, Erika and Stephen, Maria J. 2011. *Why Civil Resistance Works: The Strategic Logic of Nonviolent Protest*, Columbia University Press, New York.

Chong, Dennis. 1991. *Collective Action and the Civil Rights Movement*, University of Chicago Press, Chicago.

Clark, Elizabeth B. 1989. "Self-Ownership and the Political Theory of Elizabeth Cady Stanton." *Connecticut Law Review* 21, pp. 905–941.

Cole, David. 2016. *Engines of Liberty: How Citizen Movements Succeed*, Basic Books, New York.

Congleton, Roger D., Grofman, Bernard, and Stefan Voigt. 2019. *The Oxford Handbook of Public Choice*. Oxford University Press, Oxford, UK.

Coyne, Christopher J. and Hall, Abigail R. 2018. *Tyranny Comes Home: The Domestic Fate of U.S. Militarism*. Stanford University Press, Palo Alto, CA.

Diani, Mario. 2015. *The Cement of Civil Society: Studying Networks in Localities.* Cambridge University Press, Cambridge, UK.

DiMaggio, Paul J. 1988. "Interest and Agency in Institutional Theory," in Lynne Zucker (ed.), *Institutional Patterns and Organizations: Culture and Environment.* Ballinger, Cambridge, MA, pp. 3–22.

Earl, Jennifer. 2011. "Political Repression: Iron Fists, Velvet Gloves, and Diffuse Control." *Annual Review of Sociology* 37, pp. 261–284.

Ellickson, Robert C. 2001. "The Market for Social Norms." *American Law and Economic Review* 3, no. 1, pp. 1–49.

Enikolopov, Ruben, Makarin, Alexey, and Maria Petrova. 2020. "Social Media and Protest Participation: Evidence from Russia." *Econometrica* 88, no. 4, pp. 1479–1514.

Eskridge, William N. Jr. and Riano, Christopher. C. 2020. *Marriage Equality: From Outlaws to In-Laws.* Yale University Press, New Haven, CT.

Feinberg, Matthew, Robb, Willer and Chloe Kovacheff. 2020. "The Activist's Dilemma: Extreme Protest Actions Reduce Popular Support for Social Movements." *Journal of Personality and Social Psychology: Interpersonal Relations and Group Processes* 119, no. 5, pp. 1086–1111.

Fitzgerald, Kathleen J. and Diane M. Rodgers. 2000. "Radical Social Movement Organizations: A Theoretical Model." *Sociological Quarterly* 41, no. 4, pp. 573–592.

Fligstein, Neil and Doug McAdam. 2012. *A Theory of Fields*, Oxford University Press, New York.

Gamson, William A. and Gadi Wolfsfeld. 1993. "Movements and Media as Interacting Systems." *Annals of the American Academy of Political and Social Sciences* 528, no. 1, pp. 114–125.

Goodwin, Jeff, Jasper, James M., and Francesca Polletta. 2001. *Passionate Politics: Emotions and Social Movements.* University of Chicago Press, Chicago.

Granovetter, Mark. 1978. "Threshold Models of Collective Behavior." *American Journal of Sociology.* 83, no. 6, pp. 1420–1443.

Habermas, Jurgen. 1981. "New Social Movements." *Telos* 49, pp. 33–37.

Haines, Herbert H. 1984. "Black Radicalization and the Funding of Civil Rights: 1957–1970." *Social Problems* 32, no. 1, pp. 31–43.

Hayek, Friedrich A. 1960. *The Constitution of Liberty*, Routledge and Kegan Paul, London.

Hayek, Friedrich A. 1972. *A Tiger by the Tail: The Keynesian Legacy of Inflation.* Institute of Economic Affairs, London.

Heaney, Michael T, and Fabio Rojas. 2015. *Party in the Street: The Antiwar Movement and the Democratic Party after 9/11.* Cambridge University Press, New York.

Hillman, Arye L. and Ngo Van Long. 2019. "Rent Seeking: The Social Cost of Contestable Benefits." in R. D. Congleton, B. Grofman. & S. Voigt (eds), *The Oxford Handbook of Public Choice*. Oxford University Press, Oxford. UK, 489–518.

Holdo, Markus. 2019. "Cooptation and Non-cooptation: Elite Strategies in Response to Social Protest." *Social Movement Studies* 18, no. 4, pp. 444–462.

Hutt, William H. 1964. *The Economics of the Colour Bar: A Study of the Economic Origins and Consequences of Racial Segregation in South Africa.* Andre Deutsch, London.

Irving, Sean. 2020. *Hayek's Market Republicanism: The Limits of Liberty*, Routledge, London.

Jasper, James M. 2011. "Emotions and Social Movements: Twenty Years of Theory and Research." *Annual Review of Sociology* 37, pp. 285–303.

Johnson, Charles W. 2013. "Women and the Invisible Fist: How Violence Against Women Enforces the Unwritten Law of Patriarchy," viewed 13 August 2022, http://charleswjohnson.name/essays/women-and-the-invisible-fist

Kashwan, Prakash, Mudaliar, Praneeta, Foster, Sheila R. and Floriane Clement. 2021. "Reimagining and Governing the Commons in an Unequal World: A Critical Engagement." *Current Research in Environmental Sustainability* 3, 100–102.

King, Brayden G. and Sarah A. Soule. 2007. "Social Movements as Extra-Institutional Entrepreneurs: The Effect of Protests on Stock Price Returns." *Administrative Science Quarterly* 52, no. 3, pp. 413–442.

King, Hanna. 2010. "U.S. AIDS Coalition to Unleash Power (ACT-UP) Demands Access to Drugs, 1987–89." Global Nonviolent Action Database, viewed 12 April 2022, https://nvdatabase.swarthmore.edu/content/us-aids-coalition-unleash-power-act-demands-access-drugs-1987-89

Kinna, Ruth, Prichard, Alex, and Thomas Swann. 2019. "Occupy and the Constitution of Anarchy." *Global Constitutionalism* 8, no. 2, pp. 357–390.

Klein, Daniel B. and Charlotta Stern. 2006. "Sociology and Classical Liberalism." *Independent Review* 11, no. 1, pp. 37–52.

Kolev, Stefan. 2019. "The Puzzles of a Triumvir: Friedrich von Wieser as Political Economist and Sociologist." *European Journal of the History of Economic Thought* 26, no. 5, pp. 942–972.

Lal, Deepak. 2006. *Reviving the Invisible Hand: The Case for Classical Liberalism in the Twenty-First Century.* Princeton University Press, Princeton, NJ.

Langrill, Ryan N. and Virgil Storr. 2015. "Contemporary Austrian Economics and the New Economic Sociology," in P. J. Boettke & C. J. Coyne (eds.), *The Oxford Handbook of Austrian Economics*, Oxford University Press, New York, pp. 547–562.

Lavoie, Don. 1991. "The Discovery and Interpretation of Profit Opportunities: Culture and the Kirznerian Entrepreneur," in B. Berger (ed.), *The Culture of Entrepreneurship.* ICS Press, San Francisco, pp. 33–51.

Lavoie, Don. 1993. "Democracy, Markets, and the Legal Order: Notes on the Nature of Politics in a Radically Liberal Society." *Social Philosophy and Policy.* 10, no. 2, pp. 103–120.

Lee, Francis L. F., Chen, Hsuan-Ting, and Michael Chan. 2017. "Social Media Use and University Students' Participation in a Large-scale Protest Campaign: The Case of Hong Kong's Umbrella Movement." *Telematics and Informatics.* 34, no. 2, pp. 457–469.

Lemke, Jayme and Vlad Tarko. 2020. *Elinor Ostrom and the Bloomington School.* McGill-Queen's University Press, Montreal, Canada.

Levine, Peter. 2019. "'What Should We Do?' The Bloomington School and the Citizen's Core Question," in R. Q. Herzberg, P. J. Boettke, & P. D. Aligica (eds.), *Ostrom's Tensions: Reexamining the Political Economy and Public Policy of Elinor C. Ostrom*, Mercatus Center at George Mason University, Arlington VA, pp. 105–125.

Lichbach, Mark Irving. 1995. *The Rebel's Dilemma.* University of Michigan Press, Ann Arbor.

Madison, Gary B. 1998. *The Political Economy of Civil Society and Human Rights*, Routledge, New York.

Magness, Phillip W. 2020. "The Anti-discriminatory Tradition in Virginia School Public Choice Theory." *Public Choice.* 183, nos. 3–4, pp. 417–441.

Makovi, Michael. 2015. "The Welfare Costs of Rent-Seeking: A Methodologically Individualist and Subjectivist Revision." *Journal of Philosophical Economics.* 9, no. 1, pp. 73–101.

Marx, Gary T. 1979. "External Efforts to Damage or Facilitate Social Movements: Some Patterns, Explanations, Outcomes, and Complications," in J. D. McCarthy & M. N. Zald (eds.), *The Dynamics of Social Movements: Resource Mobilization, Social Control and Tactics.* Winthrop Publishers, Cambridge, MA, pp. 94–125.

McCarthy, John D. and Meyer N. Zald. 1973. *The Trend of Social Movements in America: Professionalization and Resource Mobilization.* General Learning Press, Morristown NJ.

McCarthy John D. & Meyer N. Zald. 1977. "Resource Mobilization and Social Movements: A Partial Theory." *American Journal of Sociology.* 82, no. 6, pp. 1212–1241.

Meadowcroft, John. 2014. "Exchange, Unanimity and Consent: A Defence of the Public Choice Account of Power." *Public Choice.* 158, no. 1, pp. 85–100.

Melenovsky, Chris M. 2019. "The Status Quo in Buchanan's Constitutional Contractarianism." *Homo Oeconomicus.* 36, nos. 1–2, pp. 87–109.

Melucci, Alberto. 1985. "The Symbolic Challenge of Contemporary Social Movements." *Social Research.* 52, no. 4, pp. 789–816.

Merton, Robert K. 1936. "The Unanticipated Consequences of Purposive Social Action." *American Sociological Review.* 1, no. 6, pp. 894–904.

Meyer David S. and Nancy Whittier. 1994. "Social Movement Spillovers." *Social Problems.* 41, no. 2, pp. 277–298.

Morris, Aldon D. 1984. *The Origins of the Civil Rights Movement: Black Communities Organizing for Change.* Free Press, New York.

Morris, Aldon D. and Suzanne Staggenborg. 2004. "Leadership in Social Movements," in David A. Snow, Sarah A. Soule, and Hanspeter Kriesi (eds.), *The Blackwell Companion to Social Movements.* Blackwell Publishing, Malden, MA, pp. 171–196.

Munger Kevin, Bonneau, Richard, Nagler, Jonathan, and Joshua A. Tucker. 2019. "Elites Tweet to Get Feet Off the Streets: Measuring Regime Social Media Strategies During Protest." *Political Science Research and Methods.* 7, no. 4, pp. 815–834.

Novak, Mikayla. 2016. "Deirdre McCloskey, Kirznerian Growth and the Role of Social Networks: Comment." *Economic Affairs.* 36, no. 2, pp. 217–220.

Novak, Mikayla. 2021a. *Freedom in Contention: Social Movements and Liberal Political Economy.* Lexington Books, Lanham, MD.

Novak, Mikayla. 2021b. "Review of Sean Irving's Hayek's Market Republicanism: The Limits of Liberty." *Cosmos + Taxis.* 9, nos. 7–8, pp. 60–68.

Novak, Mikayla. 2021c. "Social Movements and Liberal Political Economy," viewed 31 March 2022, https://csgs.kcl.ac.uk/liberal-political-economy-insights-into-social-movements.

Olson, Mancur. 1965. *The Logic of Collective Action: Public Goods and the Theory of Groups.* Harvard University Press, Cambridge, MA.

Opp, Karl-Dieter. 1989. *The Rationality of Political Protest: A Comparative Analysis of Rational Choice Theory.* Routledge, New York.

Opp, Karl-Dieter. 1998. "Explaining Revolutions from Below: East Germany in 1989." *Independent Review.* 3, no. 1, pp. 91–102.

Ostrom, Ellinor. 1990. *Governing the Commons: The Evolution of Institutions for Collective Action.* Cambridge University Press, New York.

Ostrom, Vincent. 1997. *The Meaning of Democracy and The Vulnerability of Democracies: A Response to Tocqueville's Challenge.* University of Michigan Press, Ann Arbor.

Pierson, Michael D. 2003. *Free Hearts and Free Homes: Gender and American Antislavery Politics.* University of North Carolina Press, Chapel Hill, NC.

Popper, Karl. [1945] 2013. *The Open Society and Its Enemies.* Princeton University Press, Princeton, NJ.

Polletta, Francesca. 2002. *Freedom Is An Endless Meeting: Democracy in American Social Movements.* University of Chicago Press, Chicago.

Powell, Jim. 2000. *The Triumph of Liberty: A 2,000-Year History, Told Through the Lives of Freedom's Greatest Champions.* Free Press, New York.

Robnett, Belinda, Glasser, Carol L., and Rebecca Trammell. 2015. "Waves of Contention: Relations among Radical, Moderate, and Conservative Movement Organizations." *Research in Social Movements, Conflicts and Change.* 38, pp. 69–101.

Rosenthal, Naomi, Fingrutd, Meryl, Ethier, Michele, Karant, Roberta, and David McDonald. 1985. "Social Movements and Network Analysis: A Case Study of Nineteenth-Century Women's Reform in New York State." *American Journal of Sociology.* 90, no. 5, pp. 1022–1054.

Sandefur, Timothy. 2018. *Frederick Douglass: Self-Made Man.* Cato Institute, Washington, DC.

Schumpeter, Joseph A. [1934] 1961. *The Theory of Economic Development: An Inquiry into Profits, Capital, Interest, and the Business Cycle.* Trans. R Opie, Harvard University Press, Cambridge, MA.

Selby, Gary S. 2008. *Martin Luther King and the Rhetoric of Freedom: The Exodus Narrative in America's Struggle for Civil Rights.* Baylor University Press, Waco, TX.

Shaffer, Butler D. 1975. "Violence as a Product of Imposed Order." *University of Miami Law Review.* 29, pp. 732–763.

Shantz, Jeffrey. 2020. *Organizing Anarchy: Anarchism in Action.* Brill, Boston, MA.

Sharp, Gene. 1973. *The Politics of Nonviolent Action. Part 2: The Methods of Nonviolent Action.* Porter Sargent, Boston.

Smith, Adam. [1776] 1999. *An Inquiry into the Nature and Causes of The Wealth of Nations.* (ed.) A, Skinner, Penguin Classics edition, Penguin, London.

Soule, Sarah A. 2012. "Social Movements and Markets, Industries, and Firms." *Organization Studies,* 33, no. 2, pp. 1715–1733.

Staggenborg, Suzanne. 2013. "Entrepreneurs, Movement," in D. A. Snow, D. della Porta, B. Klandermans, & D. McAdam (eds.), *The Wiley-Blackwell Encyclopedia of Social and Political Movements*, Blackwell Publishing, Malden, MD.

Stern, Charlotta. 1999. "The Evolution of Social-Movement Organizations: Niche Competition in Social Space." *European Sociological Review.* 15, no. 1, pp. 91–105.

Storr, Virgil H. and Arielle John. 2020. *Cultural Considerations within Austrian Economics.* Cambridge University Press, Cambridge, UK.

Thrasher, John J. 2019. "Democracy Unchained: Contractualism, Individualism, and Independence in Buchanan's Democratic Theory." *Homo Oeconomicus.* 36, nos. 1–2, pp. 25–40.

Tilly, Charles. 2008. *Contentious Performances.* Cambridge University Press, New York.

Troncoso, Stacco. 2015. "The commons as a common paradigm for social movements and beyond," viewed 1 December 2022, https://commonsstrategies.org/the-commons-as-a-common-paradigm-for-social-movements-and-beyond

Tullock, Gordon. 1967. "The Welfare Costs of Tariffs, Monopolies, and Theft." *Western Economic Journal.* 5, no. 3, pp. 224–232.

Udehn, Lars. 1996. *The Limits of Public Choice: A Sociological Critique of the Economic Theory of Politics.* Routledge, London.

Vanberg, Viktor J. 2020. "J. M. Buchanan's Contractarian Constitutionalism: Political Economy for Democratic Society." *Public Choice.* 183, nos. 3–4, pp. 339–370.

van Dyke, Nella and David S. Meyer. 2014. *Understanding the Tea Party Movement.* Routledge, London.

von Mises, Ludwig. [1949] 2007. *Human Action: A Treatise on Economics.* Liberty Fund, Indianapolis, IN.

van Winden, Frans. 2007. "Affective Public choice." in J. C. Pedro and P. Schwartz (eds.), *Public Choice and the Challenges of Democracy.* Edward Elgar, Cheltenham. UK, pp. 45–61.

Wagner, Richard E. 1993. "The Impending Transformation of Public Choice Scholarship." *Public Choice.* 77, no. 1, pp. 203–212.

Wagner, Richard E. 2016. *Politics as a Peculiar Business: Insights from a Theory of Entangled Political Economy.* Edward Elgar, Cheltenham, UK.

Wagner, Richard E. 2018. "Buchanan's Liberal Theory of Political Economy: A Valiant But Failed Effort to Square the Circle," in P. J. Boettke and S. Stein (eds.), *Buchanan's Tensions: Reexamining the Political Economy and Philosophy of James M. Buchanan.* Mercatus Center of George Mason University, Arlington, VA, pp. 9–33.

Wall, Derek. 2017. *Elinor Ostrom's Rules for Radicals: Cooperative Alternatives Beyond Markets and States.* Pluto Press, London.

Warburg, Jennifer. 2017. "The Rise of the YIMBY Movement." The Urbanist. January 11, viewed 12 April 2022, https://www.spur.org/publications/urbanist-article/2017-01-11/rise-yimby-movement.

Welzel, Christian. 2013. *Freedom Rising: Human Empowerment and the Quest for Emancipation.* Cambridge University Press, Cambridge, UK.

Williams, Dana M. 2017. *Black Flags and social movements: A Sociological Analysis of Movement Anarchism.* Manchester University Press, Manchester, UK.

Williams, Rhys H. 1995. "Constructing the Public Good: Social Movements and Cultural Resources." *Social Problems.* 42, no. 1, pp. 124–144.

Chapter 7

Freedom in Economic Sociology

Patrik Aspers

Liberalism's core aim is a state of affairs in which "coercion of some by others is reduced as much as is possible in society" (Hayek 1960, 11). The constraints under which actors live and act, for example, property rights, are codified in law. It is the state's task to monitor behavior and impose negative sanctions against whatever is not in accordance with the law. In the liberal tradition the state and its formal institutions, including laws, are seen as an outcome of a "contract"—in practice, the "unspoken agreement to abide" by it—between the state's citizens (Dahrendorf 1985, 89).

The classical liberal tradition can be understood as a reaction to its respective societal problems. Early liberal thinkers were living in an era of rising individualism (Calhoun et al. 2007, 6), which gives the sociological background to their ideas (Collins 1998). The tradition of liberalism is rooted in the works of Montesquieu, Locke, Hume, Rousseau, Kant, Smith, Tocqueville, and Mill. Hayek and Popper, as well as more neoliberal thinkers, such as Friedman, Buchanan, and Nozick, have also made contributions to the, broadly speaking, liberal tradition (Festl 2021).

Some liberal authors stress contractual solutions, alluded to by Hobbes, to problems of order by referring to formal institutions, such as property rights, and to coordination, which primarily occurs in markets. Implied is the idea of actors who possess some civic virtues, such as participation in the public realm and contractual capacity. Given these conditions, actors can utilize and express their political freedom.

This chapter points, in addition to political freedom, to the need for resources and intervention by a central authority to safeguard the resources, in a broad sense, necessary to enable actors' use of politically available freedom. This typically implies that people must have access to basic resources, such as health care, housing, and education, so they at least get to the age at which they can provide for themselves (cf. Dahrendorf 1983, 132).

But even under conditions of political freedom and resource availability people may be unable to act freely. This chapter focuses on the third aspect of freedom, namely, actors' social conditioning because of their structural positions and cultural priming. This conditioning enables people to act freely, but it may also prevent them from doing so. The social conditions discussed here imply more than just freedom guaranteed by a well-functioning legal system that safeguards freedom. This sociological idea of societal priming and the relational constitution of human beings to friends and society at large, with its corresponding implicit and sometimes explicit critique of liberalism, is to some extent heralded by the communitarians, who argue for the importance of contextual factors (Beckstein 2021). The issue of how relations and resources are important for agency is also touched upon by Berlin (1969) with his discussion of positive versus negative freedom. However, sociology proper offers a more detailed and more research-grounded view of human beings and action conditions. This leads to the question of how classical liberal ideas fare when encountering sociology. Put differently, is there something that the liberal tradition could learn from sociology?

To address this question, action in the market economy (Smith 1981) is chosen as a case in point for analyses, because it is often considered by liberals to be the arena in which contracts are signed between free individuals. It may thereby be possible to see how structural and cultural factors constitute human beings, and how these enable and constrain their actions.

SOCIOLOGY'S EGOLOGICAL STARTING POINT

Sociological ideas emerged at a time when people in Western countries were becoming free in the classical etymological sense, namely, not slaves.[1] Though sociology has never been inherently liberal, individualism served as its starting point. This idea that that individuals, like atomistically existing egos or monads, operate in solitude and only occasionally are social, is a presumption in many theories. This assumption is no surprise because Christian and Cartesian streams of individualistic thought dominated the academic scene, implying a reflexive and knowing subject destined to investigate and dominate a world given by God. Early formulations in Descartes (Steel 2004) were later developed into a more general individualist perspective (Udehn 2002), which were taken over and refined by the early political economists (Hirschman 1986).

The connection with liberalism and early economic thinking is clear, and it is obvious that economics and, more generally, rational choice theory start with the egological assumption (Olson 1971) of atomistic actors. It is, moreover, not difficult to trace an egological starting point to utilitarianism and ideas about another key libera idea, namely, contracts. Moreover, economists view actors and their preferences as essentially unaffected by others' preferences (Becker and Murphy 2000). Sociology, in contrast, is about how the environment affects the individual, and, as Duesenberry says, "economics is all about how people make choices [and] sociology is about why they don't have any choices to make" (1960, 233). Though his view is exaggerated, it is not wrong; it will also serve as a reference point for my analysis.

Early sociologists, many of whom carved out their discipline as a critique of economics, nonetheless took over the idea of atomistic actors who become social only when they interact with others or when they orient themselves toward others. This is the position of the perhaps most prominent sociologist, Max Weber, who started out as an economist. Weber assumes that man is essentially rational, existing as an atom, and only occasionally social. He says, "We shall speak of 'action' insofar as the acting individual attaches a subjective meaning to his behavior—be it overt or covert, omission or acquiescence. However, action is 'social' insofar as its subjective meaning takes into account the behavior of others and is thereby oriented to its course" (Weber 1978, 4). Put differently, many actions are not, according to Weber, social. Several texts point at the egological-atomistic root of social science (R. Connell 2019; R.W. Connell 1997; Lepenies 1988; Aspers and Kohl 2013), which blends social constitution out.

FREEDOM IN SOCIOLOGY

The notion of freedom is not central in sociology, neither as an analytic-scientific term nor as a theme of empirical investigation. Moreover, sociologists and sociology as a discipline is not associated with liberal discussions (Klein and Stern 2006). A 1977 review concluded that "freedom is a topic more often studied in other fields than sociology" (Hillery, Dudley, and Morrow 1977, 685). In this review, 30 different definitions of freedom in both anthropology and sociology are analyzed, and out of these 13 refer to social structure and 17 to subjective factors. We learn that social scientists try to explain and understand freedom, and sometimes also measuring it indirectly. Few sociological texts published after 1977 do not offer a detailed analysis of freedom.

There are, however, a few sociologists who deserve to be mentioned in relation to liberalism. The position of Herbert Spencer and his warnings about a large state are well known. But Spencer has long been out of fashion and is rarely referred to in contemporary sociology, clearly a lot less than Durkheim, Simmel, Weber, Malinowski, and Marx. Some later sociologists have developed their ideas in direct connection to the period after the Second World War, and typically in relation to communism and fascism. Some have addressed issues of liberalism, but it has rarely been the focus of their academic work. Peter Berger is one sociologist who has shown interest in the notion of freedom, for example, religious freedom. Also worthy of mention is French sociologist Raymond Aron, who is claimed to be a social liberal by Dahrendorf (1994, 122). But Aron's writings are not directed toward liberal discourse.

The German sociologist Ralf Dahrendorf (1926–2009) has written extensively on freedom. He was inspired by Popper and Hayek, among others, although he by no means supported the kind of minimal state suggested by Nozick or any other of Dahrendorf's contemporary liberals. According to Dahrendorf, people need the means to access the opportunities that exist in a free society. But society always implies a form of sociality that can be seen as constraints from which "no one is free, and which may therefore be regarded as 'data' or constants" (Dahrendorf 1968, 183). Dahrendorf goes on and lists these "constants": "man's possibly unfree will, his bodily nature and its consequences, and indeed the fact that man is a social being and as such necessarily exposed to alien control and sanctions." Accordingly, freedom is not just freedom from the state—real freedom requires means to make use of the available alternatives in a free society. To accomplish this, political interventions may be necessary, not just to make available a large set of opportunities, but also to enable actors to achieve their ends practically, such as redistribution of resources and education. Put differently, even liberal sociologists like Dahrendorf (1966) clearly identify how the market economy must be planned and controlled, at least partially. In addition to political freedom, which is based on formal institutions, this second aspect of the resources necessary to use available freedom is sometimes discussed by liberals, but, to my knowledge, it plays a relatively minor role. The rest of this text focuses on the third aspect of freedom, its social conditions, namely, the extent to which our socially conditioned—due to structure and culture—position both enables and hinders freedom.

ENABLING AND CONSTRAINING: THE SOCIALITY OF HUMAN BEINGS

The sociological project during the period after Spencer became increasingly empirical and produced studies of how human beings—intentionally and unintentionally—both construct the social fabric and are largely products of its sociality. There are many examples of sociological findings that show how human beings are socially constituted and conditioned, already in classic sociology. Despite his inherently "non-social" starting assumption, mentioned above, Weber, for example, develops a sociological apparatus that studies values, norms, and structures. American pragmatism stressed the interactional necessity for human beings to be constituted. In other words, what one is, or rather becomes, cannot be reduced to individual capacities; it is a product of social interaction (Mead 1964). The idea of socialization is made explicit in Parsons (1977). One consequence of socialization through social interaction is that people become more like others; one learns from others, because one takes over ideas, preferences, virtues, and much more from older generations. Similar ideas are summarized and developed in the sociological classic *The Social Construction of Reality*, by Peter Berger and Thomas Luckmann (1991). One of its key ideas is that objective meaning is created out of the interaction by actors, who over time internalize it. Meaning is the basic term that captures everything that is socially codified, for example, in language, values, knowledge, virtues, and practices. In a second step this objective meaning is transferred to new members of society by means of socialization. Put differently, children learn socially constructed meanings by internalizing the objective meanings that prevail in the society of which they gradually become members. They learn these meanings in a way that makes them part of themselves, because much of the learning is done without reflection.

Pierre Bourdieu, to take a sociologist who has studied how we become social without necessarily noting it, shows how meanings are internalized also in the body of human beings. He speaks of "habitus," which refers to how the social history of a human being is inscribed in the body. This idea also means that peoples' different histories result in different "habiti," and Bourdieu also discusses class habitus (Bourdieu 1984) to capture the similarity of peoples' trajectories that can be observed in society. Bourdieu emphasizes how social structure constrains individual actions, and he has empirically investigated how these trajectories of social mobility in society function, which leads him to question the idea of free choices in forming one's own societal destiny. The main reason for this is the second aspect of freedom, resources. The notion of social capital—connections with others, seen as a resource—is an important aspect of how people can enable actions. The priming is so deeply rooted that one cannot say that there are first egos who only later become social. It is more accurate, when describing Bourdieu's analysis, to say that to be a human being is to be socially conditioned, and that such conditioning is a function of the social environment.

Bourdieu's theoretical analysis is grounded in his anthropological fieldwork. It is not surprising that the constitutive element of the social is even more observable in anthropological work investigating "traditional" societies. If we look at the work of Malinowski (1922), for example, it is clear that social relations are constitutive. Malinowski analyzes how structural positions in the social network are even inherited. This means that actors are not only enabled and constrained by these ties, but they *are* those ties. These ties are confirmed in trade and trade again confirms actors' identities. All these activities are part of their culture. These insights later led sociologists to talk of "social constructions" (Berger 1964), a phenomenon that today has very wide scope and is largely accepted. Because human beings are inherently social they have internalized society, its values, practices, and knowledge, that is, in terms of structure and culture (Giddens 1984), which both enables and blocks their actions. But this sociological idea can be enriched by looking at it through a philosophical lens. The reason is that also philosophers have addressed how human beings internalize social values. But because some of them are critically examining this sociality, their analysis shows what sociologists look at in a different light. Thus, when the philosophical and sociological analyses of socialization are put next to one another, we get a good understanding of the sociality of human beings.

NIETZSCHE AND HEIDEGGER ON THE SOCIAL

The sociological position that human beings are inherently social is confirmed by the work of Nietzsche and Heidegger. But they also qualify this idea. Nietzsche is critical of sociology, which in his view reduces individuality by forcing it into a collectivistic framing. Having said that, Nietzsche's critique extends to most thinkers; even liberal thinkers such as Mill and Spencer are clearly not seen in a positive light (Antonio 1995). Comte and Spencer are criticized for adhering to a crowd-based sociology, which plays down the realization of the individual, especially the "overman" (Aspers 2007, 479). Sociology, Nietzsche says, denies activity and embraces reactivity (Friedrich. Nietzsche 1994, II, §12). He also claims that mechanical and organic sociological theories lack meaning and purpose, and they cannot guide man in life (Friedrich Nietzsche 1980, 11:564–565, §618). In Nietzsche's view, "individualism" is not rooted in similarity, but in man's uniqueness. Nietzsche is critical of sociology's view of what makes man social, as he is of all ideologies and ideas that equalize people, including liberal ideas.

Nietzsche argues that sociologists promote what he calls "herd virtues" ("*Heerdentugenden*") (Friedrich Nietzsche 1980, 12:357 §901). He regards the sociological focus on the mediocre man ("*mittlere Art Mensch*") as problematic. A more fundamental problem, however, is that Comte, Spencer, and others put the collective first when discussing development. Comte, according to Nietzsche, got it completely wrong: "Not Mankind, but the overman [*Übermensch*] is the goal! Misunderstanding by Comte!" (Friedrich

Nietzsche 1980, 11:210). Spencer is accused of the same mistake (Friedrich Nietzsche 1980, 12:525; 13:475 §944).

Moreover, Nietzsche says that "[o]ur entire sociology simply does not know any other instinct than that of the herd, that is, that of the sums of zeroes—where every zero has 'equal rights,' where it is virtuous to be zero" (Friedrich Nietzsche 1980, 13:238, §53). Nietzsche argues that in the end sociology becomes "a doctrine of the forms of domination" (Friedrich Nietzsche 1911, §462). He means that the morals of the majority are manifested in sociology, and that theories and "discovered" laws are simply forms of domination. It is clear from the above quotations that Nietzsche thinks that sociology represents a threat to the development, and the possibility of freedom, of the individual, and that the discipline is a theory of domination that blocks man from individual development.

Heidegger, in contrast to Nietzsche, actually goes further than sociologists in his analysis of how deeply social human beings are. Though Nietzsche's critical analysis may be useful, it is only with Heidegger that the idea of a totally enmeshed subject is analyzed ontologically. Heidegger is critical of the egologism discussed above, and the corresponding pseudo problems to which it gives rise. Heidegger's historical review of the individualistic fallacy penetrates deep into philosophy, and he is explicitly critical of those social science and philosophical approaches that stress the individual as an "ontic" assumption, namely, those that assume that the atomized individual is the natural point of departure (Aspers and Kohl 2013, 10–11). To him it is self-evident that human beings are part of a larger whole, in which other beings are essential. For Heidegger, it is our practical life and experiences that are the starting point, not a world somehow independent of us (Heidegger 2001b, 83–84). It is this "relational" system of, for example, relations to others and to tools which constitute the ontological structure (also referred to as the "care [*Sorge*] structure") by which man is both conditioned and a part. According to Heidegger (2001b, 84), this whole is more than the parts that make it up. To be in the world means that relations constitute man, to others and to things. This leaves us with the question of the other(s): who are they and what is their role in the ontological edifice?

Man is "living in the world," but it is of course the same for all; in other words, there are not different worlds for different people, but the same one. What Heidegger calls *Dasein* (being—literally, "being there"), he argues, is "always already" in the world together with other *Daseins,* who are called (under that aspect) *Mitseins* (being-with). Heidegger thereby rejects methodological individualism and sees "the social context as the ultimate foundation of intelligibility" (Dreyfus 1991, 7). Other *Daseins*—relations with whom are designated *Mitsein*—constitute what he calls an "*existentiale*"—their existence and a particular Dasein's relations to them permeate all things.

People trade with other people, the camping ground in the forest is used by someone, and the neighbors whose voices I can overhear on my balcony are all examples of the fact that one is never alone. But the relations we have to others also constitute us more indirectly. How we read the newspaper, the ways we react to a funny story, the way we do business, and much more structure our behavior, even when one is alone. In contemporary language Heidegger is talking about institutions. One eats as one (*man . . . das Man*) eats, one behaves as one behaves, one greets others as one greets others, to take a few additional examples of institutions. These institutions—or to simplify, norms and activities—can never be excluded or isolated from how *Dasein* acts: if they were, man would no longer be man. Dasein is in-the-world (Heidegger 2001a, 138), involved in activities with others, for others, in the position of others, and with tools and knowledge generated by others (2001b, 167), even when involved in deviant behavior and oriented toward social norms. Heidegger's analysis becomes a critique of the idea of free will because he shows how deeply rooted people's socially conditioned traits are. Indeed, he argues that they constitute man ontologically.

Because of the combined effort of the social sciences and the human sciences, already at the beginning of the twentieth century we had, at least if one looks in the direction presented here, a good understanding of human beings as inherently social. Man is socially integrated, and one cannot speak of "autonomous actors." Human action is contingent not just on "external" factors, but also on factors that are inseparable from human being, because human being is social, a sociality which is played out and conditioned by publicness (Arendt 1988; Habermas 1989; Heidegger 1988, 31–33). Heidegger, like Nietzsche, analyzes the actual conditions of human beings, and both find that man is not free. If we take these general points and criticisms of how action and freedom are viewed in sociology, it is possible to explore this matter in a concrete field, and here a field is selected that thematically addresses an area that is not alien to many liberal thinkers, namely, economic sociology.

FREEDOM IN ECONOMIC SOCIOLOGY

The discussion so far has brought up general ideas about freedom in relation to sociology and the topics that sociology covers. I will now analyze how contemporary economic sociologists think about freedom. Their views are a continuation of the general sociological analysis conducted above. Economic sociology (Swedberg 2003) is a broad field of research, and it is easy to identify researchers who focus primarily on structure, for example, White (2002) and those who put the emphasis on culture, such as Zelizer (2011). Neither of these two economic sociologists focus on formal property rights. In fact, property rights are assumed, and are not the focus of research, though this topic has also been discussed by sociologists (Carruthers and Ariovich 2004). In the case of Zelizer it is a study of how property rights have expanded into a domain not previously considered "economic," namely, life insurance for children.

CULTURAL ANALYSIS: ZELIZER ON LIFE INSURANCE

Cultural analysis of the economy shows how economic decision-making depends on cultural frames (Goffman 1974). Viviana Zelizer (1979) has analyzed how it took a cultural reframing to establish life insurance in the USA as something that is as "normal" as other forms of insurance, such as fire insurance. She argues that at the beginning of the nineteenth century it was still unusual to have life insurance. There was a public debate on why. The point here is that the existence of rational, free, and independent human beings is valid in some cases, but not in others. This change in the ways people perceive life insurance can be explained by gradual reinterpretation of what is accepted, and Zelizer outlines the causes of this process. Gradually, traditional religious values of life were understood in terms of risk and speculation. The companies selling life insurance, Zelizer shows, adjusted their sales strategies and advertisements to counteract resistance from potential customers. These activities promoted the reframing of life insurance. This meant that what used to be the "safety net" of friends, neighbors, and relatives was replaced by the economic bureaucracy of large insurance companies.

Zelizer's analysis clarifies how deeply rooted human beings are in cultural frames. One may say, following Zelizer, that human beings are not free to choose; or put differently, the freedom of their choices are explained by actors' culturally given framework. The argument is not that frames determine actions, or that they are fixed—Zelizer's analysis shows that they are not—but that they must be considered when analyzing what people do. Human beings are primed by cultural frames. Contractual freedom, a premise of classic liberalism, was present to only a marginal degree in early nineteenth century US society. A hundred years later this domain of life, too, could be treated as contract based. Zelizer's idea has gained support from similar studies in other contexts, for example, China (Chan 2009). What the cultural analysis of insurance shows is that human beings do not act on preset preferences; the preferences are acquired in a process. Furthermore, this is a social process. Taken together, any approach stressing free individuals who "just" decide on whether life insurance is good or not naively represent its own presumption of the world, rather than investigating and explaining human beings' actions.

NETWORK ANALYSIS: WHITE ON MARKETS

Harrison White, like Zelizer, belongs to the first generation of economic sociologists. White studies markets, or more precisely, producer markets, which are characterized by the production of goods that are sold to consumers. A central point White makes (1981) is that these markets are emergent and self-reproducing social structures. Based on an assumption of rational actors, the social structures and identities of producers generate a stable market order. It is the mutual adjustment of actors that explains the social outcome, but once there is a social order, it conditions future actions. Added to this is a business culture that is rooted in history (White 2002, 299).

In White's view, markets are "no more inhuman than your family or than cliques or clans" (White 2002, 303). The market is one arena in which identities emerge and actors operating under the condition of "Knightian uncertainty . . . coalesced out in production markets with distinct identities" (White 2002, 302). White argues that market trade in the private sphere provided "a basis for the trust needed in commercial calculative connection" (White 2002, 303). So markets are one arena among others for social forms (White 1992), and these social structures grow over time without central planning. Rather, uncertainty and confusions are the triggers of markets (White 2008, 57).

In White's analysis of market interaction, the state is frequently absent. Contracts are not the focus, and cannot be seen as a starting point that is given by nature (White 2008, 173). The focus is on actors, who themselves are formed in the social interaction, "Persons come into existence and are formed as the result of overlaps among identities from distinct network-populations" (White 2008, 129). Hence, White acknowledges a social constructivist approach, but gives much space to agency, although within structural boundaries. The structural approach shows clearly that what some may see as "free actions" are conditioned by their position in the social structure. These structures thus enable actors to act, but also limit what they in practice can choose to do. It is worth noting that though White cannot be seen as a classical liberal, he surely stresses the social interactional side, and his work does not focus on the state and its politics. Though the state sets the basic conditions for the market economy, White does not give it a major explanatory role when it comes to markets. Whereas Zelizer puts the emphasis on the cultural embeddedness of human agency and freedom, White stresses how agents are part of social structures. These two analyses, the cultural and the structural, however, must not stand in opposition; from the perspective of this chapter, they rather complement one another and reinforce the idea that human beings are socially conditioned.

CONCLUSION

The liberal idea of freedom is primarily concerned with legal matters, to safeguard that coercion of some by others in society is not occurring more than necessary. Sociology addresses primarily not this formal aspect of freedom but the resources that enable actors to make practical use of the opportunities that a liberal society—in principle—offers. Both of these are central aspects of freedom. This chapter addresses the third aspect of freedom, namely, the social conditioning that both enables and constrains actors. Social conditioning refers to the social-structural, social-cultural, and social-cognitive aspects that underline the sociality of this conditioning. To put it differently, human beings can make a lot of decisions, and for many of these decisions they are free. The point here is twofold: the social context is partly making people free, but their idea of freedom and the conditions of freedom are also framed in social processes. This to a large extent empirical topic is not discussed by either classical or modern liberals. Even Hayek (1960, 1–20), who talks about various aspects that may limit actors' freedom, does not engage with the social conditioning of human action.

Given that social constraints and the process that leads to social conditioning are not much discussed within the liberal tradition, freedom should not be seen as given. It is here proposed, and to be further investigated in future studies, that freedom must be acquired in the process of transcendence of the self, an enterprise that must partly be directed against resistance of what one is and one's social conditioning. Knowledge to reflect on what one is and what one has become are necessary conditions of becoming free, and not inherent human capacities. Reflection can occur in contexts in which people are exposed to new ideas and to some extent also struggle against one another, and more fundamentally struggle with what they take for granted. George Herbert Mead (1934, 354–78) has discussed the notion of reflection in general, though his more behavioristic approach stresses how stimuli are challenged, such as when one fails to open a drawer made of wood (1934, 355–56). But Mead also suggests that our "social self reflective conduct" (1934, 124n) makes men free. By this he means that we become free in processes in which we, more profoundly, become social. Heidegger's notion of reflexivity is more strongly connected to the socially produced world, but he too thinks that reflection reveals itself when things do not work, when things work differently from what one expected, or when we do not know what to do in a new situation. It is partly by reflection that, Heidegger says, one can find oneself (Aspers and Kohl 2013). One interpretation of Heidegger is that the insight that one is not free is a condition of freeing oneself (Ruin 2008). Malinowski (1922) shows how difficult it was for those participating in the complex Kula-Ring form of trade to reflect on and understand it, though they lived in it. It was only with modernity that role switching and its correlated reflexivity that switching between different roles and settings became possible outside a small elite. Durkheim ([1895] 1984) catches this transformation by describing how mechanical solidarity, defined by similarity, gave way to organic solidarity in industrial society, based on the interdependency between people who are occupying different roles. This idea has been refined and connected with switching between networks in domains (Mische and White 1998). Accordingly, education and structural conditions of role and domain switching help people to reflect. Seen in this light, knowledge of what makes us less free is a condition for making us free. To enable this reflection requires access to education in order to be(come) a free human being.

Where does this leave us? It would be naïve of liberals to neglect the mounting empirical and philosophical evidence that human beings are socially conditioned. Most liberals are aware of the social conditioning and its consequence, but a closer connection and use of empirical research would and probably should be an integrated part of a liberal research agenda. This chapter is an invitation to study the relations between liberalism and sociology to the mutual benefit of both traditions, but also to outline paths to how sociological knowledge can provide insights into the social conditioning of the self and its position in social life. A systematic analysis and coverage of the liberal tradition in sociology and a more detailed analysis of the relative absence of liberal notions in sociology could be a good starting point. In more concrete terms this entails launching research that empirically studies freedom, perception, and ideas of freedom in societies. A theoretical research agenda may address questions concerning the extent to which freedom can be combined with the fact that man is social.

REFERENCES

Antonio, Robert. 1995. "Nietzsche's Antisociology: Subjectified Culture and the End of History." *American Journal of Sociology* 101 (1): 1–43.

Arendt, Hannah. 1988. *The Human Condition*. Chicago: Chicago University Press. 1958.

Aspers, Patrik. 2007. "Nietzsche's Sociology." *Sociological Forum* 22 (4): 474–499.

Aspers, Patrik, and Sebastian Kohl. 2013. "Heidegger and Socio-ontology: A Sociological Reading." *Journal of Classical Sociology* 13 (4): 487–508.

Becker, Gary, and Kevin Murphy. 2000. *Social Economics, Market Behavior in a Social Environment*. Cambridge: The Belknap Press of Harvard University Press.

Beckstein, Martin. 2021. "Kommunitarsmus." In *Handbuch Liberalismus*, edited by Michael Festl, 321–27. Berlin: J.B. Metzler.

Berger, Peter. 1964. "Review of 'Truth in the Religions: A Sociological and Psychological Approach' by W. Montgomery Watt." *American Sociological Review* 29 (2): 291–292.

Berger, Peter, and Thomas Luckmann. 1991. *The Social Construction of Reality, A Treatise in the Sociology of Knowledge*. London: Penguin Books. 1966.

Berlin, Isaiah. 1969. "Two Concepts of Liberty." In *Four Essays On Liberty*, 118–172. Oxford: Oxford University Press.

Bourdieu, Pierre. 1984. *Distinctions: A Social Critique of the Judgement of Taste*. Cambridge, MA: Harvard University Press. 1979.

Calhoun, Craig, Joseph Gerteis, James Moody, Steven Pfaff, and Indermohan Virk, eds. 2007. *Classical Sociological Theory*. Oxford: Blackwell.

Carruthers, Bruce, and Laura Ariovich. 2004. "The Sociology of Property Rights." *Annual Review of Sociology* 30: 23–46.

Chan, Cheris C.S. 2009. *Invigorating the Content in Social Embeddedness: An Ethnography of Life Insurance Transactions in China. AJS; American Journal of Sociology*.

Collins, Randall. 1998. *The Sociology of Philosophies: A Global Theory of Intellectual Change*. Cambridge: Harvard University Press.

Connell, R. W. 1997. "Why Is Classical Theory Classical?" *American Journal of Sociology* 102 (6): 1511–1557. https://doi.org/10.1086/231125. http://www.jstor.org/stable/10.1086/231125.

Connell, Raewyn. 2019. "Canons and Colonies: The Global Trajectory of Sociology." *Estudos Históricos (online)* 32 (67): 349–367. https://doi.org/https://doi.org/10.1590/S2178-14942019000200002.

Dahrendorf, Ralf. 1966. *Markt und Plan: zwei Typen der Rationalität*. Tübingen: J.C.B. Mohr.

———. 1968. *Essays in the Theory of Society*. Stanford: Stanford University Press.

———. 1983. *Die Chancen der Krise*. Stuttgart: Deutsche Verklags-Anstalt.

———. 1985. *Law and Order*. London: Stevens and Sons.

———. 1994. *Liberale und andere: Portraits*. Stuttgart: Deutsche Verlags-Anstalt.

Dreyfus, Hubert. 1991. *Being-in-the-World, A Commentary on Heidegger's Being and Time, Division 1*. Cambridge: The MIT Press.

Duesenberry, James. 1960. "Comment on an Economic Analysis of Fertility." In *Demographic and Economic Change in the Developed World*, edited by National Bureau of Economic Research, 231–40. Columbia: Columbia University Press.

Durkheim, Émile. [1895] 1984. *The Division of Labour in Society*. London: Macmillan. 1893.

Festl, Michael. 2021. *Handbuch Liberalismus*. Berlin: J.B. Metzler

Giddens, Anthony. 1984. *The Constitution of Society, Outline of the Theory of Structuration*. Berkeley: University of California Press.

Goffman, Erving. 1974. *Frame Analysis, An Essay on the Organization of Experience*. Cambridge: Harvard University Press.
Habermas, Jürgen. 1989. *The Structural Transformation of the Public Sphere*. Cambridge: MIT Press. 1962.
Hayek, Friedrich. 1960. *The Constitution of Liberty*. Chicago: Chicago University Press.
Heidegger, Martin. 1988. *Ontologie. Hermeneutik der Faktizität, Gesamtausgabe II. Abteilung: Vorlesungen 1919–1944, Band 63*. Frankfurt am Main: Vittorio Klostermann.
———. 2001a. *Einleitung in die Philosophie, Gesamtausgabe, II Abteilung: Vorlesungen, Band 27*. Frankfurt am Main: Vittorio Klostermann.
———. 2001b. *Sein und Zeit*. Tübingen: Max Niemeyer Verlag. 1927.
Hillery, George A., Charles J. Dudley, and Paula C. Morrow. 1977. "Toward a Sociology of Freedom." *Social Forces* 55 (3): 685–700. https://doi.org/10.2307/2577463. http://www.jstor.org/stable/2577463.
Hirschman, Albert O. 1986. *Rival Views of Market Society and Other Recent Essays*. New York: Viking. 1982.
Klein, Daniel B., and Charlotta Stern. 2006. "Sociology and Classical Liberalism." *The Independent Review* 11 (1): 37–52. http://www.jstor.org/stable/24562033.
Lepenies, Wolf. 1988. *Between Literature and Science: The Rise of Sociology*. Cambridge: Cambridge University Press. 1985.
Malinowski, Bronislaw. 1922. *Argonauts of the Western Pacific, An Account of Native Enterprise and Adventure in the Archipelagoes of Melanesian New Guinea*. London: Routledge.
Mead, George. 1934. *Mind, Self, and Society, From the Standpoint of a Social Behaviorist*. Chicago: Chicago University Press.
———. 1964. *George Herbert Mead on Social Psychology*. Chicago: University of Chicago Press. 1938.
Mische, Ann, and Harrison White. 1998. "Between Conversation and Situation: Public Switching Dynamics across Network Domains." *Social Research* 65 (3): 695–724.
Nietzsche, Friedrich. 1911. *Der Wille zur Macht. Band XV-XVI in Nachgelassene Werke*. Leipzig: Alfred Kröner Verlag.
———. 1980. *Sämtliche Werke, Kritische Studienausgabe*. Berlin: Walter de Gruyter.
Nietzsche, Friedrich. 1994. *On the Genealogy of Morals*. Translated by Carol Diethe. Cambridge: Cambridge University Press. 1887.
Olson, Mancur. 1971. *The Logic of Collective Action, Public Goods and the Theory of Groups*. Cambridge: Harvard University Press. 1965.
Parsons, Talcott. 1977. *Social Systems and the Evolution of Action Theory*. New York: The Free Press.
Ruin, Hans. 2008. "The Destiny of Freedom: in Heidegger." *Continental Philosophy Review* 41 (3): 277–299. https://doi.org/10.1007/s11007–008–9087–4. https://doi.org/10.1007/s11007–008–9087–4.
Smith, Adam. 1981. *An Inquiry into the Nature and Causes of the Wealth of Nations*. Indianapolis: Liberty Press. 1776.

Steel, Valerie. 2004. *Encyclopedia of Clothing and Fashion*. New York: Charles Scribner's Sons.

Swedberg, Richard. 2003. *Principles of Economic Sociology*. Princeton: Princeton University Press.

Udehn, Lars. 2002. *Methodological Individualism: Background, History and Meaning*. London: Routledge.

Weber, Max. 1978. *Economy and Society: An Outline of Interpretive Sociology*. Translated by Guenther Roth and Claus Wittich (ed.) 2.volumes. Berkeley: University of California Press. 1921–22.

White, Harrison. 1981. "Where Do Markets Come From?" *The American Journal of Sociology* 87 (3): 517–547.

———. 1992. *Identity and Control, A Structural Theory of Social Action*. Princeton: Princeton University Press.

———. 2002. *Markets from Networks, Socioeconomic Models of Production*. Princeton: Princeton University Press.

———. 2008. *Identity and Control, How Social Formations Emerge*. Princeton: Princeton University Press.

Zelizer, Viviana. 1979. *Morals and Markets: The Development of Life Insurance in the United States*. New York: Columbia University Press.

———. 2011. *Economic Lives: How Culture Shapes the Economy*. Princeton, NJ: Princeton University Press.

NOTES

1. The term "free" refers to "having a free throat" ("*Freihals*," in German) (Dahrendorf 1968, 183). It means that one is not fettered. Freedom thus initially meant not to be physically fettered. But today freedom is used metaphorically.

Chapter 8

Classical Liberalism vs. Populism and Authoritarianism

The Struggle for Modern Democracy

Jack A. Goldstone

Classical liberalism is lost.[1] This may be no surprise. Classical liberalism developed in the seventeenth and eighteenth centuries, paving the way for the Enlightenment and then growing with it. This was a world of monarchies, state monopolies on religion, strict patriarchy, and slavery. Classical liberalism opposed the first two of these institutions immediately, and then later opposed the latter two as well. Classical liberalism sought to create societies of general prosperity and personal freedom, with elites and governments limited in their authority. The classical liberal ideal fostered open, pluralistic societies, market competition, and equality under the law, while opposing privilege, that is, privileged firms, guilds, ethnicities, religions, rulers, and elites.

The world of the twenty-first century, however, is a world of republics and authoritarian states (including military, party, and personalist regimes). It is a far richer and more technologically advanced world than that of the seventeenth and eighteenth centuries, and one where private enterprise and market pricing have triumphed over state-led central planning, even (for the most part) in formerly communist states such as Russia, China, and Vietnam.

So perhaps it is logical that the classical liberal principles, developed in one age, should be superseded by other principles of governance more suited to a fast-changing, technology-driven, and individualistic one. Yet what has in fact taken the place of classical liberalism in guiding the structure of governments is producing outcomes very much at odds with any ideals of general prosperity and freedom. What we see gaining strength around the world is the old Romantic ideal of ethno-nationalist states, ruled by leaders claiming to strengthen the nation by putting national unity and loyalty to the state above personal freedoms, and state power above constitutional limits. These include military or party-run states, as well as populist republics with elected but largely unaccountable leaders.

In addition, as Francis Fukuyama has recently pointed out, in the realm of ideas the classical liberal ideal of free, prosperous, and relatively equal individuals under a limited state protecting private property is being assaulted from two directions (Fukuyama 2022). On the right, it is giving way to advocacy for a libertine freedom to accumulate wealth without regard for the welfare of the society as a whole, while stripping the state of any capacities or role except to protect and privilege the accumulations of wealth; on the left it is giving way to advocacy for submerging individuals into group identities, with groups placed along a spectrum of historical injustices and the state being harnessed as an engine to rectify or even reverse that spectrum in the name of greater justice.[2]

To be sure, there is some justification for each assault. Where the market rewards innovation and efficiency by creating accumulations of wealth, government should not excessively interfere to forcibly eliminate inequality. And where certain identity groups have experienced a history of exclusion and discrimination, ending such unfair and unequal treatment of the group is essential for those who comprise it to lead free and equal lives as individuals. Yet if both efforts are carried to extremes they become distortions that produce societies that are wholly at odds with the classical liberal ideal of a free, equal, and generally prosperous society.

What has been lost in these recent trends is the classical liberal belief that governments have major responsibilities for which they must be empowered, while at the same time governments must be held accountable and so must be restrained. A thoughtful, rational, nuanced understanding of the proper role of government and of freedom as created and maintained by the proper institutions of government has been replaced by one of two simple, emotional views: "Government is the problem and the less government the better" or "Government is the protector of society and the more government the better."

These extremes, however, have not provided us with government that is more adapted to the current global condition and better suited to maintain freedom and prosperity. Rather they have recreated massive inequality and renewed privilege, blunted general prosperity, and encouraged damaging and dangerous conflicts. Instead of moving societies forward from classical liberalism, they have moved societies *backwards* toward the kind of polities that prevailed in the late nineteenth and early twentieth century Romantic/nationalist backlash against Enlightenment principles. The aggressive, militarizing, ethno-nationalist regimes of 1930s Germany and Japan are echoed today by those of Russia and China. In the West, the increased focus of politics on issues of race, gender and immigration echo the era of imperialism and struggles over slavery and citizenship.

If freedom, peace, and prosperity are reasonable social goals, then the classical liberal ideals are still the best basis for realizing them. However, the political institutions created by classical liberalism, namely, representative democracy and constitutional regimes, cannot be relied upon to maintain classical liberal principles intact. Those institutions are too easily turned to other purposes, and molded into vehicles for romanticist, populist, and personalist rulers. What is required for classical liberal ideals to guide a society are not only classical liberal institutions, but also a commitment by elites to ensure that those institutions are run according to those principles, and that society values and protects those principles in its core actions. That in turn—and here is where I differ from Fukuyama—requires not only commitment to a set of ideas, but also a specific material and social context that incentivizes allegiance to classical liberalism. Republican democracy is rare in history, and has emerged only in particular socio-economic contexts. Without that context, elites are strongly incentivized to distort or overturn classical liberal principles, to reinstate privilege and foster ethnic identification and social divisions to preserve their elite position. There is a reason that democratic republics have been historically rare, and that America's Founding Fathers were skeptical whether their experiment in creating a national liberal regime could endure. Daron Acemoglu and James Robinson are correct that producing and maintaining liberal democracy requires active engagement by elites and the population to keep governance within a "narrow corridor," in which government is strong enough to protect individuals and their property from external threats and internal crimes, and skilled enough to oversee the investments and institutions required to facilitate innovation, commerce, and public health, yet is also sufficiently accountable to the laws and to its citizens for the latter to retain a substantial amount of freedom, civil liberties, and diversity (Acemoglu and Robinson 2019). If conditions facilitate elites shifting governance out of that "narrow corridor," then democracy is likely to falter or fade away.

Simply put, extreme inequality gives elites great economic and political power to bend the institutions of government, and incentivizes them to privilege their position so that it can be indefinitely increased and maintained against popular demands for a larger portion of society's wealth. The best path for doing that, as we have seen throughout history, is for elites to promote popular fears of unrest, violence, and overthrow by external and internal enemies. This produces a xenophobic, ethno-nationalist response that favors strong leaders and unshackled state power. By contrast, with only moderate inequality, elites' welfare more strongly tracks that of society as a whole, so they are more inclined to promote overall prosperity and have less incentive to insulate themselves by taking control of the state and expanding state power. Moreover, insofar as in this case popular voices are likely to be stronger, elites' concerns about loss of their property and position is best met by *limiting* state power, so that popular control of the state does not threaten them. Elites then are incentivized to support constitutionally limited state authority and strict adherence to the rule of law.

Sociology has a vital role to play in this regard. Sociological research can document the operation of existing institutions and their effects on society; it can measure and demonstrate the decline of social mobility and the re-emergence of privileged, semi-hereditary elites; assess the extent and impact of inequality on social life; and highlight the loss of pluralism and rise of ethno-nationalist and religious exclusion. In short, sociology can identify the loss of those conditions that support classical liberalism, and suggest ways to restore them.[3] For that reason, sociology—and not just its Marxist manifestations—has been seen as an enemy of those seeking to recreate privilege and harness government to protect it. Yet without understanding patterns of social change, without sociology's ability to track the relationship between society, institutions, and ideas, we lose the ability to see and trace the changes that can undermine classical liberal societies from within, and to rectify those adverse trends.

This chapter will first discuss the most misunderstood aspects of classical liberalism: its definition of freedom and the proper role of government. I will then examine how neoliberalism and populism have distorted and corrupted classical liberalism, replacing its ideals of personal freedom under law and private property for all with a neo-feudalism of privilege and authoritarian governance. I will note how modern communications technology has empowered these latter tendencies, and made it more difficult to sustain classical liberal ideals. I will conclude with thoughts on how sociological research on institutions and social change can lead the way back to a revival of classical liberalism as the basis for organizing modern societies.

THE CLASSICAL LIBERAL TRILEMMA: EQUALITY, DEMOCRACY, AND FREE MARKETS

When classical liberalism arose, its goals were quite clear: to free human ingenuity, expression, and action from the multiple shackles placed upon them by hereditary aristocracies, absolute rulers, and the religious leaders and merchant guilds that sought to prevent innovation and competition. The opponents being so evident, the goals and methods of overturning them were also clear: replace hereditary aristocracies with legal equality and fluid hierarchies open to all on the basis of talent and achievement; replace absolute rulers with democratic, constitutional republics; and eliminate the power of religious leaders and guilds to prevent free thinking and competition (Davies 2022). Although there were sudden and stunning victories, as in the Atlantic Revolutions of the eighteenth century, there were also reversals and setbacks, so that these victories were often more partial and incomplete than they seemed at the time. As a result, the struggle to overturn the opposition to classical liberalism lasted for centuries.[4]

Yet by the late twentieth century, Lords and Ladies, absolute monarchs and emperors, nationally enforced religions, and monopolist guilds had been relegated to a few corners of the modern world, and were but historical memories elsewhere. Some countries, like the United States, Australia, and most new states in Africa and Asia had never had one or more of these historic enemies of liberalism. Yet without these solid opponents to push against (and push back), a problem arises if equality, democracy, and free markets become ends in themselves, rather than part of a system to provide freedom and prosperity.

This is because if pushed to extremes, they are not all simultaneously compatible. If equality is to be pushed to create a fundamentally egalitarian society, that can only be maintained by control and limitation of free markets, as unfettered free markets will generate great inequality in favor of those who have critical skills or command critical resources. Such wholly free markets and the resultant inequality are incompatible with full democracy, which would, through voting, seek to limit free markets and/or redistribute income and wealth. Indeed, unfettered free markets and the extreme inequality that they tend to produce are inimical to democracy, as the elites are then incentivized to strengthen government but to limit democracy to maintain their position. When democracy and free markets coincide, that is usually where citizenship is systematically limited to certain groups, so that democratic citizens vote for government to tilt market power in favor of the citizen groups and thus maintain systemic inequality. Thus, one can say that South Africa under apartheid, the US with slavery and Jim Crow, and Britain in the eighteenth century had democratic institutions that elected leaders under free elections, and also had a high degree of free markets, but they certainly did not have equality. In these cases, rather than redistribute income and wealth away from the rich, citizens are more concerned to vote to sustain the formal inequality from which they benefit.

So wholly free markets, a high degree of economic equality, and full and universal democracy cannot coexist. This means that over time, in any classical liberal society, compromises must be made. Either democracy must be limited so that voters cannot fend off extreme inequality by limiting the operation of free markets; or equality must be systematically limited so that even the lower portion of the dominant groups accept free market outcomes;

or free markets must be limited so that extreme concentrations of wealth do not undermine equality and democracy.

In sum, the paradox of classical liberalism is that once it has vanquished its original foes of monarchy, state religion, hereditary privilege, and state-supported monopolies it no longer makes sense to seek wholly unfettered free markets, maximal social equality, or unlimited power for democratic government. Rather, the goals of preserving a balance of liberty, prosperity, and equality must be achieved with some degree of limits on free markets, on the enforcement of economic equality, and the power of democratic governments.

CLASSICAL LIBERALISM REQUIRES STRONG BUT CONSTRAINED GOVERNMENT, AND PERSONAL FREEDOM UNDER SOCIETY-WIDE LAWS

For John Locke and other classical liberals, the ideal of freedom was not simply freedom from the authority of government. Such freedom left men in a state of nature, in which they were prey to violence, unable to cultivate and accumulate property, and in the words of Thomas Hobbes, faced with a life that was likely to be "nasty, brutish and short." True liberty, they argued, was only to be found *under* government, for only then could life, property, and choices on how to live be made secure. But not any kind of government would do, as a government that was arbitrary, unaccountable, and wedded to its own interests or those of a privileged elite would not provide general liberty and prosperity. Instead, liberty was to be found in living under laws that were *freely chosen by the members of society for themselves* (or chosen by their designated representatives). In classical liberalism, freedom is not freedom from government *as such*, but freedom from government by arbitrary and privileged elites.

Alexis de Tocqueville, in the early nineteenth century, described seventeenth-century Europe as a place where "absolute monarchy had everywhere triumphed over the ruins of the oligarchical and feudal liberties of the Middle Ages. Never were the notions of right more completely confounded than in the midst of the splendor and literature of Europe; never was there less political activity among the people; never were the principles of true freedom less widely circulated." By contrast, he found in America, that:

> those principles, which were scorned or unknown by the nations of Europe, were proclaimed in the deserts of the New World, and were accepted as the future creed of a great people. The boldest theories of the human reason were put into practice by a community so humble, that not a statesman condescended

> to attend to it; and a legislation without a precedent was produced offhand by the imagination of the citizens. In the bosom of this obscure democracy, which had as yet brought forth neither generals, nor philosophers, nor authors, a man might stand up in the face of a free people and pronounce the following fine definition of liberty:
>
> ...'There is a liberty of corrupt nature, which is affected both by men and beasts to do what they list; and this liberty is inconsistent with authority, impatient of all restraint; by this liberty "sumus omnes deteriores." [Translation: "all are ruined"] It is the grand enemy of truth and peace, and all the ordinances of God are bent against it. But there is a civil, a moral, a federal liberty which is the proper end and object of authority; it is a Liberty for that only which is just and good: for this liberty you are to stand with the hazard of your very lives, and whatsoever crosses it, is not authority, but a distemper thereof. This liberty is maintained in a way of subjection to authority; and the authority set over you will, in all administrations for your good, be quietly submitted unto by all [that] have a disposition to . . . true liberty.' (de Tocqueville 1835, Book One, Chapter 2; the definition of liberty that de Tocqueville presents in this passage came from a speech by the American colonial leader John Winthrop).

The founders of classical liberalism, from Locke to Adam Smith to J. S. Mill, recognized that strong and effective government is needed not only to enforce contracts and protect private property, but to break up monopolies and ensure the competitiveness of free markets, to ensure and protect the free flow of information, to provide public goods (roads, schools, parks), to protect the majority from oppression by elites, and to protect the minority from the whims and passions of the majority. A government that lacks the capacity to do these things effectively cannot promote and maintain a classic liberal society. Far from "government is the problem," the classical liberal view is that the proper use of government authority is absolutely essential, and there is no true liberty without it.

The reasons for this were quite obvious to the founders of classical liberalism because as Tocqueville noted, they lived in a world where privilege was taken for granted and readily accepted as the "normal order" by most people in most societies. They knew that human beings were such that even if a society began with equality and free competition, those who initially gained would seek to entrench their gains and preserve them for their own benefit and that of their families and heirs, by turning the government and the laws to protect their elite status. To avoid this, government and law had to be designed and used to constantly break up monopolies, undermine the entrenchment of privilege, and protect the opportunities and equal legal status of all citizens. That is why the US Constitution banned all titles and essentially banned all privileges for government officials; why it divided power among state and local governments and among the branches of the federal one; and why it consistently required building diverse coalitions to act and planted assorted vetoes to prevent narrow or momentary groupings from acting with haste or oppression.

At the same time, the Founding Fathers replaced the weak and ineffective government of the Articles of Confederation with the much stronger Federal government of the Constitution. They knew the national government needed to be strong enough, and well financed enough, to take on monopolies, prevent the accumulation of elite privileges, and empower the citizenry to protect *true* liberty by implementing a fair and equal enforcement of the laws. *Limited* government could not mean *weak* government, or the liberal order would not survive (Fukuyama 2015).

LIMITS ON CLASSICAL LIBERALISM IN THE UNITED STATES

"A republic, if you can keep it" Ben Franklin is reported to have said, to describe the product of the Constitutional Convention. The Founders' work was guided by the knowledge of the previous republics of human history: that of Athens in classical Greece, the Roman Republic, and the city-state republics of Italy, all of which produced stunning civilizations with brilliant art, literature, and military success. Their work was also informed by the knowledge that all of those republics had failed; that Athenian democracy gave way to oligarchic rule and the empire of Alexander; that the Roman Republic fell under the absolutism of the Caesars; and that the great and powerful republics of Venice, Florence, and Genoa fell under the rule of dukes and emperors. What enabled the republics that inspired classical liberals to succeed, and why did they fail?

The answer is that they failed to maintain a balance of limited inequality, limited free markets, and limited democracy. In Athens, the unfettered democracy of the Assembly eventually fell under the sway of the demagogic Alcibiades, who led the city into a massive defeat in Syracuse. In Rome, the Republic was eventually eroded by the great concentrations of wealth in the hands of the leading senators, who fought ruinous civil wars over control of the empire. In Florence, Pisa, and other Italian city states, efforts by workers and popular parties to achieve full democracy led to repeated civil wars and revolutions as popular and elite parties struggled for control; eventually they reverted to autocracies (as the Medici rule in Florence) or merchant republics that were in fact oligarchies (as in Venice and Genoa).

America's Founding Fathers therefore sought to limit democracy by having only members of the House of Representatives directly chosen by citizen voters. They could not foresee, of course, the nineteenth- and twentieth- century rise of great concentrations of industrial wealth, so did little to limit free markets (including the trade in human beings), and assumed that legal and citizenship equality among white males would suffice to keep society basically egalitarian. To be sure, Thomas Jefferson went further, wanting to keep the US more equal by encouraging a society of journeyman farmers, and discouraging the financial, legal, and business centers of Philadelphia, New York, and Boston from becoming too powerful.

By the twentieth century, however, it was clear that free markets had created such great inequality that democracy and equality under the law were in danger. The actions of the two Roosevelts—trust-busting and national-park creating Teddy Roosevelt, and labor-supporting and commerce-regulating Franklin D. Roosevelt—sought to restore a balance in which corporations would not become all-powerful monopolies, and workers could effectively challenge corporate and finance leaders to obtain a fair share of business profits. Also early in the twentieth century, following the growth in both the middle class and women's education, efforts to promote equality led to the direct popular election of senators and women gaining the right to vote. Franklin D. Roosevelt's support for unions and public works was rooted in the view, expressed in his second inaugural address in 1937, and anathema to wealthy elites even then, that "The test of our progress is not whether we add more to the abundance of those who have much; it is whether we provide enough for those who have too little."

The Great Depression and World War II, as Walter Scheidel has shown, greatly aided the reduction of severe inequality (Scheidel 2018). After the war, the US emerged in the 1950s as a society with a national government that imposed extremely high marginal tax rates, was highly active in supporting highways, innovation, and education, and regulated a wide range of commercial and media activities, with an alphabet soup of Federal agencies who regulated drugs, securities, railways, airlines, banking, labor relations, media, meat-packing, and more. In the 1960s and 1970s, civil rights and environmental regulation further increased the scope of the national government to assert equality and intervene in markets for labor, housing, and land-use.

The result of all these market restrictions was, perhaps surprisingly, the greatest period of broad gains in income and wealth for ordinary Americans that the country had ever seen, what John Kenneth Galbraith in 1958 deemed "the Affluent Society." To be sure, the 1960s and 1970s saw significant turmoil, as the battles for student rights, civil rights, women's rights, and the anti-war and anti-nuclear movements produced not only protests but riots and assassinations. Yet through the 1970s, the general prosperity of most Americans continued to grow.

SOCIOLOGICAL RESEARCH DEMONSTRATES THE DECLINE OF CLASSICAL IDEALS AND QUALITY OF LIFE

This began to change in the 1980s. The late 1970s saw a debilitating spike in inflation, due mainly to the quadrupling of energy prices as the OPEC cartel was founded and began to exercise monopoly power over global energy pricing. The 1980s solution was not only to raise interest rates, but to attack what admittedly had become excessive anti-market actions, not only in the US but also the UK, where Margaret Thatcher paired with Ronald Reagan as heroes of free enterprise and opponents of unions and regulation. Both reduced their extremely high marginal income tax rates, deregulated many segments of their economies, and attacked the unions that had come to preserve jobs, salaries, and benefits that were no longer feasible to maintain.

Yet these pro-market measures produced not general prosperity, but a concentrated increase in the income and wealth of the richest, while leading to a prolonged stagnation in median worker's incomes. According to the US Bureau of Labor Statistics (Richter 2019), real hourly earnings for production and nonsupervisory employees, which had risen from $20 per hour to $23 per hour from 1964 to 1973, then began a long decline to $19 per hour in the 1990s, and only recovered to $23 an hour by 2019. Another way of looking at this is to consider the median usual weekly real earnings of wage and salary workers (16 years and older). The St. Louis Fed gives this as $332 per week (in 1982–84 dollars) in 1979; it was $368 in 2021, a total increase of only 10.8% over forty-two years, or an average increase of only one-quarter percent per year across these decades (Federal Reserve Economic Data 2023). Meanwhile, as Emmanuel Saez and Gabriel Zucman have shown, between 1978 and 2018, the share of pre-tax national income earned by the top 1% rose from 10% to about 17% and the share of wealth owned by the top 0.1% rose from 7% to about 18%; moreover the share of wealth owned by the ultra-wealthy (the top .00001%), rose twelvefold, from about 0.1 to 1.2% (Saez and Zucman 2020).

This trend was not arrested by the British Labor or US Democratic Parties when they came to power in the 1990s. Instead, their embrace of free markets meant encouraging the globalization of trade and outsourcing as ways to widen markets and lower manufacturing costs and consumer prices, continuing to whittle away labor regulations, freeing financial and securities markets from regulation, and reducing welfare spending and government support for education, all of which led the trend to greater inequality to continue and strengthen.

Moreover, as manufacturing jobs fell to automation and outsourcing, while white-collar and professional jobs that required a college degree continued to show wage and income gains, the nature of inequality changed. Rather than the main class divide being between business owners and workers, or even between whites and minorities, economic fortunes were divided between the populations of rural and small-town locations with older and less-educated workers, and the populations of major metro areas, with younger populations (assisted by in-migration), higher education levels, and concentrations of the "creative" jobs in higher education, finance, management, law, accounting, medicine, engineering, communications, computing, and other high technology (Florida 2019).

The stagnant income of average workers posed a problem for both households and businesses. The purchasing power of households was, however, augmented by two trends: the entry of women into the market as full-time workers, and the wide extension of credit through credit cards, home equity credit, and more generous loans on cars, homes, and other purchases. These allowed households to acquire consumer goods immediately, but in the long run transferred more of their incomes to financial services firms, greatly expanding the size and profits of finance in the economy (Krippner 2012). Over decades, the shifting of all kinds of financial risks to consumers while increasing the profits of firms further increased the trend to inequality (Hacker 2019; Smith 2012). Defined-benefit pensions, protected-low-cost mortgages (provided by heavily regulated Savings & Loans banks), publicly subsidized nearly free college tuition even at the flagship state universities; all these nearly disappeared from the 1980s to the early 2000s.

While inequality *per se* has rarely been seen as a problem in America, compared to the animus against inequality in other countries, this level of inequality eventually became fatal, in the literal sense. Not only did median income stagnate, life expectancy also stagnated and then even began to decline. What Anne Case and Angus Deaton call "Deaths of Despair"—suicides, drug overdoses, alcohol-related liver diseases—as well as accidents and gun violence, started to outweigh gains in health and nutrition. Some populations in the US have the life expectancies of third-world countries, and the US as a whole now has among the lowest life-expectancy of any developed nation—less than Turkey or Greece, and about seven years less than the OECD leaders (Woolf 2023).

To be certain, the "deaths of despair" label may be overblown: most of these deaths are not voluntary, but the result of gun violence, cardio-pulmonary disease due to obesity and diabetes, and accidental drug overdoses due to fentanyl. Nonetheless, US suicide rates reached a record high in 2022 (Singh 2023). Moreover, overall life expectancy has clearly become far more tilted by income inequality: For cohorts born in 1930, men in the top income quintile who reached age 50 lived 5.1 years longer than males in the bottom income quartile. By contrast, for cohorts born in 1960, who became adults after 1980, that gap had more than doubled: men in the top income quintile who had reached age 50 lived 12.7 years longer than their counterparts in the bottom income quartile. This was the result of men in the top income quintile in the cohort born in 1960 enjoying 7.1 years of additional life expectancy compared to the 1930 cohort; while in the second-lowest income cohort the gain for the 1960 cohort was only 1.1 years, while the lowest-income quintile actually had a half-year *shorter* life expectancy than the lowest income quintile born thirty years earlier (Congressional Research Service 2021).

In addition, deregulation and globalization led to a revival of the frequent booms and busts that economists had once dismissed as banished by "the great moderation." The 2001 dot-com bubble was followed by the 2008–2009 housing bust and the 2021–2022 post-Covid inflation. Every ten years, ordinary workers had to face a financial upheaval.

At the same time, concentrations of great wealth unseen in America since the "gilded age" of the nineteenth century have provided the wealthy with extraordinary political influence. America's intended society of citizen-voters is now dominated by oligarchs whose wealth can be put at the service of unlimited political messaging and support for political candidates who will enact their agenda. Countervailing forces, like the funds and manpower that unions once provided to political campaigns, are weak or absent. Under current laws (enacted since the 1980s) the wealthy can conceal much of their wealth from taxation in domestic or foreign tax shelters, and anonymously contribute unlimited amounts to Political Action Committees to support their political and economic goals. (In the 2022 mid-term elections, 38 percent of campaign spending was contributed by the top 1 percent income group (Weisman and Shorey 2022).) Inequality thus affects not only material circumstances, but also affects the political equality of citizenship to the extent that the concentrated wealth of individuals is permitted to pour, anonymously and with few or no restrictions, into the media and politics.

Perhaps most distressing was that the divide in income and wealth was accompanied by a sharp, even shocking, decline in social mobility in the United States. The justification for inequality of income in the US, lacking any historical or hereditary justification for why some should be richer than others, was always that the US had a relatively open system of social mobility. Those who worked harder, used their talents, and achieved more would earn higher incomes; those with lower incomes were not systemically disadvantaged. This highly individualistic view of inequality certainly fit the classical liberal ideal, as long as opportunity was indeed open and anyone willing to work hard and apply their talents could rise.

For the most part, this was the situation for the US in the 1950s through 1970s. A vast expansion of cheap higher public education meant that the baby-boomers could easily become the first of their families to attend college. Baby-boomers with college degrees could then readily find white-collar jobs as teachers, government workers, or in the professions as all of these expanded with the strong population and economic growth of these decades. But blue-collar workers were not left behind; their unions provided rising wages and benefits that often matched those of white-collar workers. Social mobility, even for minorities (though at a lesser rate) was widespread, and when combined with generally rising real wages, this meant that children could almost certainly count on higher real incomes (at the same age) than their parents. For cohorts that entered the labor force from the mid-1950s to the mid-1970s, over 80% made more money than their parents at the same age. But this too ended: for cohorts that entered the labor force from 1980 to the mid-2000s, the fraction that did better than their parents was only 50–60%. Currently about half of workers make less than their parents at the same age (Chetty et al. 2017). The decline in social mobility is also geographically uneven: it is particularly marked in the South, the desert southwest, and the industrial heartland of Michigan, Indiana, Missouri, and Ohio (Reeves and Krause 2018). Unable either to compete with the college-educated elite, nor be confident that their children would be able to do better, it is unsurprising that among the older and less-educated in these regions, distrust and anxiety about the future (theirs and that of the country) became common currency.

Naturally, Americans—and workers in other countries with similar trends—turned bitterly against the "liberal" elites who had presided over the globalization of free markets, financial deregulation, and the enormous surge of inequality. As voters sought major changes, many of the core centrist parties that had led the United States, the United Kingdom, Canada, France, Italy, and other countries simply dissolved in the early twenty-first century, abandoned by voters in favor of new parties promising new approaches, or transformed into new, radical versions with different leaders and programs.

Surges of immigration provided an additional scapegoat for disenchanted workers, leading to wide support for ethno-nationalist parties that promised a return to more prosperous times for working and lower-middle class workers. Indeed, support for the populist Donald Trump in the USA was greatest precisely in those counties that had seen the worst trends in life expectancy and health. Yet to be sure, it was not economic hardship *per se* that led to populist fervor; when polled, Trump voters were not so much concerned about their income but about their place in America and America's place in the world—their anxieties were that people like themselves (White, Christian, farmers, and blue-collar workers) were losing their status and respect within America compared to urban professionals, losing their numerical and social dominance in their country due to immigration from non-European countries, were being unfairly treated by policies that favored ethnic and gender minorities, and that globalization and unfair foreign competition were eroding American workers' dominant place in the world (Mutz 2018). Hence the powerful appeal of Trump's campaign slogan to "Make America Great Again" by reversing all of these processes. Similar trends and beliefs dominated the counties that voted for Brexit in the United Kingdom (Kaufmann 2019).

The result has been a striking wave of support for markedly illiberal policies: closing off immigration, ending free trade, officially supporting the nationally dominant religion, limiting access to voting, enforcement of traditional gender roles, and reduced tolerance for pluralism of all sorts.

PUPPIES, PORN, AND POPULISM

One of the cardinal tenets of classical liberalism is tolerance of pluralism. As long as peacefully expressed, different viewpoints are seen as essential to the free dialogue and contestation of ideas that allows truth to emerge and spread, rather than being controlled for the benefit of the few. Yet this tolerance has been strikingly eroded by the shifts in the character and control of the media in the twenty-first century.

In the twentieth century, the ideal of a "free press," seen as vital to democracy by the Founding Fathers and classical liberals in general, was made compatible with the free market by a limited amount of regulation, designed to ensure open competition. Ownership of media was primarily local, and strictly limited, so that most locations had their own newspaper or several of them, and their own news stations on radio and TV. They might share content across networks and from wire services, but ownership was dispersed. Moreover, content in print and commercial broadcast media was regulated by strict liability laws and professional standards, which ensured fact-checking and editorial review before publication or broadcast (Rauch 2021). Flat-earthers and other idiosyncratic views might have their own societies, but they had no easy way to access and influence millions, as the wider networks and major media outlets would not broadcast such views.

This began to change with the spread of the internet as a new medium to broadcast news and opinions. In the 1990s, it was hoped that the internet—as a wholly democratic medium of expression, in which any person was now empowered, at virtually no cost, to reach an unlimited audience—would foster free and open discussion and thus advance pluralism, democracy, and the emergence of truth. In short it would be an ideal support for the classical liberal ideal. It is hard to imagine any view of a new technology that was more naïve and misguided.

Begun as a way for scholars and scientists to quickly exchange information, private corporations arose to facilitate the use of the internet by ordinary folks as a way to share pictures, stories, videos, and communications. Facebook, Twitter, Instagram, Snapchat, Tik-tok, Wechat, and browsers with easy-to-compose professional-looking web-pages made it easy to reach millions of viewers, with little editing or filtering, at almost no cost. The problem was that with unlimited and unfiltered content available, how could one find and choose one's preferred content? The solution was provided by for-profit companies who monetized, and thus promoted, those sites that drew the most engagement. Of course, experience with other media has shown that in order to avoid obscene content, deception and lies, and hate-speech targeting all kinds of groups, strict liability, regulation, and editing is necessary before content is published or aired. And media moguls also know that emotionally grabbing, passion-inflaming content is most engaging and draws the most return views.

Yet this wisdom was conveniently set aside when it came to the internet and the new companies that rose to compete for on-line engagement. The result was that the most inexpensive, wide-reaching, and accessible media ever invented became subject to content prioritization on the basis of emotional and passion-inflaming content. Of course, rational political discussion and scientific discourse continued to be found on-line, just as C-span broadcasts of congressional hearings and public TV documentaries find a place among the hundreds of channels of television content. But just as it is "Game of Thrones" and "Breaking Bad" that draw orders of magnitudes more viewers than educational or intellectual content, so it is more emotional and passion-inflaming sites that are most profitable on the internet. Yet unlike television and conventional newspapers and magazines, the internet has virtually no liability, regulation, or editorial restrictions. Lies and deceptions, anonymous platforms and statements, violence and hate porn run rampant, alongside videos of cute animals and apocalyptic warnings of political disaster.

The distortion of the information field by the internet has been accompanied by a transformation of the overall media field. Newspapers have died out by the hundreds and thousands, leaving a print media landscape owned by a few large corporations that favor the positions of their billionaire owners. More and more people get their news and information mainly from internet sources or television. Television news has shifted from a small number of networks seeking the broadest audience by appealing to the average viewer and eschewing the extremes, to many niche-channels carried by cable and satellite (and the internet) that seek to build their audience by cultivating a loyal base devoted to their channels' particular world-view.

Instead of a single wide-ranging information field, with strong regulation and editing of content for accuracy and suppression of obscene hate-filled content, we have arrived at a fractured information field, where people are encouraged to select and indulge in the repetition of lies that they favor, and soak in hate-filled content that targets those they dislike. The result is a social media landscape dominated by puppies, porn, and populism. That is how pets Buddy and Boo had 16 million Facebook followers (half again more than President Biden), or how Esther the Wonder Pig has more Facebook followers than Democratic House Majority leader Nancy Pelosi. More important, that is how approximately one-third of American adults have come to express beliefs that Donald Trump actually won the 2020 US presidential election, and that President Biden's victory was "stolen" or "illegitimate" (Swann 2022), while smaller numbers, but still hundreds of thousands, believe in wild conspiracy theories about Democrats being pedophiles, Satanists, and agents of Jewish globalists who want to destroy America.

Instead of tolerance of diversity among a single national community, the US (and many other countries) has been ripped asunder, going forward as distinct, mutually hostile, and distrusting communities inhabiting their own opposite and incompatible information worlds. This renders the classical liberal ideal of shared discourse to sift divergent views against a grounding of shared facts and standards for adjudicating truth virtually impossible.

NORMATIVE SOCIAL SCIENCE: THE RETURN OF UTOPIAS

The conditions for classical liberal society to function—a high degree of material and political equality; an open discourse subject to mutually agreed-upon facts and rules for sifting truth from falsehood and unsupported opinion; a strong but constrained government, accountable to citizens by free, fair, and equal-citizenship based elections free from excessive influence by the wealthy; and limits on free markets to prevent inequalities of wealth and income from depriving average workers of hope for the future or their political voice—no longer obtain in the United States or much of the world. Indeed, for billions of people in China and areas that receive Chinese investment, the illiberal system of single-party authoritarian government offered by China as a model has great appeal as a more stable, efficient, and effective system of government than the current U.S.'s version of liberal democracy.

Social science is often expected to be "objective" and simply analyze the present and past, and avoid polemical advocacy of different visions for the future. Yet the latter was once an honored way of discussing basic principles of social organization, from Plato's *Republic* to Moore's *Utopia.* Moreover, certain analyses of social trends, if they are clearly adverse, implicitly call for suggestions about how they may be altered for the future.

For example, when Foucault and his followers argue that elites in power frequently promulgate falsehoods to legitimize and preserve their power, which those elites claim are truths, that is accurate. But different normative conclusions can be drawn from that observation. One can conclude that there is no truth, only the claims of elites, which need to be countered by subaltern groups expressing their own views as truth. Or, one can conclude that it is necessary for those committed to exposing falsehoods and lies to seek an objective truth through standards of evidence and argument that all can agree on (Rauch 2021). To a large degree, the progressive left has adopted the former position, insisting on their own views as truths, and being hostile to those who do not accept them. The right has adopted this view even more so, to the extent of pushing a renewed wave of book banning and restrictions on what can be taught in state-supported universities to suppress ideas and facts they find offensive. In both cases, that is an illiberal position. In classical liberalism, truth is what results from a fair contest among ideas and arguments according to objective rules of evidence, logic, and demonstration, and even those propositions proven in this way to be false or harmful should be disdained, not banned.

In finding a way to reinvigorate classical liberalism, sociologists (and the other social sciences) not only need to document the loss of the functional perquisites and conditions of classical liberalism—that has been achieved in abundance, as the above sampling of research results makes clear. Sociology also needs to identify what must be done to restore the critical social conditions that are foundational for classical liberal society to function, even if that seems like a utopian enterprise.

Francis Fukuyama, in his recent work on classical liberalism, concluded with a simple message for restoring classical liberalism: moderation. Certainly moderation *is* a virtue of classical liberalism, and moderation in inequalities of wealth and income, in discourse, and in government regulation is certainly to be desired. But in some areas, moderation is simply a slippery slope to dictatorship. Should rule of law be only moderately applied to all equally? It is the very weak application of the law to wealthy and especially white-collar crimes that has undermined the trust in government and toleration of inequalities of wealth necessary to liberal society. Should Congress be only moderately capable of checking the executive branch? The repeated failures of Congress to impeach President Trump, due to party identification outweighing the need to punish wrongful executive actions, only encouraged and empowered executive disregard for the law. Should the courts be only moderately objective, as opposed to striving for the maximum impartiality in respect for precedent and application of the law? No. In certain fundamentals, it is *only* by insistence on strict fidelity to classical liberal ideals of equality under law and accountability of government and officials that freedom can be maintained.

For the United States to again be a model of classical liberalism and how a classical liberal society can combine freedom and prosperity, a large number of changes will have to be made from our current conditions. But these changes will need to occur by a combination of popular organization, dispersed power, and perhaps state-by-state changes, rather than by centralized, top-down state action which would obviate the classical liberal goal.

1. Means will have to be found—for example, restoring unions (likely both private and public sector) to improve bargaining strength, raising minimum wages, or redistribution through taxes and benefits—that check and partly reverse the great rise in inequality of the last forty years. This may be a realistic goal: In 2022, we have in fact seen a resurgence of union action and success, with unions from the screenwriters' and actors' guilds to the United Auto Workers winning significant victories from their employers. Yet more radical efforts to tax wealth and the highest incomes more heavily will almost certainly also be needed.[5]
2. Means will have to be found—for example, greater access to high-quality low-cost education, regulation of wages, public investments in varied projects especially in lower-income areas—to provide access to reasonably well-paid and dignified work for people of all abilities and education. Here, too there are signs of progress, with more than half the US states having raised the minimum wage, in some places to double the Federal minimum (which remains at $7.25/hour) (Economic Policy Institute 2023).
3. Means will have to be found—for example, preschool education, more flexible zoning and housing transfers, access to credit for education and/or business investment, more secure health and welfare benefits—to restore opportunities for economic mobility in all regions and income groups.
4. Means will have to be found—for example, regulation, strict liability, anti-trust—to restore a public information field where truth is prized while false and passion-inflaming content is easily labeled and downplayed, and fortunes cannot be built on fraud. While we are far from real progress in this regard, there may be a model for advance in the Biden Administration's executive order on Artificial Intelligence, which makes companies that develop AI tools liable for any foreseeable costs of the misuse or flaws in their AI programs that cause losses or harm.

5. Means will have to be found—for example, housing benefits, zoning changes, child benefits, education benefits, health insurance, public safety, pensions—to ensure that all Americans who work have access to the core elements of a dignified life.
6. Means will have to be found—for example, regulation of campaign finance, automatic voter registration and ballot delivery for citizens, election day holiday—to ensure that voting for citizens is easy, equally accessible, and not excessively influenced by inequalities outside the political sphere.
7. Means will have to be found—for example, reinstating the filibuster, perhaps with time-limits, for appointment of Federal judges; strengthening Congressional subpoena power and Inspector Generals (who should not serve at the pleasure of the branch they are appointed to inspect)—to ensure that checks and balances are effective between co-equal branches of government, and that the judicial branch is widely respected as impartial and objective.

That this is a huge, even utopian, list of reforms is true. It resembles the list of reforms made by Franklin D. Roosevelt's administration in response to the twin disasters of the Depression and WWII. But what is important is not the specific reforms, which can be amended from the above list and seriously debated. What is vital is the recognition that the conditions for a classical liberal society to be realized are now substantially lacking and under threat, even in states that call themselves liberal democracies, and that if freedom and general prosperity are to be reclaimed, those conditions must be restored.

Will such changes also only arise in response to some disaster? In fact, the undoing of the critical conditions for classical liberal society has probably gone too far to otherwise be overthrown. The demographic-structural model of social instability that I developed has been applied to the United States by Peter Turchin, and it both details how conditions in the mid-nineteenth century led to Civil War, and shows how conditions at present are more similar to those of the mid-nineteenth century than any other time in US history (Goldstone and Turchin 2020). Political polarization, mistrust of media, inequality, declining social mobility, declining life expectancy—all are at exceptional levels and will not easily be reversed simply by seeking reforms. Elites who benefit from the current situation are well entrenched and unlikely to yield. It thus may take another major catastrophe, in the economic or public health or military sphere, as noted by Scheidel (Scheidel 2018), to so weaken dominant elites and force the search for new solutions that the necessary changes will be welcomed, and utopian ideas accepted as useful goals.

The Founding Fathers, steeped in classical liberal ideals, designed the US Constitution with several goals in mind. Their design sought to keep

Congress dominant over the executive, to bridge national divisions through balancing popular and regional power bases in a bicameral legislature and federal system, to prevent an intolerant minority from lording over the majority of citizens, and—above all—to avoid a petty, selfish, and incompetent demagogue from coming to power and evading punishment for such behavior if they should somehow come to office.

It is now clear that the efforts of the Founding Fathers—again perhaps unsurprisingly after nearly 250 years of technological change and growing social complexity—have failed. The executive has grown to extreme dominance, even defiance, of Congress; the nation is again divided into two hostile nations based on identity-defining but contrary beliefs; and intolerant minorities on both the right and the left are claiming the right to dictate truths and policies for all Americans. Numerous books on the Trump presidency have documented his self-serving and incompetent behavior in office, from the slapdash and intentionally deceitful handling of an epidemic that cost over a million American lives, to giving Russia's president precedence over the US military and intelligence services in interpreting Russian actions and setting US policy on Ukraine, to orchestrating an attack on the US Congress when they were in the act of declaring the presidency of his opponent, and even stealing hundreds of US government documents—many of them critical to US security—when leaving his official position (Woodward 2018). Yet what is important is not the peccadillos of an individual, or the fact of political divisions, but the fact that the American political system has been so badly bent that the leaders of one of the major parties, and a vocal and large fraction of the citizens, applaud these acts and continue to treat Trump as the savior of the nation.

All of this cannot be easily reversed. But scholars can do what scholars have done in dark times throughout history: preserve the understanding and ideals of a better social order, document how things have changed and fallen away from those ideals, and map a path back that may be pursued when conditions allow. This creates a reserve of intellectual capital for policy reform; attempting to sketch out better futures is not merely utopianism, it is necessary to motivate and equip those who will plan and implement changes to restore classical liberal institutions and habits.

There is reason for optimism. Marx once said that history repeats itself, the first time as tragedy, the second time as farce. If our current era repeats a previous time when classical liberalism gave way to ethnic nationalism and authoritarianism, namely the 1930s, then Trump may be the appropriate individual to lead the farce. His re-election may lead to disaster, but not so grave as in WWII, and be followed, as was WWII, by an unprecedented era of freedom and prosperity. If one had told Europeans in 1940, during the depths of war, widespread dictatorship, and genocidal violence, that less than a decade hence, they would enter on decades of far greater democracy, freedom, peace, and prosperity than they had ever imagined, they would have found it unfathomable. Yet it occurred. So we may hope, if we keep clear on the social changes that have undermined classical liberalism, and the conditions that can restore it, that we may lay templates for another resurgence of freedom and well-being in the near future.

This volume is addressed to elites, whose leadership will be essential to achieving the seven goals listed above. Yet the point of this chapter is that elites cannot create a classical liberal society without working with, and respecting the dignity and equality of, everyone in it. As the title of this volume observes, freedom is something we do together, for everyone's benefit.

SUGGESTED ADDITIONAL READINGS

Fukuyama, Francis. 2022. *Liberalism and Its Discontents*. New York: Farrar, Straus and Giroux.

Piketty, Thomas. 2022. *A Brief History of Equality*. Translated by Steven Rendall. Cambridge, MA: Belknap Press.

Smith, Hedrick. 2012. *Who Stole the American Dream*. New York: Random House.

Turchin, Peter. 2023. *End Times: Elites, Counter-Elites and the Path of Political Disintegration*. New York: Penguin.

REFERENCES

Acemoglu, Daron and James A. Robinson. 2019. *The Narrow Corridor: States, Societies and the Fate of Liberty*. Westminster, UK: Penguin.

Case, Anne, and Angus Deaton. 2021. *Deaths of Despair and the Future of Capitalism*. Princeton, NJ: Princeton University Press.

Chetty, Raj, David Grusky, Maximilian Hell, Nathaniel Hendren, Robert Manduca, and Jimmy Narang. 2017. "The Fading American Dream: Trends in absolute income mobility since 1940." *Science* 356, Issue 6336 (April): 398–406.

Congressional Research Service. 2021. "The Growing Gap in Life Expectancy by Income: Recent Evidence and Implications for the Social Security Retirement Age." Updated July 6, 2021. https://crsreports.congress.gov/product/pdf/R/R44846.

Davies, Stephen. 2022. "Classical Liberalism." In *The Routledge Companion to Libertarianism*, edited by Matt Zwolinki and Benjamin Ferguson, 216–19. New York: Routledge 2022.

de Tocqueville, Alexis. 1835. *Democracy in America.* Vol. 1, Chapter 2.

Desmond, Matthew. 2023. *Poverty in America*. New York: Crown.

Economic Policy Institute. 2023. "Minimum Wage Tracker." Last modified July 1, 2023. https://www.epi.org/minimum-wage-tracker/.

Federal Reserve Economic Data. 2023. "Employed full time: Median usual weekly real earnings: Wage and salary workers: 16 years and over." Last modified January 19, 2023. https://fred.stlouisfed.org/series/LEU0252881600A.

Florida, Richard. 2019. *The Rise of the Creative Class*. New York: Basic Books.

Fukuyama, Francis. 2015. *Political Order and Political Decay from the Industrial Revolution to the Globalization of Democracy*. New York: Farrar, Straus and Giroux.

Fukuyama, Francis. 2022. *Liberalism and Its Discontents*. New York: Farrar, Straus and Giroux.

Garton Ash, Timothy. 2020. "The Future of Liberalism." *Prospect*, December 9, 2020.

Goldstone, Jack A., and Peter Turchin. 2020. "Welcome to the Turbulent Twenties." *NOEMA*, September 10, 2020. https://www.noemamag.com/welcome-to-the-turbulent-twenties/.

Grusky, David, and Jasmine Hill, ed. 2017. *Inequality in the 21st Century: A Reader.* New York: Routledge.

Hacker, Jacob S. 2019. *The Great Risk Shift: The New Economic Insecurity and the Decline of the American Dream, Second Edition*. New York: Oxford University Press.

Harrington, Brooke. 2016. *Capital Without Borders: Wealth Managers and the One Percent*. Cambridge, MA: Harvard University Press.

Kaufmann, Eric P. 2019. "Can Narratives of White Identity Reduce Opposition to Immigration and Support for Hard Brexit? A Survey Experiment." *Political Studies* 67, Issue 1 (February): 31–46.

Krippner, Greta. 2012. *Capitalizing on Crisis: The Political Origins of the Rise of Finance*. Cambridge, MA: Harvard University Press.

McCloskey Nansen, Deirdre. 2006. *The Bourgeois Virtues*. Chicago: University of Chicago Press.

McCloskey Nansen, Deirdre. 2010. *Bourgeois Dignity*. Chicago: University of Chicago Press.

McCloskey Nansen, Deirdre. 2016. *Bourgeois Equality*. Chicago: University of Chicago Press.

Mutz, Diana C. 2018. "Status Threat, Not Economic Hardship, Explains the 2016 Presidential Vote." *Proceedings of the National Academy of Sciences* 115, no. 19 (April): E4330–39.

Piketty, Thomas. 2017. *Capital in the Twenty-first Century*. Cambridge, MA: Belknap Press.

Piketty, Thomas. 2021. *Time for Socialism: Dispatches from a World on Fire, 2016–2021*. New Haven: Yale University Press.

Rauch, Jonathan. 2021. *The Constitution of Knowledge: A Defense of Truth*. Washington, DC: Brookings Institution Press.

Reeves, Richard V., and Eleanor Krause. 2018. "Raj Chetty in 14 charts: Big findings on opportunity and mobility we should all know." *Brookings*, January 11, 2018. https://www.brookings.edu/blog/social-mobility-memos/2018/01/11/raj-chetty-in-14-charts-big-findings-on-opportunity-and-mobility-we-should-know/.

Richter, Felix. 2019. "50 Years of US Wages, in One Chart." *World Economic Forum*, April 12, 2019. https://www.weforum.org/agenda/2019/04/50-years-of-us-wages-in-one-chart/.

Saez, Emmanuel and Gabriel Zucman. 2020. "The Rise of Income and Wealth Inequality in America: Evidence from Distributional Macroeconomic Accounts." *Journal of Economic Perspectives* 34: 3–26, Figures 1 and 3.

Scheidel, Walter. 2018. *The Great Leveler, Violence and the History of Inequality from the Stone Age to the Twenty-First Century*. Princeton, NJ: Princeton University Press.

Singh, Kanishka. 2023. "US suicide deaths reached record high in 2022, CDC data shows." *Reuters*, August 11, 2023. https://www.reuters.com/world/us/us-suicide-deaths-reached-record-high-2022-cdc-data-shows-2023-08-11/.

Smith, Hedrick. 2012. *Who Stole the American Dream?*. New York: Random House.

Swann, Sara. 2022. "No, Most Americans Don't Believe the 2020 Election was Fraudulent." *Politifact*, February 2, 2022. https://www.politifact.com/factchecks/2022/feb/02/viral-image/no-most-americans-dont-believe-2020-election-was-f/.

Weisman, Jonathan, and Rachel Shorey. 2022. "Fueled by Billionaires, Political Spending Shatters Records Again." *The New York Times*, November 3, 2022. https://www.nytimes.com/2022/11/03/us/politics/midterm-money-billionaires.html.

Woodward, Bob. 2018. *Fear: Trump in the White House*. New York: Simon & Schuster.

Woolf, Stephen. 2023. "Falling Behind: The Growing Gap in Life Expectancy Between the United States and Other Countries, 1933–2021." *American Journal of Public Health* 113, no. 9 (September): 970–980. https://doi.org/10.2105/AJPH.2023.307310.

NOTES

1. I thank Fabio Rojas and Lotta Stern for inviting me to contribute and helpful edits; Bill Glod for carefully going over the entire volume and raising good questions about the chapters, including my own; and Steven Fish for detailed and thought-provoking comments on my chapter that pushed me to revise many particulars. I am indebted to all of them but all errors are my own.

2. These points were also cogently made by Timothy Garton Ash (2020).

3. Notable work on increasing inequality and declining social mobility, and their impact on the quality of life—some of it by economists as well as sociologists—includes Matthew Desmond (2023), Thomas Piketty (2017), David Grusky and Jasmine Hill (2017), Brooke Harrington (2016), and Anne Case and Angus Deaton (2021).

4. For a good history of the struggle, see Deirdre Nansen McCloskey (2006; 2010; 2016).

5. Some of the most radical ideas for reducing inequality in modern industrial states can be found in Thomas Piketty (2021). However, classical liberalism requires

that inequality be reduced by popular organization for reform, moderate government action, and popularly supported law (e.g., to restore the tax structure of the US in the 1950s/1960s) rather than a socialist regime.

Chapter 9

The Problem on Campus is How We Think

Ilana Redstone

THE QUESTION

One chilly afternoon in the spring of 2022, I drove to campus and parked down the street from a modern and sleek brick building.[1] The air was brisk as I walked the short distance from my car to the glassy doors of the main entrance. After a few minutes of wandering through hallways that seemed indistinguishable from one another, I found Room 256—the clean, brightly lit, seminar room I was looking for. It was unoccupied when I entered, so no one was there to watch as I slid my laptop from its sleeve, opened it up, and began to page through the slides that I would not finish that day. Faculty and graduate students trickled in and took their seats.

I was there to give a talk that had been scheduled several months earlier. The topic was how certainty quietly drives the way we judge and demonize people who disagree with us, especially when it comes to heated and contentious issues. Certainty makes it difficult to cultivate a culture that is open to a wide range of viewpoints and it makes communication across ideological divides all but impossible.

There are three main ways this can happen. One is that certainty leads us to stop asking questions. After all, why would we continue asking questions when we already have all the answers? Two is that it lets us believe that there are no questions *someone else* could ask. This leads us to judge harshly anyone who *does* ask a question. And three is that it tricks us into thinking that the principles and values on which we're basing our judgments are obvious to everyone around us and therefore don't need to be stated out loud. Its effects are so pervasive, I've come to call it the Certainty Trap. It refers to a resolute unwillingness to consider the possibility that we're wrong or that we're not right in the way we think we are.

For this particular talk, I was focused on college campuses, but the observation applies more broadly. My main point was—and still is—that the instinct to judge a person, idea, or position as ignorant, stupid, or morally bankrupt comes largely from one factor: an unwillingness or an inability to identify, name, and question the underlying belief, value, or moral that we treat as inviolable.

My talk that day didn't go well. There are probably multiple reasons for this—for one thing, the audience expected a research-based talk and I gave one that consisted almost entirely of theory and commentary. But, it is also the case that I simply wasn't prepared for some of the questions that were asked. I was only a few minutes into my talk when a few hands went up.

I am no stranger to discussing my work and I am familiar with the many of the things people ask. They often include things like: Are you saying there's *nothing* we can be certain of? Or, where does the acknowledgment of uncertainty end? Am I saying we have to teach intelligent design alongside evolution in our elementary schools? I'm prepared to tackle all of these challenges.

When it comes to the physical world, nothing is certain. The next time I turn on my kettle to boil water, it might not boil. If I drop a glass on the tile floor, there's some chance it won't break. This is different from an abstract world where the rules are completely and exhaustively defined—as in the world of mathematics, for instance. This is why the following statement on its own is certain (provided I've specified base 10 math): 2+2=4.

This is why, when it comes to the question of: Where does it end?, the answer is: it doesn't. Any line we draw about what kinds of ideas can be questioned and what can't is ultimately unjustifiable. This brings us to the third question, do we have to then teach intelligent design alongside evolution? There's nothing about understanding the provisional nature of our knowledge that suggests that any explanation is as good or as likely as any other. And, at some point, we bump up against practical considerations of time. In a 15-week introductory biology course, does it make sense to spend six weeks talking about intelligent design? Probably not. Might it be interesting to take 15 minutes of one class period and walk through the thinking? If I were in that class, the answer would be yes.

But, that day, we didn't even get to these kinds of questions. One that I wasn't expecting came from the back of the room. The faculty member who raised her hand, cleared her throat, peered over her glasses and said: "How do you know this is a problem?" In other words, she challenged: Was I offering a diagnosis and a solution that no one really needed?

I paused for a moment as the question caught me off guard. I confess I wondered to myself briefly how anyone in higher education paying even the slightest attention could think there *wasn't* a problem when it comes to how we think and communicate on tough and heated issues. But I pushed that thought out of my mind. I tried to focus on what she was asking and how I might answer it coherently.

THE ANSWER

As I understood it, she was asking for evidence, or even proof, that the symptoms of the problem of certainty were real, and not something I made up. It's a completely fair question that I wasn't entirely sure how to answer. Often, when people talk about the challenges of ideological conformity or a lack of political or viewpoint diversity on campuses, they point to things like self-censorship, infringements on free speech, or the number of shoutdowns and disinvitations in the previous year. In many ways, these are natural things to focus on because we can measure them. We can count the lawsuits people file when they feel their first amendment rights have been violated. There are surveys asking people how often they feel they self-censor and there is at least one database that catalogs disinvitations and shoutdowns (FIRE 2023). Because we can measure each of these components, we can observe how they change over time and we can compare them across contexts.

However, while each of these metrics has some value, they can also be a distraction. After all, the lack of ideological diversity on campuses doesn't become a problem only when the level of self-censorship rises above a particular level. It's not just worrisome when we go beyond a certain number of speaker invitations rescinded due to protesting students or faculty. It's a problem because we're at a point where ideological narrowness is woven into higher education in general—and, given the focus of this book, I'll add—and to my home discipline of sociology in particular. A student made this point one day in class, perhaps more clearly than I could have.

During the first few weeks of the semester, I introduced the class to the work of Thomas Sowell—an economist and prolific writer who, when I asked, none of them had previously heard of. For my course, they had watched—and we had discussed at some length—an interview Sowell did about his book, "A Conflict of Visions." In that book, in the simplest terms, Sowell describes two fundamentally different ways of understanding the world. He argues that these visions, while they're almost never articulated or acknowledged, run in the background of our thinking and shape our views on a wide range of social policies. The first vision is what Sowell calls "constrained." In this view of the world, human beings are inherently flawed. We are imperfect, hierarchical, and competitive by nature. In this sense, the role of our social institutions is to keep our baser instincts in check and to keep us from descending into anarchy. (To be clear, that summary contains my words, not Sowell's, but it captures the general idea.)

This stands in contrast to what he calls the "unconstrained" vision. With the unconstrained vision, human beings' natural state is largely egalitarian and peaceful (Sowell refers to the famous quote from Rousseau: "Man is born free but everywhere is in chains" as the epitome of this perspective.) In this line of thinking, the extent to which we've fallen from this state is due to the failures of our socially constructed institutions. And, importantly, this vision suggests that our institutions can be *re*constructed in a way that supports a return to our natural state. Loosely speaking, the "constrained" vision maps onto conservative political ideology and the "unconstrained" vision maps on to liberal or progressive political ideology.

Suffice it to say that these are two radically different ways of understanding the world and human nature. Let's get back to the student I mentioned—the one who put her finger on the lack of ideological diversity in sociology. After hearing Sowell's interview and listening to the class discussion, she raised her hand, with a pensive look, and asked, "If we think Sowell's framework makes sense, then doesn't that mean that sociology is irrelevant?" Surprised by the question, I asked, "Do you mean the current sociology class specifically or the discipline more generally?" She meant the discipline more generally.

There might well be an expression more precise than "irrelevant" that fits what the student was getting at. "Ideologically one-sided" was probably closer to her intent. Regardless, she'd made a connection that was important. She observed that the entirety of the discipline grew forth from only one of Sowell's two visions: the "unconstrained" one. What's more, rather than basing her conclusion on a single experience, she was drawing from her time in a range of sociology classes.

The student is right. Sociology is built around the idea of perfecting institutions—both minimizing the harm that they can create and maximizing the good they can do. In fact, it's a discipline that uses as one of its core tenets something called "The Sociological Imagination"—the idea that sociology's main contribution is in the way it looks at the impact of the structures in which individuals live. In other words, it sounds a lot like it's rooted in Sowell's "unconstrained" vision.

Sociology isn't the only field that's emerged from within this singular vantage point. Much of the social sciences and the humanities have too. But I'm not sure that emerging from within a constrained vision is even the problem. In fact, I can imagine an argument where this one-sidedness is a feature, not a bug. Planting a metaphorical stake in the ground when it comes to what you stand for—looking for structural causes to social problems—and what you don't—blaming individuals for their lot in life—can be empowering and provide clarity.

So how was I to answer the question that emerged during the seminar I was giving that crisp spring day? What evidence did I have that this is a problem? Do I talk about Sowell's unconstrained vision and the student's astute observation? Should I rattle off the rates of self-censorship from the latest survey? Should I talk about how those rates are higher among conservative students than among liberal students? Should I open up a discussion about free speech concerns and discuss why they're warranted? Do I show a chart of time trends of disinvitations?

Perhaps those are the kinds of answers the person asking the question was looking for. But they all sidestep the real problem. Each of the metrics listed above is an outward manifestation of the much deeper, more systemic, cause outlined at the beginning. This means that a reliance on those metrics to demonstrate the extent of the problem misses the point because they don't get to the root. Let's back up for a moment.

When people feel they can't speak their mind on a heated issue, it's often out of a concern that they're going to be judged negatively—whether by their peers, online, or somewhere else. The tendency to reflexively judge harshly someone who disagrees sits underneath many of the arguments over limits on free speech, levels of self-censorship, and whether a particular speaker should be platformed. And it comes from a problem that runs deep: how we think.

We reflexively judge others who disagree because our position or opinion is driven by a value, belief, or principle that we see as beyond questioning—or as certain. And, while this often happens subconsciously, it drives the judgment that keeps us from thinking about and engaging on many of the most contentious issues we face. Too often, we fail to understand how this works.

This leads to two potential solutions. One is to simply recognize the limits of what we know and understand that our knowledge is provisional. This is the case whether we're talking about the relationship between gender and biology, the causes of or solutions to inequality, or any number of other third-rail issues. The other solution requires a level of clarity and precision in our language that many of us are not used to having.

Avoiding the Certainty Trap means committing to this clarity. It means understanding that talking about the "right" or "best" immigration policy isn't meaningful until or unless we're clear about who immigration is supposed to benefit in the first place. Is it for people fleeing worse situations in other countries or is it to strengthen the economy for the people already living in the US? It means being clear that a person could oppose affirmative action because they're racist, but they could also oppose it for other reasons too. And understanding that, if all you know about someone is that they have an opinion you don't like, you can't tell what's driving them. And it means a willingness to leave character condemnation aside because we understand the costs of getting it wrong.

Ultimately, recognizing that a belief, value, or principle should be open to questioning and criticism doesn't necessarily require letting it go or changing our minds. And when this recognition is combined with the understanding that no ideas get a free pass when it comes to being examined or questioned, it leads to something new.

The importance of being clear, precise, and explicit in our thinking is difficult to overstate. Putting that into practice, however, isn't always straightforward.

THE POWER OF UNCERTAINTY

In many of the classes I teach, we end up spending a lot of time talking about inequality. I suppose this isn't too surprising for a sociology professor. What are inequality's causes and solutions, what level is acceptable, why do outcomes differ systematically across groups, etc . . . ?

Here's one of the exercises I'll do with students to try to highlight the importance of uncertainty. I'll say "Let's talk about educational success and educational inequality." And I'll start by asking this room full of U of I undergraduates, "How did you get here?" Not how did they get to the classroom that day, but how did they get to the U of I? They all know people from their high schools who didn't get into the U of I or who didn't go to college at all. So, to what do they attribute their success?

In some ways, the exercise is a way into a broader conversation about the dual roles of structural forces and individual choices in the generation of inequality. As a discipline, sociology tends to focus almost entirely on the former, while rarely, if ever, invoking the latter. Sociology's general resistance to considering individual level factors may stem from a—largely reasonable—concern that doing so can easily slide into "blaming the victim." As in, people are only poor because of their own bad choices. At the same time, focusing only on structural causes limits our understanding of what is a deeply complex problem.

When we do this activity in class, students will often say things like, "I studied really hard," "I went to class," "I got a scholarship," "I had an inspirational teacher," and "My parents would have killed me if I didn't do well." I often have to assure them that my role is simply to note what they say.

If, through the course of this exercise, no one mentions the potential role of structural or systemic causes, I'll bring it up myself—bracketing for the moment whether the concept of "structural causes" is sufficiently well-defined. When I bring up its potential relevance, the students will often nod, suggesting that the absence of, for instance, systemic racism probably mattered too.

So, I'll point out, now we have a list of different factors we think might contribute to educational success. And I'll note how, sometimes, in conversations on this topic, the only factors that are mentioned are the structural ones—often with the idea that pointing to individual level determinants is a thinly veiled way to blame those who don't succeed in a way that feels callous. And I'll ask them, given the conversation we're having now and the factors you all have listed, what does it mean for how we talk and think about educational inequality if we only focus on structural causes as we often do in, for instance, sociology? They quickly understand that this is perilously limiting.

Sometimes the conversation about inequality can become so challenging to think through that it's helpful to consider an extreme case. For this, every once in a while, I'll turn to "Harrison Bergeron," a short story by Kurt Vonnegut, Jr. It opens with this description:

> THE YEAR WAS 2081, and everybody was finally equal. They weren't only equal before God and the law. They were equal every which way. Nobody was smarter than anybody else. Nobody was better looking than anybody else. Nobody was stronger or quicker than anybody else. All this equality was due to the 211th, 212th, and 213th Amendments to the Constitution, and to the unceasing vigilance of agents of the United States Handicapper General. (Vonnegut 1961).

While various things occur over the course of the story, I usually focus on the world Vonnegut had imagined. It was a world where equality in every dimension was socially engineered. If a person was smarter than average, they were forced to wear a contraption that disrupted their thoughts so they couldn't string ideas together. If a person was too graceful, they were forced to wear weights. If a person was too attractive, they were forced to make themselves appear uglier. And so on and so forth.

Usually the article is a jumping off point for a conversation that starts with the acknowledgment that the society described in Harrison Bergeron isn't one that we would want to live in. This generally leads to an interesting conversation about what the "right" level of inequality is, who should decide, and how we should think about it. However, one day when I brought this up, ready to raise the usual questions, a student in the front row raised her hand.

She quietly challenged, "Maybe it's not such a bad way to live after all. Maybe it's the son [in Vonnegut's story] who's out of line for trying to go against a system that seems to be working for most people." I thought for a moment before a smile came over my face. In all the time I'd discussed this story in class, no one had ever raised this question. Now, it's true that the characters in Vonnegut's story hardly seem like they're in a position where they're free to decide or make a choice about whether they want to remain in that world or not. And yet, her question, as we look at the story analytically, is fascinating.

I said, "You're one hundred percent right to ask this." Even in a context as dystopian as the one that Vonnegut created, we should be open to exploring and understanding why the world of Harrison Bergeron is presumed to be such a bad one. What is the principle, value, or belief that drives that judgment? Once again, we can ask that question without endorsing (or, for that matter, condemning) the principle itself.

In response to my prompt to name the principle, I suggested that the judgment is driven by a core belief in the sovereignty of the individual and the individual's right to pursue their potential. We can name and examine that value *without letting it go*. We can also ask the question: What would it be like to have a different one?

The recognition that we can name and examine any belief, value, or principle has powerful implications. It lets us explore ideas in a way that doesn't commit us to anything, doesn't require us to change our minds, and doesn't require us to let go of core beliefs.

Thinking in this manner opens up the space for conversations on even, or especially, the most heated and contentious topics we face. We can pick any hot issue and talk about different questions that come up. For instance, how should we think about a particular social problem when sources tell different stories? Do we focus on people's lived experiences or do we focus on what the data tell us? What is the "right" amount to lean into identity groups? Whose interests should be prioritized when those of two groups conflict? What's the "right" way to divide ourselves into groups in the first place? And, for all of these: Who should decide and why?

If I could go back to that seminar Room 256 that day, I would take the time to give an answer to the question of how do I know it's a problem that sounds more like the one I'm describing here. I would talk about the limitations in how we think and the way we tend to judge people who disagree. I don't know if it would have convinced the person who asked the question, but it would have been more precise than stumbling around with survey data on self-censorship. After all, the numbers only tell part of the story. We need to look at the judgments that drive them and the certainty that, in turn, drives those. Ultimately, the relevant question isn't whether free speech or self-censorship on campus is in a bad enough state to warrant attention—it's a call to look and think about how we make judgments in the first place.

FURTHER READING

For readers who would like to do a deeper dive into the problem of certainty described here, *The Certainty Trap* book will be out in summer 2024 and thecertaintytrap.substack.com is free to all. More information about Ilana Redstone's work is available at www.ilanaredstone.com.

REFERENCES

FIRE. 2023. *Campus Disinvitation Database*. https://www.thefire.org/research-learn/campus-disinvitation-database.

Vonnegut, Kurt, Jr. 1961. "Harrison Bergeron" originally published in *The Magazine of Fantasy and Science Fiction*. Accessed 2024-01-05 at https://www.tnellen.com/westside/harrison.pdf.

NOTE

1. I am deeply grateful to my brother, Joshua Redstone, who has tirelessly helped me think through the problem of certainty.

Conclusion

Fabio Rojas and Charlotta Stern

REFLECTIONS AND TRAJECTORIES

One of Pierre Bourdieu' and Loïc Wacquant's (1992) great lessons is that sociology is a reflexive endeavor. We never sit completely outside of the social reality that we study, and we should strive to consider our place in it. The knowledge that researchers create is a relational act. The questions we ask and the data we seek are situated in the connections between the researchers and those they study. Thus, Bourdieu urged, it's always important to incorporate an element of reflexivity in sociological writing, a sensitivity for how historical processes have created the structures that sociologists observe and are part of.

Motivated by this call, we offer this concluding chapter as a reflection where we think about ourselves and how the classical liberal dialogue fits into larger professional and cultural contexts. We start by considering the current state of sociological research and how "classical liberal sociology" sits in that knowledge structure. Then, we discuss how this project reflects current understandings of speech and freedom, and then conclude with a few personal reflections on our intellectual journey.

THINKING ABOUT SOCIOLOGY AS A PROFESSION TODAY

Our aim in editing this book has been to enthuse more sociologists about classical liberal ideas and intuitions because we think those ideas and intuitions deserve to be appreciated by the profession and they would improve sociology. Another aim has been to show how sociology can contribute to classical liberal scholars, such as Novak's chapter on social movements. This bridge building raises an important question. In what ways does this connection affect the intellectual landscape of academic sociology? Does this knowledge work increase the variety of theory and empirical work found in the sociological world?

We can address this question by looking at the constellation of ideas within modern sociology. Researchers Vincent Traag and Thomas Franssen (2016) visualized thousands of sociology publications drawn from the World of Science database from 2010–2015 and posted the results on their blog. They presented readers with a "sociogram," a diagram illustrating how various idea cluster together based on whether an article's author included both terms in an article's title. The results are telling, with two broad groups of articles reflecting parallel understandings of sociology. Traag and Franssen describe the split in the following manner: "The universe of quantitative sociology consists of terms like 'survey,' 'data' and 'scale' but also of 'socioeconomic status,' 'women,' 'men' and 'career' (in blue). The universe of qualitative sociology consists of terms such as 'discourse,' 'practice,' and 'meaning' but also of 'power,' 'identity,' and 'masculinity' (in red)."

The mostly quantitative side of sociology, the highly positivist wing, is where you find sociologists who study stratification, health, and demography using large-scale data and statistics. The other side of the discipline deploys qualitative evidence in a description and critique of power and inequality.

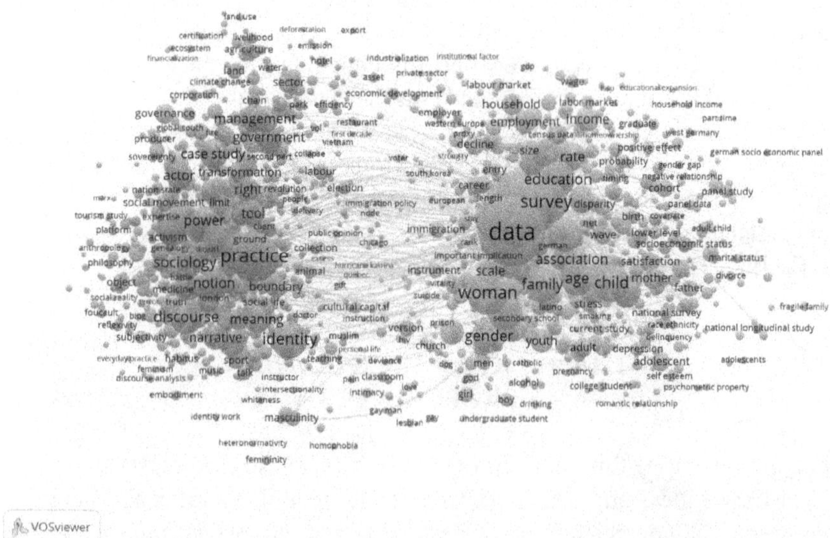

Figure C.1. Map of the field of sociology 2010–2015. Traag and Franssen (2016) map of the field of sociology 2010–2015.

CWTS Meaningful Metrics. https://www.cwts.nl/blog?article=n-q2v294

It might be useful to think of these two sociologies as the wings of "post-modern" sociology. We call current sociology post-modern since few sociologists would hold an unmodified positivist stance built on appeals to strong notions of scientific Truth, falsification, and cumulative science. Contemporary sociologists know their Kuhn (1962), and they accept that social science is not natural science. The post-modern sociologists are aware that social science as a truth-seeking social practice is embedded in a larger social reality. Scientific theories are always at risk of being overturned as each generation brings novel perspectives to long-standing scientific problems.

Still, the quantitative and qualitative wings of post-modern sociology differ in important ways. Quantitative sociologists tend to be sympathetic to norms of intersubjectivity, truth, and universalism. While they are cautious about the contingent findings of social science, post-modern quantitative sociologists do act in ways that belie a technocratic optimism. Using proper survey methods, carefully constructed experiments, and proper statistical techniques, the contingent findings of social science might find a place in public discourse and produce better policy.

The mostly qualitative side of sociology, the post-modern critical wing, is where sociologists embrace critical race theory (e.g., Ray 2022), feminism (e.g., Smith 1990), and post-colonialism (e.g., Go 2017).The post-modern critical wing is not so keen on traditional science and its norms, and here we find scholars sympathetic to subjectivity, relativism, and constructivism (see Reed and Weinman 2019 for a review of these issues). The two wings are separated by preferred methods, but often also by different views on knowledge, science, theory, and what counts as scholarship. Thus, adding more complication to the mix can be questionable, and our students tend to say that there are too many different theories already.

From the professional sociologist's standpoint, the richness of theories is a comparative advantage. Students are exposed to a variety of theoretical perspectives throughout their training, which broadens one's perspective. One way to practice critical thinking is, after all, to have access to more than one interpretation. Exposure to multiple viewpoints allows students, and scholars as well, to understand that scientific and ethical stances are constantly subject to debate and alternatives need to be considered. Adding freedom as a perspective in sociology would enrich sociological theorizing further, and it would certainly sharpen our critical thinking skills. In addition to having liberal technocratic and critical theory viewpoints, sociologists could explore the implications of centering individualism, which points a different style of social science focused on a strong ethical commitment to voluntary action.

The "freedom" perspective in sociology acts as a counterpoint to the technocratic impulse of many quantitative sociologists who are often drawn toward strong policy conclusions based on experiments or survey data, while overlooking how broader social contexts would complicate such prescriptions (Nair and Howlett 2016). Classical liberal sociologists can ask how proposed policy solutions take into account individual autonomy and how liberalized economies and free communities can create bottom-up solutions to social problems. A classical liberal stance would also help reduce the "automatic leftism" of the profession where it is often assumed that market failures are the presumed explanations for phenomena as varied as wage differences (Weeden and Grusky 2014), health disparities (Vassiliev et al. 2017), or mortality variation (Schreker, Birn, and Aguilera 2018). Rather than assume a given disparity as an outcome produced by market failures, classical liberals would ask if liberalized economies produced broader positive trends and if markets, civil society, and other forms of voluntary action can provide further relief.

Ultimately, the key question for classical liberal sociologists is, "What is the alternative?" (Sowell 2000) It is not assumed that markets are the worst outcome. Instead, it may be possible that markets, and other spontaneous orders, produce imperfect, yet highly desirable outcomes. Another argument is that the known alternatives, such as command economies, leave much to be desired. Furthermore, automatic leftism leaves under-theorized alternative explanations behind differences, and this has led to a profession that under-appreciates ideas of liberty, spontaneous order, and markets. Market failures are assumed and market successes ignored. The theme is comparative institutional analysis (Greif 1998).

A classical liberal approach to sociology would enhance our understanding of agency and social structure. For classical liberals, the most important freedom is the freedom from coercion or what Isaiah Berlin (1969) called negative freedom. Born out of a concern for how states and private entities forcibly restrain people (Courtland, Gaus, and Schmidtz 2022), classical liberalism has always had a disproportionate focus on negative freedom. To most sociologists, however, freedom often denotes positive freedom. Positive freedom focuses on outcomes and builds on the fact that individuals are not entirely free from constraints, be they social or material. For example, in discussions of poverty, classical liberals will focus on economic liberalism because it allows people to pursue wealth, while sociologists often focus on positive freedom by looking at the things that people at low income levels aren't able to do, even though they may be free from coercion.

It is important to think about this imbalance. Most sociologists seem not to care too much about negative freedom, perhaps because they tend to think that "freedom from" is related to selfishness, atomistic individualism, unrealism, or to regard it as beyond sociology's purview (see the discussion by Aspers, in this volume). As freedom-loving sociologists we agree that freedom from all constraints is unrealistic, as we are all born into social settings and are constrained by them. However, sociologists' neglect of negative liberty is unwarranted and excessive. Realizing that freedom is not perfect and never will be, or that individuals are constrained by their embedding in social contexts, does not mean that negative freedom is unimportant to a good life. Au contraire, the right to your body, your mind, and soul is a freedom that is essential for a good life and a just society. Just think of the alternative. A life lived under coercion is demeaning and inhumane. If one cares about positive freedoms, one must also embrace negative freedoms because they underlie much of the culture and institutions that make positive freedoms possible.

Sociologists, eager to turn a critical eye toward inequalities in outcomes, often underplay the most important source of coercion in Western societies today, nation-states. Brandon Davis's chapter is an excellent corrective to this tendency because it puts government-coercion at front stage. His scathing critique of the predatory state illustrates what an unfree life is like in a society where formal freedom, or negative freedom, is promised but not delivered. One can read Davis's chapter to imply that government agents are the villains creating and upholding what he terms systemic racism. After all, the legislation, courts, the police, and the legislator are all state agents.

In contrast, in much contemporary sociology, market society is the villain. In fact, former ASA President Michael Burawoy (2005) has argued many times that the natural position for a sociologist is to oppose the excesses of markets and defend civil society against their harms. This impulse is reflected in the substantial research that focuses on market imperfections as an explanation for compensation differentials (Weeden and Grusky 2014), obesity (Dolezal and Spratt 2023), and life course outcomes such as marriage (Randles and Woodward 2018). Disparate effects between social groups are documented and dissected. Perfect equality is the norm to which markets processes are held and any deviation from absolute equality is unjust. A classical liberal sociology offers an important rejoinder to this position. For example, the power of exit is often under-valued in sociological analyses of markets and labor processes. No employer in a free economy can force you to stay on in a job you dislike. Exit is always an option, even when it is costly and hard. Exit is also a strong signal that something is wrong (Hirschman 1970). A signal that an entrepreneur, a volunteer organization, or just folks in the neighborhood pick up and it may motivate them to figure out some way to improve the situation. That is not to say that the mechanism is perfect, and it is a process that takes more time than the top-down government commando does. However, such voluntary exchange of goods or services, a contract defining future collaboration to build a car, a bake sale in the neighborhood are two examples of market collaborations. People engaging with each other in their respective pursuits of happiness. As the chapter by John Iceland and Eric Silver on market liberalism clearly documents, the result is greatly reduced poverty and creation of wealth. The result is what Adam Smith studied in *The Wealth of Nations* and named the order of the invisible hand. The distinction between freedom and coercion is worth keeping in mind.

Jack Goldstone's chapter reminds us that wealth creation may entail social and economic inequalities that demand critique and further evaluation. The classical liberal perspective suggests that we should examines institutions that employ voluntary means for mitigating these trends. Another perspective that a classical liberal sociology might bring to the study of inequality is to understand trade-offs. Economic liberalization might create inequality, but it also reduces absolute rates of poverty, as argued by Iceland and Silver. A classical liberal sociology would enrich the field by adding more nuance and complexity to the study of social stratification.

These comments, and the arguments made by various authors in this volume, are meant to move sociologists away from a strong reliance on market failure as a starting point for social theory. In one way, expecting the market to be perfect suggests sociologists are holding markets to higher expectations than they are market interventions. On the other hand, it is a double standard when the same high expectations are not expected by government interventions. It is not so much that sociologists hold their views in bad faith as they focus so much attention on market failures and so little on government failure. We argue that a more balanced argument can be made.

FREEDOM IS DONE TOGETHER!

Another theme that we wish to reflect on is that freedom can never be completely divorced from its social context. In a very real sense, freedom is something we do together. After all, culture, social norms, and social change regulate what we can do, yet they are spontaneously emerging orders. They are seldom designed from above and all human groups interact in ways that generate rules that enable, or limit, what people in that community can do. Freedom is a group project, and various chapters illustrate this crucial point.

The chapter on social movements by Mikayla Novak shows how social change occurs in society when people get together and work toward it. Freedom must be built. The same general message can be seen in Rojas's chapter on race and ethnicity. If people are free to enter and exit social groupings, with little coercion, they may enter into fruitful collaboration. In the chapter by Lauren Hall on health care, she documents how "bottom-up" health care, such as minority doulas and midwives, emerge to care for minority women during pregnancy and birth giving. Again, freedom and voluntary action make it possible to try new things. These new things are what innovation and entrepreneurship are all about. It is unfortunate that economics, with its ideal typical model that focuses on homo economicus' utility maximization, has shaped so much of our thinking about markets. Markets are people working together. Sometimes for profit, other times to care for themselves and others. A broader type of utility, and far from selfish maximization!

On a deeper level, this book represents classical liberal inquiry as something to be done by the collective. This volume does not present a single voice, but a cacophony where each author brings a different perspective. Some chapters are written by scholars with strong liberal commitments, while others are written from a critical point of view. Most importantly, we asked each author to approach the intersection of sociology and classical liberalism in their own way. This resulted in an impressive spectrum of essays that range from detailed reviews of empirical data, explorations of social theory, and personal reflections. If this diversity and dynamism is what emerges from our efforts, then classical liberal sociology has a bright future.

TOLERATION AND THE LIBERAL PRINCIPLE OF FREE SPEECH

This volume is an exercise in scholarly inquiry as well as an assertion of free speech and toleration. We do not expect all our authors to concur with our views. Dissent is expected and celebrated. For example, Jack Goldstone's chapter declares classical liberalism to be dead in a world where populism, nationalism, and social media erode democratic deliberation and rationality. Mental and physical walls are built and politicians are rewarded for dividing ideas, individuals, and phenomena into good and evil. Goldstone's chapter reminds us that liberalism as a living and meaningful social practice is at risk in such a world.

Similarly, in her micro-sociological essay on interaction on campus, Ilana Redstone discusses the increasing intolerance for talking about, listening to, or reading about topics that challenge one's values or norms. Openness and toleration seem to be dwindling left and right. The pressure to outlaw or regulate actions or speech by person A because it violates person B's norms or values is intolerant and conflicts with a free society. On a macro-level, intolerant politicians threaten societal freedoms. On a micro-level, a new definition of violence is corroding norms of toleration. Underlying both developments seems to be vulnerability: in the name of protecting the vulnerable or returning to an orderly society, freedoms are under threat. Freedoms of conscience, thought, and speech are fundamental rights of individuals, they are after all considered human rights, and protecting these rights is the duty of the government.

We also recognize that freedom is a complicated thing as it entails an important discussion of competing interests because the strong defense of speech and viewpoint diversity can lead to damaging social conflict. In Europe, we can see how strong speech protections can lead to controversy and even violence. In 2023, for example, xenophobic groups in Sweden gained permission to publicly burn the Qur'an, which resulted in protests and clashes with the police (Syed 2023). In the US, crowds of angry students have injured faculty members who wished to host controversial campus speakers (Read 2017). We hope that the discussions of liberalism, toleration, and free speech found in this volume can help scholars and policy makers understand the social processes that allow for the non-violent expression of dissent and viewpoint diversity.

INDIVIDUALISM AND COLLECTIVISM: A CLASH OF PERSPECTIVES?

We conclude this volume with a consideration of individualism-collectivism dichotomy in sociology. It is often thought that sociology must rely on a collective foundation that rejects individualism. Sociological thinking, in contrast, often emphasizes collective identities. Much of Emile Durkheim's corpus, for example, is an attempt to establish "social facts" that supersede accounts of individual agency. Talcott Parsons, the dominant figure of mid-twentieth century sociology, began *The Structure of Social Action* with a thorough attack on utilitarian social theory, which tried to describe society as the outcome of individual actions. In contrast, individualism is a core attribute of classical liberal thinking where rights and duties are based in one person and the pursuit of happiness is an individual project. Still, individualism does not in itself preclude adhering to a collective, only in the most analytical rational-choice version is that true. The individual freedom of Smith and de Tocqueville did not preclude duties to the collectives or the importance of group belonging; in contrast, other-regarding desires, duties, and moral principles are parts of our identities, of what it means to be a human.

What at first may seem a clash of perspective turns out to be a difference in perspective. Rational choice sociology is one example of how theorizing on sociological topics from individual action can contribute to our understanding of such collective topics as group solidarity, religion, or social problems such as segregation and discrimination. Anthony Giddens's (2014) structuration theory or Mark Granovetter's (1985) embeddedness theory might be another approach, where it is understood that individual action and social structure mutually constitute each other. These examples suggest that there is no necessary contradiction between classical liberalism and sociology.

To conclude, we think much can be achieved by adding discussions of freedom and markets to the sociological arsenal. To judge markets and governments on the same scale, and for more sociologists to learn to also appreciate the spontaneous order of individual interaction and the force it brings to society.

REFERENCES

Berlin, Isaiah. 1969. "Two Concepts of Liberty." in I. Berlin, *Four Essays on Liberty.* London: Oxford University Press: 118–72. New ed. in Berlin 2002: 166–217.

Burawoy, Michael. 2005. 2004. "American Sociological Association Presidential Address: For Public Sociology." *The British Journal of Sociology,* 56: 259–294.

Bourdieu, Pierre and Loïc Wacquant. 1992. *An Invitation to Reflexive Sociology.* The University of Chicago Press.

Courtland, Shane D., Gerald Gaus, and David Schmidtz, "Liberalism," The Stanford Encyclopedia of Philosophy (Spring 2022 Edition), Edward N. Zalta (ed.), https://plato.stanford.edu/archives/spr2022/entries/liberalism/. Retrieved August 28, 2023.

Dolezal, Luna and Tanisha Spratt. 2023. "Fat Shaming under Neoliberalism and COVID-19: Examining the UK's Tackling Obesity Campaign." *Sociology of Health & Illness,* 45 (1): 3–18.

Giddens, Anthony. 2014. "Structuration Theory: Past, Present and Future." In *Giddens' Theory of Structuration* (pp. 201–221). Routledge.

Go, Julian. 2017. *Postcolonial Thought and Social Theory.* The University of Chicago Press.

Granovetter, Mark. 1985. "Economic Action and Social Structure: The Problem of Embeddedness." *American Journal of Sociology:* 481–510.

Greif, Avner. 1998. "Historical and Comparative Institutional Analysis." *The American Economic Review*, 88 (2): 80–84.

Hirschman, Albert O. 1970. *Exit, Voice, and Loyalty: Responses to Decline in Firms, Organizations, and States*. Harvard University Press.

Kuhn, Thomas. 1962. *The Structure of Scientific Revolutions*. The University of Chicago Press.

Nair, Sreeja and Michael Howlett. 2016. "Meaning and Power in the Design and Development of Policy Experiments," *Futures,* 76: 67–74.

Randles, Jennifer and Kerry Woodward. 2018. "Learning to Labor, Love, and Live: Shaping the Good Neoliberal Citizen in State Work and Marriage Programs." *Sociological Perspectives, 61* (1): 39–56.

Ray, Victor. 2022. *On Critical Race Theory*. Penguin/Random House.

Read, Brack. 2017. "A Scuffle and a Professor's Injury Make Middlebury a Free-Speech Flashpoint." *The Chronicle of Higher Education.* https://www.chronicle.com/article/a-scuffle-and-a-professors-injury-make-middlebury-a-free-speech-flashpoint/. Retrieved August 28, 2023.

Reed, Isaac Ariail and Michael Weinman. 2019. "Agency, Power, Modernity: A Manifesto for Social Theory," *European Journal of Cultural and Political Sociology,* 6 (1): 6–50.

Schrecker, Ted, Anne-Emanuelle Birn, and Mariajosé Aguilera. 2018. "How Extractive Industries Affect Health: Political Economy Underpinnings and Pathways," *Health & Place,* 52: 135–147.

Smith, Dorothy E. 1990. *The Conceptual Practices of Power: A Feminist Sociology of Knowledge*. The University of Toronto Press.

Sowell, Thomas. 2000. *Basic Economics*. Basic Books.

Syed, Amrani. 2023. "Why Quran Burning Is Making Sweden and Denmark So Anxious." *Time.* https://www.msn.com/en-us/news/world/why-quran-burning-is-making-nordic-leaders-so-anxious/ar-AA1fj6vQ. Retrieved August 28, 2023.

Traag, Vincent and Thomas Franssen. 2016. "Revealing the quantitative-qualitative divide in sociology using bibliometric visualization." *CWTS Meaningful Metrics*. https://www.cwts.nl/blog?article=n-q2v294. Retrieved August 26, 2023.

Vassilev, Ivaylo, Rogers, Anne, Todorova, Elka, Kennedy, Anne and Poli Roukova. 2017. "The Articulation of Neoliberalism: Narratives of Experience of Chronic Illness Management in Bulgaria and the UK." *Sociology of Health and Illness,* 39: 349–364.

Weeden, Kim A. and David B. Grusky. 2014. "Inequality and Market Failure." *American Behavioral Scientist,* 58 (3): 473–491.

Index

About the Editors

Fabio Rojas is the Virginia L. Roberts Professor of Sociology at Indiana University, Bloomington. His research focuses on social change, activism, and organizational behavior. He is the author of *From Black Power to Black Studies: How a Radical Social Movement Became an Academic Discipline* (2007, Johns Hopkins University Press) and *Party in the Street: The Antiwar Movement and the Democratic Party after 9/11* (2015, Cambridge University Press). He has also published in venues such as the *American Journal of Sociology*, the *Academy of Management Journal*, and the *Proceedings of the National Academy of Sciences*.

Charlotta Stern is the CEO of Ratio and a professor of sociology at Stockholm University, Sweden. Her research interest includes labor market issues at the intersection of human resources and industrial relations, and particularly aspects of the Swedish labor market model.

About the Contributors

Patrik Aspers is chair of sociology at the University of St. Gallen and has previously been chair at Uppsala University. He holds a PhD (2001) from Stockholm University. His research is oriented to economic sociology, qualitative research, sociological theory, uncertainty reduction, and organizational sociology. Aspers's work draws on phenomenology. His most recent book, *Uncertainty: Private Problems and Public Solutions*, will appear in 2024 by Oxford University Press. He is the author of numerous books, including *Markets* (Polity Press, 2011), *Orderly Fashion: A Sociology of Markets* (2010), and *Orders of Worth* (2011, with Jens Beckert).

Brandon Rudolph Davis is an assistant professor in the Department of Political Science and the Murphy Institute at Tulane University. Brandon earned an MSW from Alabama A&M University, an MA in gender and race studies, and a PhD in political science from The University of Alabama. He is also a former postdoctoral research associate at the Political Theory Project at Brown University. His research focuses on American politics, law and society, and race and ethnic politics. Brandon is interested in normative and empirical approaches to institutions, representation, and criminal justice.

Jack A. Goldstone (PhD Harvard) is Hazel Professor of Public Policy and a Fellow of the Mercatus Center of George Mason University. He is the author of *Revolution and Rebellion in the Early Modern World* (winner of the 1993 Distinguished Contribution to Scholarship Award of the American Sociological Association) and has authored or edited fifteen additional books and more than 200 book chapters and journal articles on comparative history, political conflict and social change. Goldstone has won Fellowships from the J.S. Guggenheim, Carnegie, and MacArthur Foundations, and has received career awards for distinguished achievement in both political sociology and comparative and historical sociology.

Lauren Hall is professor of political science and Associate Dean of Academic Affairs in the College of Liberal Arts at the Rochester Institute of Technology. She is the author of *The Medicalization of Birth and Death* (Johns Hopkins University Press, 2019) and *Family and the Politics of Moderation (*Baylor University Press, 2014) and the co-editor of a volume on the political philosophy of French political thinker Chantal Delsol. She has written extensively on the classical liberal tradition, including articles on Edmund Burke, Adam Smith, and Montesquieu and she serves on the editorial board of the interdisciplinary journal *Cosmos+Taxis*. Her current research is on the moral and political implications of regulations, the importance of political and social moderation, and gender and the family. She writes for popular audiences at https://radicalmoderatesguide.substack.com/.

John Iceland is distinguished professor of sociology and demography at Penn State University. His research and teaching interests focus on demography, social inequality, and polarization in the United States. He is co-author of the book *Why We Disagree about Inequality: Social Justice vs. Social Order* with Eric Silver and Ilana Redstone.

Mikayla Novak is a senior fellow with the F. A. Hayek Program for Advanced Study in Philosophy, Politics and Economics, Mercatus Center at George Mason University. Her research interests include fiscal and economic sociology, social movement studies, entangled political economy, public finance, and social theory. She is the author of numerous peer-review research articles and of two books, including *Freedom in Contention: Social Movements and Liberal Political Economy* (Lexington Books).

Ilana Redstone is a professor of sociology at the University of Illinois at Urbana-Champaign and the co-director of the Mill Institute at UATX. She's also the author of The Certainty Trap, coming out in September 2024. You can find out more about her work at www.ilanaredstone.com.

Eric Silver is professor of sociology and criminology at Penn State University. His research focuses on morality, deviance, punishment, and public opinion. He teaches an award-winning course on morality called "Knowing Right from Wrong" with more than 700 students enrolled each semester.

www.ingramcontent.com/pod-product-compliance
Lightning Source LLC
LaVergne TN
LVHW051505080126
829330LV00002B/16